The World Turned

The World Turned

Essays on Gay History, Politics, and Culture

John D'Emilio

DUKE UNIVERSITY PRESS   *Durham and London*   2002

Designed by Amy Ruth Buchanan
Typeset in Carter & Cone Galliard
by Keystone Typesetting, Inc.
Library of Congress Cataloging-in-
Publication Data appear on the last
printed page of this book.

THE DISTRIBUTION OF THIS
BOOK IS SUPPORTED BY A
GENEROUS GRANT FROM THE
GILL FOUNDATION.

FOR JIM

Contents

Preface

Something happened in the 1990s. Something dramatic and, I expect, irreversible in its consequences.

There is hardly a nonfiction gay book that does not make an obligatory nod to the Stonewall Rebellion, that myth-enshrouded event when the queens fought back in Greenwich Village and the fighting spirit of gay liberation was born. The world seemed to turn that evening. The darkness of the closet was left behind forever, the fearful secrecy of gay life discarded, the shame associated with it repudiated.

But, truth be told, Stonewall, gay liberation, and radical lesbian feminism touched very few. I say this even though I am someone whose life was thoroughly remade by the thrilling intensity of those years. In the 1970s, marching through the streets of New York, or Washington, or Montreal, or San Francisco, I was convinced that the eyes of all were on us, and that we were making everything different than it had been. The self-transformations accomplished by those early waves of men and women coming out publicly reached so deeply into our psyches that of course we thought everyone was watching and nothing would ever be the same again.

Looking back from the vantage point of the early twenty-first century, I now see Stonewall mostly as potential, as the harbinger of changes still way in the distance. The devastating intrusion of AIDS into our lives, the rise of aggressive fundamentalist religious movements, and the triumph of Reaganite conservatism in American politics all meant that the road from Stonewall held twists and turns and curves and bumps that no one could ever have suspected.

By contrast, the changes that the 1990s brought—their nearness to us notwithstanding—look to me to have a durability and a reach that go far beyond what the Stonewall generation was able to accomplish. For in the 1990s, the world finally did turn and notice the gay folks in its midst.

The evidence for it comes from a host of phenomena large and small. Staid American corporations like Motorola and Chevron provide domestic partnership benefits for their gay, lesbian, and bisexual employees. In Chicago, the city government has constructed rainbow towers along the main street of the chief gay neighborhood. *People* magazine puts on its cover a lesbian rock star, her lover, and their baby (who was conceived with the sperm of a straight male singer). One of the top network comedies at the end of the decade, honored with a long string of Emmy nominations, was *Will and Grace*. Gay/straight alliances are sprouting up in the nation's high schools. Heterosexual parents are taking their children out of the Boy Scouts rather than countenance the antigay discrimination the organization is wedded to. The Web site of the University of Minnesota includes two lesbians in a series of staff couples. In Iowa, a gay male couple received the "foster parents of the year" award.

Or, just take some evidence from my own life. My parents, God-fearing Italian Catholics who never have missed Sunday Mass and say the rosary every day, send birthday and Christmas gifts to my partner, Jim. Whenever I call home, they never fail to ask how "big Jim" (to distinguish him from "little Jim," my younger brother) is doing. When I was hired in 1983 to teach at the University of North Carolina in Greensboro, a local newspaper referred to me as "the fag doctor" and claimed that Greensboro was on its way to becoming the "leading center for faggotry" in the state. When I was hired at the University of Illinois at Chicago in 1999, the *Sun-Times* called it "a recruiting coup among academics," and the university promised to make a good-faith effort to find a job for my partner. I receive fellowships and grants and awards for my work in gay studies, where once upon a time I was virtually unemployable.

Now don't misunderstand me. I am *not* saying that some kind of gay utopia has arrived. The evidence to refute such a claim is as abundant as the examples of mind-boggling change are numerous. But profound change for the better can coexist with a litany of very real grievances. And, since the grievances have a long, long history while the spectacular advances of recent years are fresh and new, forgive me if I choose to emphasize the hopeful.

If I had to summarize succinctly the nature of the difference between the present moment and the Stonewall era, I would describe it in this way. Pretty much every gay man or lesbian of the Stonewall era came of age believing that we were the only person like us in the world, and that what we were was not good. A whole train of assumptions about life's possibilities flowed from that beginning. Today, when I listen to the undergraduates in my gay studies and U.S. history courses, I hear something very different. However much my queer students may be struggling with their emerging identities (and they do still struggle), and however uninformed about gay life my heterosexual students may be, all of them begin with the assumption that gays and lesbians are very much a part of the world in which they are reaching maturity. It's a starting point much to be preferred to the conditions that prevailed a generation ago. It offers more openings for dialogue, more possibilities for continuing change, more hope for the future. And this transition came about in the course of the 1990s.

*   *   *

The essays in this volume were all written in the nineties. While they do not, individually, each chart the changes that the decade brought, I think that they do, collectively, provide a sense of movement from there to here.

The essays were composed in a variety of locales, under a variety of circumstances, and for a variety of audiences. In the course of the 1990s, I lived in Greensboro, North Carolina; Palo Alto, California; Canberra, Australia; Washington, D.C.; and Chicago. I taught U.S. history at a small state university in the South; did policy work for a national gay organization inside the infamous Beltway; supported my writing habit for long stretches through various grants; and taught gay and lesbian studies courses at a large public urban university in the Midwest. Some of the essays were the product of years of research and were written for history journals and anthologies. I composed others originally as lectures for campus audiences, keynote speeches at large conferences of movement activists, or informal presentations on panels at community forums. One was delivered at a memorial service, and another began as private scribblings intended to help me make sense of changes in my own life.

Part One, "Interpretations," contains a series of essays that each deal with an aspect of gay history since the 1940s. The first essay looks at the life of Bayard Rustin, a courageous and visionary civil rights leader and pacifist, and explores how American homophobia constricted and reshaped his public career from the 1940s through the mid-1960s. Chapter 2 looks at the 1960s and asks how our understanding of this watershed decade might change if we saw things gay as being integral, rather than marginal, to those years. In "Still Radical After All These Years," I return to the vibrant polemical literature of the early years of gay liberation and lesbian feminism and assess the nature and depth of its insights. "A Meaning for All Those Words" looks at the work of Larry Kramer — novelist, playwright, AIDS activist, cultural critic and, sometimes, general pain in the butt — and tries to understand why controversy swirled around him in the 1970s and 1980s. Chapters 5 and 6 focus on the gay and lesbian movement. The first of the pair offers a broad overview of political activism from the early 1950s to the late 1990s, and the second one zooms in on the work of a single organization, the National Gay and Lesbian Task Force. Taken as a whole, the essays in this part move us forward in time from the 1940s, when gay life was deeply in the closet, to the end of the century, when a structurally complex and visible community stretched across the country.

Part Two, "Interventions," consists of pieces that I composed in response to particular events or noticeable trends in the decade. Chapters 7 and 8 were written in the fall of 1992, the former before the election in the midst of the intense gay-baiting of the campaign season and the latter right after the Clinton victory. I drafted chapter 9, "Stonewall," as the hoopla over the approaching twenty-fifth anniversary was gathering momentum. "Born Gay" emerged in reaction to the growing preoccupation with biological theories of homosexuality; it started as a talk before small groups of activists. "What Does Gay Liberation Have to Do with the War in Bosnia?" originally took the form of a keynote speech before a conference of activists. It was an attempt to ground the gay community in a long sweep of history *and* simultaneously to ring a warning bell about the perils of identity politics. The final essay in this section was a talk that I gave before many audiences in the mid-1990s and sought to explain the rapid rise of family issues to the top of the gay agenda.

The final part consists of a series of reflections on parts of my own life and work. In "Visions of Leadership," I pay tribute to Ken Dawson, a dear friend and colleague with whom I worked closely on a number of projects and whose contributions to the gay community were vast. "My Changing Sex Life" represents an effort on my part to admit the ways that my view of gay liberation has been tightly bound with this most intimate aspect of my life, and how both have changed symbiotically over time. "Then and Now" was an attempt to assess, retrospectively, my early efforts at writing gay history, and to comment on how our knowledge has expanded enormously since the

1970s, when I first began to do research. The closing essay brings us back to the point where the collection began, with the life of Bayard Rustin, but this time in the form of a meditation on the ways that the life of a biographer and his subject inevitably become entwined.

* * *

Making proper acknowledgment for all the help and support I have received over the years that these various pieces were composed is a daunting task. For the most part, I have chosen to offer thanks, in an opening footnote to each essay, to individuals who have played a role in the evolution of particular pieces. But there are some organizations and individuals who, in one way or another, have figured more centrally in my work and my life across the whole decade.

The University of North Carolina at Greensboro, Australian National University in Canberra, the National Endowment for the Humanities, and the John Simon Guggenheim Memorial Foundation provided me with grants and fellowships that made possible long stretches of research and writing. Peter Nardi and Nancy Stoller each read my first effort to pull together a collection of essays; their helpful comments and welcome encouragement convinced me to keep at it. In various ways, the National Gay and Lesbian Task Force served as an organizational home for me through the entire decade. All the board and staff members — even the ones with whom I had the most bruising fights — contributed to a view of gay liberation bigger than I would have achieved without them, but I especially want to single out and thank Urvashi Vaid, Sue Hyde, and Helen Gonzales.

Ruth Eisenberg, Estelle Freedman, Nan Hunter, and Torie Osborn have provided sustained friendship, political comradeship, and intense conversation over the decade in which these essays were written. Sometimes they commented on what I was writing; at other times they were unaware of my work. But in either case they were pillars of my world and I thank them for everything.

Finally, there is Jim Oleson, to whom this book is dedicated. My partner for more than two decades now, he makes life very sweet.

PART I *Interpretations*

I

Homophobia and the Course of Post–
World War II American Radicalism:
The Career of Bayard Rustin

Since the 1970s, gay and lesbian history has emerged as a vibrant new area of knowledge. Combining the inventiveness of the skilled detective with the insight of the finest cultural critic, a relatively small group of historians has opened unexpected startling vistas on the past. Although the better part of the job of recuperating these lost worlds is still to come, enough has been done to justify a heady sense of accomplishment.[1]

While lesbian history has forged strong intellectual ties with women's history and thus travels across the broad terrain mapped by gender studies, the historical literature on male homosexuality, at least that written about the United States, has for the most part remained curiously centered on itself. Not only is it, as one would expect, primarily about men whose erotic desire draws them toward other men, but it also focuses relentlessly on those aspects of their lives in which gayness is central — on the construction of identity, the evolution of urban subcultures and communities, the forging of a political emancipation movement. Even when the literature moves beyond these topics, into areas such as cultural representations and the elaboration

Research for this essay was supported by grants from the JFK Library and the American Philosophical Society. I wrote a first draft while a fellow at the Humanities Research Centre of Australian National University in 1993. Thanks to Graeme Clarke, John Ballard, and Jill Matthews of ANU, and to Henry Abelove, Diane Chisholm, Gary Dowsett, Lisa Duggan, Cindy Patton, Gayle Rubin, and Carole Vance, for helpful responses. An expanded version appeared in *Radical History Review* 62 (spring 1995): 80–103. This is a slightly edited version of the *RHR* article.

of scientific theories of sexuality, the point has generally been to assess how these men have been oppressed.

To characterize the writing of gay American history in this way is not to fault it. It seems almost foreordained that these would be the topics initially to capture attention; they are the ones that most readily could be excavated through scholarly digging. But it is also true that the steady focus on gay-ness — either gay life or gay oppression — threatens to obscure the bulk of gay historical experience. Most men who desired men did not lead queer-centered social lives, and even those who did would have passed much of their time — in work, politics, worship, voluntary associations, and civic affairs — in nongay contexts. How do we draw this experience into the orbit of gay history? How do we avoid writing a history of marginalized men that, iron-ically, reproduces the very marginality gay oppression attempts to enforce?

My current project, a biography of Bayard Rustin, did not begin as an exploration in gay history. Rather, I wanted to study the 1960s. Personally, those times still resonate emotionally for me. For better or worse — though I like to think better — I am a product of the 1960s. That decade shaped irrevocably my outlook on life. Intellectually, as someone who regularly teaches courses on the sixties, I have also felt compelled to reexamine that time, as I watch the complex emotional responses of my students. Initially thrilled by the optimism, idealism, and power of the civil rights and student movements, they also become disturbed by what they see as the outcome: a nation spinning out of control, cynical, disillusioned, and fractured into separate identity movements. The sense that I carried away from those years — of a revolutionary moment greater than the sum of its individual parts — seems harder to grasp at the remove of a generation.

Rustin's career, which has not received much play in the writing about post–World War II struggles for peace and justice, caught my attention for a number of reasons. For one, the broad range of his interests offered an opportunity to explore the connections between several movements. Through his work with the Congress of Racial Equality and with A. Philip Randolph in the 1940s, and with Martin Luther King Jr. in the 1950s, Rustin was certainly as responsible as anyone for injecting Gandhian nonviolence into the heart of the struggle for racial equality. He was also at the center of the pacifist circles that kept alive a critique of Cold War militarism, sparked the first demonstrations against the nuclear arms race, and stood ready to mobilize as the Johnson administration escalated the war in Vietnam. Rustin was fiercely internationalist as well. He worked closely with European pacifists, such as those in the Campaign for Nuclear Disarmament in Britain, and, keenly attuned to the historical significance of decolonization, with African liberation leaders such as Kwame Nkrumah of Ghana, Nnamdi Azikiwe of Nigeria, and Kenneth Kaunda of Zambia. To all these efforts, Rustin brought the skills of a master strategist and a compelling vision of revolutionary possibilities. It would not be an exaggeration to claim that, more than anyone else in the postwar era, he was a bridge linking the African American freedom struggle, peace campaigns, and a socialist dream of economic democracy.

Rustin's career also intrigued me because, in the mid-1960s, he proposed a road not taken. During the critical years from 1963 to 1966, as the force of the civil rights movement provoked a wave of support for social and economic reforms not seen since the mid-1930s, Rustin argued that radicals had to engage directly the political process. Just when the line between radical and liberal was opening into an unbridgeable chasm, just when many student radicals were embarking on an eternal romance with street action, Rustin urged a transition "from protest to politics."[2] At the time, militants tended to scorn Rustin's ideas. Many of his longtime associates argued then — and have continued to claim — that Rustin's strategic call was simply one manifestation of a more generalized turn to the right. In retrospect, with our ability to see how the radical war on liberalism helped to usher in a generation-long conservative hegemony in American politics, his approach seems to me less suspect. Thus, Rustin's career appeared as a promising vehicle for exploring afresh the achievements and failures of the 1960s.

That Rustin was also a gay man, and publicly identified as such in an era when the stigma attached to homosexuality was heavy, was a bonus. But I imagined his sexuality safely contained in the corner labeled "personal life," and saw it raising interesting, but secondary, questions that were not essential to the story of politics I wished to tell.

As my research has progressed, Rustin's sexuality has resisted this ghettoization. It appears, increasingly, inescapable, injecting itself everywhere. I am coming to believe that it molded his public life and shaped the response of others to him and to his ideas. In other words, it occupies not a peripheral but a critical place in Rustin's biography and, by extension, in the history of the 1960s. Rustin's life suggests ways that gay history, by bursting out of its ghetto, can inform new ways of understanding critical moments and core topics in American history.

In the rest of this chapter, I will trace in broad outline Rustin's life and career. Along the way, I will pause to consider the moments when his sexual identity erupted into public view. Finally, I will speculate about the ways that I think his homosexuality shaped his strategic thinking in the mid-1960s, conditioned the reactions of others to him, and propelled, eventually, his alleged turn to the right.

*   *   *

Bayard Rustin was born in 1912 into an African American family in West Chester, Pennsylvania, a Quaker-settled area that had been a stop on the underground railroad for runaway slaves. His grandmother, Julia, who raised Bayard as her own child, was an early member of the NAACP. Rustin excelled in high school as a scholar, athlete, and singer, and he also displayed a willingness early on to challenge racial discrimination. In the mid-1930s, he made his way to New York City, which remained his home for the rest of his life.[3]

Living in Harlem and attending City College, Rustin found himself in the midst of the unruly politics of Depression-era New York. Along with many Americans of conscience in the 1930s, he was drawn to the Communist Party. Rustin's Quaker beliefs, expressed during these years by participation in work-study projects of the American Friends Service Committee, only added to the attractiveness of the communist movement, for during the Popular Front period the party seemed to be against both war and fascism. Rustin joined the Young Communist League (YCL) and was active in the American Student Union, a major campus-based organization in which communists were influential. Yet, like many others, he eventually found himself alienated by the party's subservience to Moscow. After Hitler's invasion of the Soviet Union in June 1941, YCL leaders told Rustin to stop his activities for racial justice. Rustin broke with the party and remained deeply distrustful of it for the rest of his life.[4]

In the months just before his split with the party, Rustin embarked on two critical political relationships. Earlier in 1941, he had met A. Philip Randolph, the black socialist labor leader who had recently called for an African American march on Washington. With Randolph leading a charge of the black masses, Rustin was naturally attracted to the older, more experienced leader, and he began working in the youth section of the organization. A. J. Muste was the other older radical to whom Rustin was drawn. Muste, whose background included years at Brookwood Labor College in the 1920s and 1930s and involvement with the American Trotskyist movement, had recently become director of the Fellowship of Reconciliation (FOR), the leading Christian-pacifist organization in the United States. He believed pacifists must engage in more than moral witness against injustice; they had to build a movement for permanent change. At Muste's invitation, Rustin joined the Fellowship's staff in September 1941 and stayed for the next twelve years.[5]

It may seem odd to describe the war years as an exciting moment for American pacifists, but such was their characterization of the times. The worldwide conflagration created an élan, an intense solidarity that drove the truest believers to ever greater sacrifices of time and energy. Rustin traveled across the country, speaking to church and student groups, signing up new members, and visiting the relocation camps where Japanese Americans were incarcerated.[6] For Rustin, a good bit of the promise of this first paying job as an agent of social change came from the knowledge that he was breaking new ground. Along with James Farmer and George Houser, two other young staff members of the FOR, Rustin was expanding the group's mission into the field of race relations. They were building a new interracial organization, the Congress of Racial Equality (CORE), dedicated to the application of Gandhian techniques to the struggle for racial equality. During the 1940s, they conducted training workshops and embarked on action projects, desegregating restaurants, drugstore lunch counters, skating rinks, and theaters.[7] Rustin also served as the FOR's liaison to Randolph's March on Washington organization. Here was an authentic working-class vehicle, and Rustin strove to inject Gandhian nonviolence into this urban mass movement. After one of its major conferences, Rustin wrote enthusiastically to Muste that "Randolph really 'hit the gong.' We had a superb meeting. . . . [he] spoke in a way that convinced me that he is really concerned to develop an understanding and use of non-violence by the American Negro."[8]

Early in 1944, Rustin was jailed for refusing induction. He entered a federal prison system that had been flooded by conscientious objectors whose hunger strikes and work stoppages were disrupting the routines of guards and inmates alike. Rustin plunged into these activities, challenging segregation and mail censorship, fomenting strikes among the prisoners, and, in the process, deepening his commitment to a hybrid of Gandhian, Quaker, and Marxist teachings. The prison years convinced Rustin that Gandhianism was the gospel of the future, and that the postwar years would require a steel-like commitment to militant action.[9]

By the time he was released from prison in June 1946, the Cold War was becoming national dogma. Pacifists found themselves increasingly isolated and were forced into symbolic forms of protest. Race relations, on the other hand, seemed to offer a more promising field of action. In 1947, Rustin and George Houser, acting through CORE, organized a test of bus company compliance with a Supreme Court decision banning segregated seating in interstate travel. Riding through the upper South, the members of the "Journey of Reconciliation" used Gandhian techniques and rallied black communities wherever they traveled. Rustin and three others also faced arrest and conviction, leading to another prison sentence.[10] In 1948, pacifists joined forces once again with Randolph, who was mobilizing against military segregation. Under prodding from Rustin, Randolph promised a campaign of civil disobedience, which opened new opportunities for Rustin's message of nonviolent resistance to sink roots into African American communities.[11] Meanwhile, Rustin spent much of his time on the road, leading workshops in which participants not only studied Gandhianism, but also exposed discrimination and instigated direct action campaigns.[12]

Because of the leadership qualities he displayed, Rustin attracted notice. Muste consciously mentored him, and strategized his development as a leader. The FOR sent him to meet with European pacifist leaders and to confer with Gandhi's followers in India. The peers with whom he worked remember the Rustin of the 1940s vividly. They were awed by the personal courage of a man who, in his solitary travels, regularly refused to comply with segregation and received beatings and jail sentences because of it. In my interviews with pacifists from this era, the two words that recurred most frequently in their description of Rustin were "prophetic" and "charismatic." Possessing a beautiful tenor voice, he could shift easily between speech and song, and he moved audiences to tears with his renditions of Negro spirituals. Rustin made an indelible impression wherever he traveled. In the eyes of one associate, Bayard was "a shining star." Another remembered "the magic about him." To many, he seemed destined to become an American Gandhi.[13]

By the early 1950s, opportunities for radical activity, even in the area of race relations, were vanishing. Aware of the rising agitation throughout Africa for independence, Rustin proposed shifting the FOR's focus to support for decolonization. The strategy was to inject nonviolent methods into the independence movements; the larger goal was to open a new space for agitation that might eventually loosen the Cold War grip on politics at home. After extended travels in Africa in 1952, Rustin returned home enthusiastic about the possibilities, and the FOR began raising money for his plans.[14]

And then the roof caved in. In January 1953, while on a speaking tour to promote his African plans, Rustin was arrested in Pasadena, California. Discovered in a parked car with two other men, he was convicted of violating California's lewd-vagrancy law and sentenced to sixty days. The Los Angeles *Times* reported the incident and, since Rustin's lectures on the West Coast had to be canceled abruptly, word spread quickly through pacifist circles.[15]

The Pasadena arrest was not the first time that Rustin's homosexuality was subjected to scrutiny. Sometime early in his tenure at the Fellowship, he and Muste discussed it. Whether Rustin raised the issue himself, or whether Muste initiated the dialogue, is uncertain, and the circumstances and content of these early talks have eluded me. Rustin's primary erotic interest was young white men in their late teens and early twenties, with whom he had ample opportunity for contact through his work. Perhaps rumors about Rustin's approaches had reached Muste. Or, the quick intense bond that A. J. and Bayard formed (almost everyone who knew them during the 1940s referred to it as a father-son relationship characterized by mutual affection and respect) may have impelled Rustin to turn to Muste for guidance. In any case, Rustin's sexuality was grist for gossip among female staffers at the FOR, some of whom were smitten by his charm and good looks. Moreover, by 1943 Bayard was in a relationship with Davis Platt, a nineteen year old whom he had met at a conference, and Platt was now a Columbia student, visiting Rustin frequently at the FOR offices across the street from the campus. Platt does not recall having to hide their intimacy from Muste and the rest of the staff, and so, before Rustin went off to federal prison in 1944, sexual matters had certainly surfaced.[16]

Incarceration sharpened the issue. In the confined atmosphere of jail, the boundary between public role and private desire collapsed. On the eve of a prisoner strike that Rustin was organizing, he found himself accused by the warden of sexual misconduct, and placed in solitary. Rustin lied to his fellow inmates about the reasons for his punishment, and the incident provoked a deeply wrenching, many-layered crisis—with his fellow inmates, with Muste, and with himself. Bayard debated what course his sexual life should take: the way offered by "Marie," a code name he employed for Platt to circumvent the prison censors, or the "challenge" offered by Helen, a Quaker woman in love with Rustin. In letters written to Platt but also intended for Muste's reading, Rustin agonized over his future:

> I must pray, trust, experience, dream, hope and all else possible until I know clearly in my own mind and spirit that I have failed [to become heterosexual], if I must fail, not because of a faint heart, or for lack of confidence in my true self, or for pride, or for emotional instability, or for moral lethargy, or any other character fault, but rather, because I come to see after the most complete searching that the best for me lies elsewhere.

Two weeks later, he was still in struggle.

> Is celibacy the answer? If so how can I develop an inner desire for it? I have a real desire for following another way but I have never had a desire to completely remove sex from my mind. What can celibacy become without such an inner desire? Does not holding M[arie] before me as an object toward whom I project these terrific impulses stifle the beam of light I saw when I spoke with H[elen]?[17]

Muste, meanwhile, wrote back, debating with Bayard the ethics of homosexual relationships. His letters were tender and affectionate, but also blunt. The issue for Muste was not the morality of homosexuality in the abstract. "On the question of a-typical relationships my position has not changed. I insist people must be understood and loved. I keep my mind open." Instead, the older man argued that everything Bayard had confided about his sexual life suggested the conflation of homosexuality and promiscuity, which for Muste represented "the travesty and denial of love . . . an impulse to use and exploit." Muste questioned whether Bayard could play a prominent role in a pacifist movement grounded in Christian ethics while leading an ethically degraded life. "Oh, Bayard, Bayard," he wrote. "No one, *no one,* has any business being self-righteous—but to *ourselves* we do apply standards and there are *some limits* to self-indulgence, to lying, to being the play-boy, for those who undertake to arouse their fellows to moral issues." He made it clear to his protégé that he would take action to protect the movement's reputation should Rustin's actions threaten its integrity. To Rustin, he urged "discontinuance of a certain type of relationship." As he put it in one of his letters, "if thy right hand offend thee, cut it off."[18]

The jail correspondence, and the clarity with which Muste sketched his position, locked Rustin into a duplicitous existence. After his release from prison in 1946, he neither pretended nor claimed to be heterosexual. But his homosexuality remained something apart, and he sought satisfaction in the ways available to gay men who did not immerse themselves in a homosexual social world—through cruising in public places. In October 1946, he was arrested on Morningside Heights for soliciting to commit an indecent act. Interviews with Rustin's associates from these years hint at other incidents, though I have been unable independently to confirm any of them. At some point, Bayard sought psychiatric help, and Muste raised money through pacifist circles to finance Rustin's therapy. Muste was led to believe that "the problem" was under control. But rumors concerning Rustin's sexuality continued to surface, and it is a measure of A.J.'s attachment to Bayard that a final crisis was always averted.[19]

Not so after Pasadena. The FOR executive board quickly issued a statement providing details of the arrest, tracing the history of the FOR's engagement with Rustin on the issue, and announcing that he was no longer on staff. The statement was distributed widely to pacifist organizations and leaders, provoking a debate not only about Rustin but about homosexuality as well.[20]

Rustin was devastated. His correspondence from this time suggests an effort to deflect criticism away from his sexuality. As he wrote to one of his associates, "I have gone deeper in the past six weeks than ever before and feel that I have at last seen my real problem. It has been pride. . . . While sex is a very real problem and while it has colored my personality, I now see that it has never been my basic problem." But, however he might interpret it, the fact remained that he had been branded and cut adrift by the world that had sustained him for twelve years. Without a discourse of homosexual affirmation and oppression, he could only attribute his predicament to personal failing. As a leader in a movement grounded in rigorous self-discipline, Rustin absorbed the blame into himself.[21]

Rustin's journey out of the wilderness began with the aid of another pacifist organization, the War Resisters League (WRL). Secular rather than religious, the WRL saw him as a skilled organizer rather than as a morally compromised soul. Despite efforts by Muste to prevent Rustin's hiring, Rustin joined the staff six months after he returned to New York and remained there for more than a decade.[22]

Rustin and his associates worked as best they could through these reactionary times. In 1955, the WRL and other peace groups initiated a public refusal to participate in civilian defense drills. By the beginning of the 1960s, they were being joined by several thousand persons, until New York State abandoned the program. Also in 1955, Rustin and a few others launched a new independent radical magazine. Grounding itself in a critique of both liberalism and classical Marxism, *Liberation* magazine was committed to economic and social justice under the banner of nonviolent revolution. It exerted an enormous influence on the American New Left, floating ideas that became hallmarks of New Left thinking and raising issues around which the young would rally.[23]

The brightest beacon in these years came from the South. Blacks in Montgomery, Alabama, were engaged in a community-wide mobilization against segregated city buses, and the leaders had stumbled on nonviolent action as their method. One could say that this was the event for which Rustin had been waiting half a lifetime. In February 1956, as the boycott was reaching a critical juncture, Rustin went to Montgomery. In obvious ways, he was an ideal emissary: the leading African American Gandhian in the nation, whose career testified to his commitment.[24]

But Rustin's trip south was no easy matter. In a cloak-and-dagger scenario whose details remain obscure, pacifists and civil rights leaders in New York met, telephoned, and dispatched letters with dizzying speed. Rustin, they argued, was a danger to the movement. It was not only, or even primarily, that he was a New Yorker who had once been associated with the Communist Party. Rather, his arrest in Pasadena, still a vivid memory to his associates, would compromise his effectiveness and subject the Montgomery movement to serious peril. The FOR's southern field secretary, Glenn Smiley, was ordered to avoid any contact with Rustin, and then upbraided when he revealed that their paths had unwittingly crossed. Randolph, Muste, and Norman Thomas, the head of the Socialist Party, were adamant that Rustin should return home.[25]

It is a tribute to Rustin's personal charm, charisma, and skill as a strategist that he survived these machinations and emerged as King's closest adviser. King was not in any sense a committed Gandhian when Rustin arrived. There were guns in his home, and the men who were guarding his house were armed. Rustin initiated the process that transformed King into the most illustrious proponent of nonviolence in the world. He also busied himself with the work of mobilizing support for the boycott, raising funds, organizing rallies, and winning labor union assistance.[26]

Rustin worked with King throughout the 1950s. He devised the plans for what became the Southern Christian Leadership Conference, King's organizational vehicle and the means by which Rustin believed a southwide nonviolent movement would be created. Rustin devoted himself to King's emergence as a national leader. As he wrote to King in 1957, "Actually, Martin, the question of where you move next is more important than any other questions Negroes face today."[27] He deliberately midwived a relationship between King and Randolph who, by this time, was the elder statesman of the black struggle. Using Randolph's stature as a legitimizing tool, Rustin organized a Prayer Pilgrimage to Washington in May 1957, at which King gave his first speech to a national audience, and two youth marches for integrated schools, in 1958 and 1959. These demonstrations gave King and the civil rights movement a national platform and forced the Eisenhower administration finally to meet with civil rights leaders.[28]

Two aspects of Rustin's work in these years deserve comment, one relating to his methods of organizing and the other to his evolving strategic vision. Throughout this period, King rarely made a decision of any consequence without consulting him. Rustin orchestrated much of what unfolded. Yet he appeared at the time, and in subsequent historical accounts, as a shadowy figure, someone deep in the background. Some of this is attributable to a leadership style, long cultivated by Rustin, that fused Quaker and Gandhian influences into a seamless modesty that never drew attention to himself. Some of this was forced on him by his sexual identity. The Baptist ministers in the SCLC did not want Rustin as director of the organization; instead, he was a "special assistant" working in New York. But I wonder to what degree his self-effacement was, all along, an adaptation to the stigma of homosexuality, a concession to the dangers to which it made him, and the causes with which he was associated, susceptible. Rustin, in other words, affected a pose — his own version of the mask that gay men of the era wore — and his dissembling fooled contemporary observers and historians alike.

Rustin's thinking in these years also took on the coloration that defined it for the next decade. Even as he immersed himself in direct action protest — and thus by the standards of the time was deviant, marginal, radical — he conceptualized it as *leading somewhere*. Protest existed not as an end in itself, but as a means to power and influence. Again and again, in his comments on the work of both the peace and the civil rights movement, Rustin called attention to the lack of a political vehicle to move beyond protest. He described the problem in different ways — as the "absence of a vital socialist movement" or, more vaguely, as the need for "a political form."[29] But what it meant for him was that protest alone would never translate into the ability directly to shape foreign and domestic policy.

In the wake of his experience in Montgomery, he came to see the outlines of a solution. "The Democratic Party," he argued, "has to remake itself radically or fall apart." If a revitalized socialist party was not on the horizon, at least the civil rights movement might provoke a political realignment. Injecting the issue directly into the Democratic Party might force a defection of white Southerners, breaking their stranglehold not only over the national party but over key congressional committees as well. The best-case scenario might lead to a thoroughly reconstituted Democratic Party, beholden to a progressive constituency.[30]

With this in mind, Rustin proposed to Randolph a major election-year project for 1960, with massive demonstrations outside the Democratic Party convention in Los Angeles and concerted efforts to shape the party's platform. King, who figured prominently in Rustin's calculations, was drawn into the scheme. Rustin's centrality to the project can be gleaned from the reaction of Randolph when a Rustin visit to West Africa to protest French nuclear testing dragged out longer than expected. Through an associate he communicated to Rustin "your indispensability for ALL non-violent action projects" and urged his immediate return to the states. The surprise eruption of a sit-in movement among southern black students in the winter of 1960, which pushed civil rights to the front page of the nation's newspapers, promised to make the work a resounding success.[31]

But Rustin's plans and influence were derailed again, this time through the manipulation of the gay issue by an African American leader. Adam Clayton Powell, the Congressman from Harlem who fancied himself the black power broker in the Democratic Party, was not prepared to have a queer radical usurp his role. In June 1960, as Rustin's convention plans shifted into high gear, Powell publicly decried the sinister hidden forces who were holding civil rights leaders "captive" and mentioned Rustin by name. Privately, he warned King that unless he abandoned the convention project and dismissed Rustin, Powell would charge that the two were having a homosexual affair. Rustin offered to resign as King's special assistant, expecting King to reject the maneuver. But King panicked, and Rustin again found himself in the cold.[32]

In important ways this incident was far more crushing than the Pasadena arrest. Dave McReynolds, who worked alongside Rustin every day at the War Resisters League and who was himself gay, remembered that "Bayard spent the most miserable time I have ever seen during those months. He was completely demoralized . . . absolutely broken. I hadn't seen Bayard, except in the [Pasadena] jail period, so destroyed. Here was a chance of a lifetime to . . . realign the political process . . . and he was paralyzed."[33] Rustin had fought his way back from pariah status, had shaped and nurtured King's career, had been the invisible guiding hand behind many civil rights initiatives for years, and yet, again, he was being discarded, this time for something that had never happened — indeed, for something that went unnamed. Interestingly, the only public criticism of King's actions that I have encountered came from James Baldwin, the African American novelist and essayist whose work addressed gay issues openly and who also was familiar with exile.[34]

Rustin returned to his peace work. It was not a completely unsatisfying alternative, since dissent from the nuclear arms race was reviving, and Rustin had helped provoke the change in political climate. In the early 1960s, he spent much time in Europe, working on antinuclear campaigns, and in Africa, assisting the Zambian independence struggle by setting up training centers for Gandhian-style resistance. But these were also the years of the civil rights movement's greatest growth, which Rustin had to watch from the sidelines.[35]

Early in 1963, Rustin and Randolph discussed a mass march on Washington for jobs and freedom. At first, their idea roused little interest among other civil rights leaders, but by late spring the situation had changed dramatically. King's Birmingham protests had gripped the nation, and Rustin apprehended a significance to them beyond the public outrage that electric cattle prods had incited. In Birmingham, the black community raised the issue of jobs; they were moving, in other words, beyond civil rights. Birmingham also unleashed a torrent of protest. Through the spring and summer of 1963, the FBI counted more than 1,500 demonstrations in thirty-eight states; it estimated that 40 percent of African Americans had participated. And Birmingham had also stoked a panic within the Kennedy administration, which finally made civil rights a priority. In June, Kennedy addressed the nation on civil rights and proposed major federal civil rights legislation.[36]

Randolph and Rustin kept pressing the march. King lined up behind it, and moderate organizations acquiesced. Early in July, at a planning meeting, Roy Wilkins of the NAACP tried to veto Rustin's role as director, dragging out, once again, the Pasadena arrest. But Randolph finessed the move by accepting the role of director on condition that he be allowed to choose his own assistants. He promptly named Rustin his deputy, and turned over the organizing to him.[37]

Rustin was by no means out of the woods. For years J. Edgar Hoover had kept an eye on the civil rights movement, secretly feeding damaging information to key segregationists. Now the FBI worked overtime, scrutinizing the Washington march as they looked for subversive connections. Early in August, Senator Strom Thurmond of South Carolina, a rabid segregationist, addressed the issue of Communist links and placed information into the *Congressional Record*. But most of it was old news, and it generated little interest, though it did spark worry in civil rights circles. On August 13, Thurmond tried again, this time targeting Rustin, who by then had been dubbed "Mr. March-on-Washington" by the press. He raised the issue of Rustin's old Communist ties and, more explosively, his conviction on "sex perversion" charges. Thurmond placed into the *Record* not only press clippings about the Pasadena incident, but also a copy of the police booking slip. Since such a document was not easily available, and since Hoover had ordered a comprehensive probe of Rustin in mid-July, it seems obvious that the FBI was Thurmond's source of information.[38]

By this time one might think that Rustin was inoculated against feeling on this issue. Yet Thurmond's charges represented something new. In 1953, pacifists had been made privy to Rustin's arrest, but the event was a throwaway item in local papers. In 1960, the conflict with Powell rippled through the nation's press, but the substance remained unnamed. Now the labeling process was clear and ubiquitous. Rustin was named a pervert before an audience of tens of millions.

But the outcome was also unique. Because the accusation was so public, because it was leveled by a segregationist, and because it came just two weeks before an event on which the movement was banking so much, civil rights leaders had to rally to Rustin's defense. Addressing a major press conference, Randolph declared that

> I am sure I speak for the combined Negro leadership in voicing my complete confidence in Bayard Rustin's character, integrity, and extraordinary ability . . . I am dismayed that there are in this country men who, wrapping themselves in the mantle of Christian morality, would mutilate the most elementary conceptions of human decency, privacy and humility in order to persecute other men.

With the elderly, dignified Randolph as spokesman, journalists did not ask probing questions about perversions.[39]

The March on Washington remains enshrined in popular memory as a glorious instant in time. Coming before the assassination of Kennedy, before ghetto uprisings, separatist rhetoric, campus rebellions, and government violence ripped the country into discordant parts, it stands as a symbol of unity, hope, and confidence. Twenty years later, James Baldwin eloquently recalled it as a moment when "it almost seemed that we stood on a height, and could see our inheritance; perhaps we could make the kingdom real, perhaps the beloved community would not forever remain that dream one dreamed in agony."[40] For Rustin, the march was the event that legitimated mass nonviolent protest. In the course of two months the Kennedys had shifted from hostility to endorsement. Members of Congress, who had initially rejected invitations to participate, ended by clamoring for a place on the platform. Labor and church groups had signed on to the cause, and all the major civil rights organizations, including the most conservative, had maintained a united front and thus explicitly had lined up behind mass action.[41]

The success of the march also transformed Rustin's persona. He was now a leader with a media profile and public recognition. He received a steady stream of interviews, invitations to speak, and opportunities to address major gatherings. The relationship with King was repaired for a time, and he was drawn back into King's inner circle. In other words, the perversion card had been played — and finally, so it seemed, trumped.[42]

In the succeeding months, Rustin was a man in motion. Early in 1964, he orchestrated a boycott of New York City's public schools; 45 percent of the system's pupils stayed home, making it the largest civil rights protest in history. He also pulled together a coalition of community, labor, and church groups to march on the New York State capital and to lobby legislators for increases in the minimum wage, funding for public employment, and expansion of job training programs. Rustin was arrested at the opening of the New York World's Fair in a protest against racial bias in hiring. Later in 1964, he organized for A. Philip Randolph a "state of the race" conference in New York City, bringing together leading activists from around the country. In 1965 and 1966, he coordinated an effort to mobilize behind a comprehensive "Freedom Budget," a progressive alternative to the more modest War on Poverty. And, as American involvement in Vietnam deepened in 1964 and 1965, Rustin appeared at rallies and strategized how Martin Luther King might most effectively deploy his influence in the service of ending the war.[43]

Rustin's evolving strategic vision also played itself out in some other political choices that puzzled his associates. In July 1964, after Goldwater's nomination as the Republican presidential candidate, Rustin engineered a call for a moratorium on civil rights demonstrations until after the November election. The following month, at the Democratic National Convention, Rustin forcefully urged the Mississippi Freedom Democrats to accept the compromise offered by Lyndon Johnson. The compromise was rejected, and writers ever since have identified this as the moment when young radicals came to specify liberalism as the enemy. And, as agitation against the Vietnam War grew, Rustin criticized the antiwar movement — for its failure to exclude Communists, for its glorification of violence, and for its anti-American rhetoric.[44]

Several common themes can be found in his actions, his speeches, and his published writing during this three-year period. One was that the Negro struggle had to move beyond civil rights. Jim Crow lunch counters were anachronisms in an advanced capitalist society, and they could be abolished by the deployment of black bodies. By contrast, structural unemployment, crumbling ghetto schools, and slum housing required the transformation of the political economy. The struggle for black equality, in other words, demanded revolutionary changes. Second, Rustin argued that African Americans could not do this by themselves. They needed coalitions. This required not only the articulation of a full social and economic program, but also action to make progressive forces the effective political majority in the United States. In the short and medium term, this was likely to happen only through the Democratic Party. Finally, Rustin believed that direct action had not to be abandoned, but tactically deployed as part of a larger political strategy.

Rustin articulated his overall perspective most succinctly in an article, "From Protest to Politics," that appeared in February 1965.[45] Even today, more than a generation later, it still stands up well as a cogent discussion of American politics, with continuing relevance. And yet "From Protest to Politics" initiated a process by which Rustin was attacked by his fellow radicals — not, this time, for his sexual identity but, instead, for an alleged turn to the right — and steadily isolated from the circles in which he had traveled for two decades.

Two examples capture the left's transformation of Rustin from exemplary organizer to enemy collaborator. Stokely Carmichael, who was widely credited with coining the slogan, "Black Power," considered Rustin in the 1950s to be "the revolution itself, the most revolutionary of men." By 1965 and 1966, he saw Rustin as sad and pathetic, an Uncle Tom whose true colors had been revealed, and in public debates fiercely criticized his former mentor. Meanwhile, in the pages of *Liberation*, the magazine Rustin had helped found, the young radical historian, Staughton Lynd, leveled blistering charges at Rustin. He accused Rustin of advocating "coalition with the marines," of embracing "elitism," and — the most damaging description of all on the left — of serving as a "labor lieutenant of capitalism."[46]

The critique of Rustin that was made then, and repeated since, can be neatly contained within the categories of left-wing political discourse. What, then, do Rustin's ideas and actions in the post-March-on-Washington, post-stigmatized-pervert period, have to do with gay history? A great deal, I think. Something more was happening here, although to speculate about it admittedly involves reaching beyond a hard base of evidence. But let me suggest some connections.

First, Rustin's political perspective was unique among those who had shared his political history in the peace and nonviolent direct action movements — those, in other words, who were self-consciously radical and who occupied a place marginal to the American political system. For instance, in the same article in which Staughton Lynd criticized Rustin for coalition politics, his own more typical "radical" proposal was to convene a people's "continental congress." Rustin, I believe, grasped the bankruptcy of radical marginality in a way that few of his peers did. Having repeatedly suffered from the stigma of the sexual-pervert label, he had lost all attachment to left-wing romanticism. His colleagues may also have been marginal to the political system, but many of them returned home at night to intentional communities grounded in heterosexual patterns of familial sociability. Not Rustin. In 1963, he was fifty-one years old, without a long-term intimate relationship, and, at least politically, he was searching for something more than a place at the periphery.

Second, Rustin argued for his political strategy without an institutional base. For years, the WRL had generously lent Rustin, its executive secretary, to the civil rights movement. But, after the March on Washington, Rustin was drawn more and more toward issues of race and economic justice, and as peace activities intensified, the WRL needed a full-time leader. Rustin was thus moving from one short-term, insecure job to another. He and Randolph tried to convert the March on Washington coalition into a permanent organization, but those plans fell victim to organizational rivalries and battles over turf.[47]

Given his level of skill and accomplishment, Rustin's free-floating status can only be attributed to the continuing stigma of his sexual identity. Even though the overt gay-baiting seemed finally to have been resolved on the eve of the March on Washington, the discomfort with Rustin's sexuality lingered. For instance, throughout late 1963 and early 1964, Martin Luther King debated with his advisers — men with whom Rustin was closely associated — whether it was now safe to bring Rustin on staff. One senses that King wanted to retain Rustin. But in the end, he backed away, and he did so by revising his own history on the issue. In these private conversations, King explained his 1960 dismissal of Rustin not as caving in to Powell's threats, but as a response to Rustin's unrestrained sexual behavior. As King explained to one associate, "I think he controls himself pretty well until he gets to drinking and he would approach these students and they started talking with people about it and there was something of a reflection on me so that was really the main problem."[48] The outcome left Rustin without an institutional home. And his lack of organizational roots made him vulnerable; it made it harder for him to implement his ideas and easier for others to dismiss him.

Third, even when one acknowledges the sharp language of leftist debates, there was a level of invective, a tone of scorn, directed at Rustin that went beyond political disagreement. An example: In September 1963, Stanley Levison discussed with his brother the state of black politics. Levison was a former Communist, a friend of Rustin, and a very close adviser to King, a relationship that they owed to Bayard. Levison's Communist past was regularly invoked by J. Edgar Hoover and the Kennedy brothers to subvert King's effectiveness. In the conversation, Levison grouped James Baldwin and Rustin together and said, "the two were better qualified to lead a homosexual movement than a civil rights movement." A few days later, to a business associate, he described Rustin as "a shrieker," a word that, to me, connotes a gay queen.[49] Coming just a month after Rustin's Washington triumph and from someone reasonably described as an armchair radical, the statements let us see the hidden homophobia in Rustin's world.

Finally, Rustin does, eventually, make something of a turn to the right. Without a base, and indeed, without a job, he accepted the offer of Randolph to head a new institute that the elder leader proposed to create specifically for Rustin. The A. Philip Randolph Institute, devoted to the building of effective alliances between labor and the civil rights movement, remained Rustin's work venue for the rest of his life. But, funded as it was by the AFL-CIO, the institute was necessarily constrained in its ability to dissent from the liberal center of the Democratic Party. During the Vietnam era, this involved fateful compromises, which Rustin made. The war, whose effect on the nation and on the left began to be felt just as the institute was being founded, would shrink the political ground that Rustin proposed to occupy, and he sought secure footing by moving to the right, not the left.

There was an element of resignation, perhaps even cynicism, in these final choices that sits uneasily alongside the profile of the younger Rustin. Shizu Proctor, who worked with Rustin at the FOR in the 1940s, remembers encountering him on the streets of New York about this time, and questioning him. "You get tired after a while," he told her, "and you have to come home to something comfortable and something you can count on."[50] Should this response surprise us? For instance, late in 1964, Rustin supervised the arrangements for King's trip to Europe to accept the Nobel Peace Prize. On his return, he described to two friends an incident in Oslo. One morning in the wee hours, Rustin was called by hotel security to deal with a potentially ugly situation. Apparently, Norwegian prostitutes were running naked through the halls, in and out of the rooms of King's brother and other members of the entourage. Rustin succeeded in keeping these events out of the papers, but what must have run through the mind of this man, whose sexuality had so often been used against him? The homophobia of American society and the response of Rustin's associates to his gay identity are deeply implicated in the political choices he made during these years.[51]

In the end, I think we can fathom at least two layers of gay meaning to Rustin's story. The first is a relatively poignant tale of one man's life and the ever widening circle of disclosure about his identity, stretching from the 1940s through the 1960s. Rustin's identity provoked a series of confrontations within the American left about homosexuality that can be characterized — at least in their *public* manifestations — as a movement from ostracism to acceptance. In that regard, the debate about Rustin foreshadowed developments within American society as a whole.

But Rustin's career offers us a story of much broader significance, a story still gay in its meanings, a story of political alternatives proposed and then abandoned. Rustin's move from margin to center — and then back again — is a tale of gay oppression whose consequences have reverberated loudly in American politics from then until now.

2

Placing Gay in the Sixties

I was born in New York City in the opening years of the Cold War. My Italian American family shared the conservative social, political, and cultural outlook of many Catholics during the crusade against Communism. My parents loved Joe McCarthy, Richard Nixon, Robert Taft, and Barry Goldwater and, as a child and an adolescent, so did I. In high school speech and debate tournaments, I delivered trophy-winning orations about the wisdom of American policy in South Vietnam and the need for the government to prevent labor strikes through a system of compulsory arbitration.

Arriving at Columbia's Morningside Heights campus as a freshman in the fall of 1966, I seemed to be immediately drawn into an unceasing effort to shed every vestige of my upbringing. In no time at all I was attending ecumenical services at which the renegade Catholic priests, Daniel and Phillip Berrigan, gave antiwar sermons; I was dodging eggs thrown at me as I marched around campus protesting the administration's cooperation with the Selective Service system; I was running through the streets of midtown Manhattan as police on horseback dispersed the crowds who had come to protest an appearance by Dean Rusk, the Secretary of State; and I was picketing in front of the residences of New York City draft board members in the hope that, through their neighbors, we could shame them into resigning from what, to me, seemed a murderous occupation.

The "sixties" are the era that shaped me. I think of them with great nostalgia. I remember those times as thrilling, exhilarating, hopeful, exuberant. The universe cracked open and revealed to me endless possibilities.

This essay originally appeared in *Long Time Gone: Sixties America Then and Now*, edited by Alexander Bloom (New York: Oxford University Press, 2001), pp. 209–229. My thanks to Alex for soliciting the piece and for his helpful comments and encouragement at every stage of the writing and editing.

True, some of what it exposed seemed to be the face of evil itself: heartless politicians who ordered the bombing of peasant villages, national guardsmen who shot to kill in America's urban ghettos, and police who beat the students who were standing up for truth and justice. But it also displayed the irrepressible human spirit, the determination of ordinary people to speak truth to power, and the capacity of a generation to reimagine the world.

The trouble with this picture is that if you press me to talk about "the sixties," almost every one of the stories that would spontaneously erupt from my memory are about events that occurred in the 1970s and are associated in one way or another with the gay liberation movement. At first glance this might seem odd, a glaring fault in the workings of my historian's mind that should, naturally, be very attuned to time and chronology. But I prefer to use it as the jumping-off point for a useful observation about historical eras: The "sixties" are less about a time period bound by the start and the end of a decade than they are about an era organically bound together by events, outlook, and mood. My guess is that for many gay men and lesbians, the sixties happened in the seventies.

Gay liberation or, more broadly, homosexuality, is largely absent from historical accounts of the 1960s. It is the forgotten — perhaps, even, the unwanted — stepchild of the era. On the surface, this exclusion seems completely plausible; there is even a certain irrefutable logic to it. History as it is written, after all, is rarely the story of everything that happens but, instead, a narrative of what is salient, what marks a period in some special way. Since the power of homophobia in post–World War II America was so strong, it necessarily forced things gay into the background. When the gay liberation movement was finally born in 1969, in the wake of riots sparked by a police raid of the Stonewall Inn, a gay bar in Greenwich Village, the sixties were just about over. Thus, a new era dawned for gay people just as the previous one was ending for everyone else.

But keeping gay out of the sixties also has an insidious, even if unintended, effect. It helps to shape a certain kind of interpretation of the 1960s and a certain kind of interpretation of homosexuality and its place in American life. The view of the sixties to which I refer has had a long shelf life. One can find it expressed in some of the first historical accounts of the decade, written in the early 1970s, and in some of the more recent assessments, published in the mid-1990s.[1] It is an interpretation framed by the idea of declension, a dizzying rise and just as dizzying a fall of social forces and political movements that initially promised a new era of peace and justice in America. This version of the sixties begins with the inspiration of black student sit-ins in the South and the idealistic rhetoric of the Kennedy presidency. It continues through the uplifting civil rights March on Washington and the historic civil rights legislation of the mid-decade, and rises to the crescendo of reform embodied in Lyndon Johnson's Great Society. It ends with ghettos burning, troops occupying urban black neighborhoods, campuses in turmoil, rioting everywhere, and a presidential administration spying on its citizens and subverting the Constitution.

For historians writing sympathetically about the great popular movements of the 1960s, this outline embodies tragedy. What started hopefully ends despairingly; what began as unifying political impulses degenerated into harsh divisiveness. The inspiration of a militant, but determinedly non-violent, civil rights movement and the vision of an early student New Left that imagined a world of peace and justice for everyone dissolved into movements whose rhetoric was polarizing and often filled with hatred and whose concept of revolution involved picking up the gun. In other words, there is a "good" sixties and a "bad" sixties.

Now stop for a moment, think about this interpretive trajectory of rise-and-fall, and consider what the exclusion of gay from the sixties inevitably does. By relegating it to the end of the story, to a brief mention of the Stonewall Riots as the country is spinning out of control, we inevitably imprison homosexuality and gay liberation in a narrative of decline. While millions of gay men and lesbians around the world look to 1969 as the dawn of a bright new age, everyone else reads it as part of the "bad" sixties and all that follows. And what is it that follows? Not the dawning of the age of Aquarius, as the young singers in the musical *Hair* proclaimed. Not the arrival of racial justice, world peace, and an equitable international economic order. Instead, the bad sixties ushers in a generation-long conservative ascendancy—the triumph of market principles, the dismantling of the welfare state, the decline of the public sector, increasing racial and ethnic polarization, a politics of greed, hatred, and resentment. This is where everything gay belongs. Thus, without exactly saying as much, gay becomes associated with reaction, backlash, and social decay. We might as well be reading Edward Gibbon's *The History of the Decline and Fall of the Roman Empire,* the classic eighteenth-century work that tied Rome's collapse to sexual immorality.

I would like to suggest some ways in which gay can be put back into the sixties. At the very least, my goal is to correct an exclusion. But I also think this exercise can lead toward more creative ways of placing the sixties in the stream of recent American history and of understanding what they were about — for those who lived through the era and for Americans today.

Gay as Echo

One of the most invidious forms that homosexual oppression took in Cold War America was the psychology of separation and marginalization it enforced. Throughout this era, society found endless ways of repeating the message that there was something deeply wrong with being gay: homosexuality was sick, sinful, criminal, depraved, menacing. That message was enacted through police harassment and arrest, firings by employers, physical beatings by thugs, institutionalization by families. For most gay men and lesbians, the result was an abiding sense of difference, reinforced and magnified by the felt need to keep one's identity hidden, secret, and invisible. During these decades, mainstream America and its gay minority engaged in a quiet conspiracy to make it seem that nothing could be more removed from the trends and currents that characterized the nation's life than the experience or aspirations of its homosexual citizens.

Yet if we look closely at one significant expression of gay experience — and of the nation's — in the 1960s, we find not difference, not a huge gaping separation, but surprising parallels. In the realm of collective political action, the gay movement seemed to echo developments in the society around it.

The African American students who initiated the Southern sit-in movement in the winter of 1960 launched a kind of political activism that was new to the era. To be sure, the civil rights movement of the 1940s and 1950s had been vigorous and assertive. But its approach to change had come largely through the lobbying and litigation efforts of an organization like the NAACP. There had been important exceptions to the NAACP's legalistic approach: A. Philip Randolph's March on Washington movement during World War II; the targeted direct action campaigns of the Congress of Racial Equality in Northern cities; the mass rallies in Washington organized by Bayard Rustin in the late 1950s; and, of course, the Montgomery bus boycott. But none of these activities seemed to provoke waves of imitators in the way that the action at a Woolworth's lunch counter did. After the Greensboro sit-in, citizen action took on a decidedly different flavor. Imbued with a conviction that justice was on their side, activists conducted themselves as if they were authorized to make change, as if their judgment about right and wrong deserved precedence over the laws and customary procedures of the society in which they lived.

At the time of the sit-ins, a fragmentary gay and lesbian movement existed in the United States. The Mattachine Society and the Daughters of Bilitis, the two primary organizations, had formed in the 1950s, had published magazines, and were setting up chapters in a few major cities. But they were also caught within the constraints of the McCarthy era in which dissent and nonconformity carried a price. Gay was so far beyond the norm that these first spokespeople for homosexual equality felt obliged to rely, as one of them phrased it, on "pillars of the community" to make their case for them.[2] The early gay movement, in other words, doubted its ability — and authority — to speak on its own behalf. Instead, it depended on the good will of enlightened lawyers, doctors, and ministers to win a hearing from society.

By the early 1960s, with the model of the civil rights movement before them, new voices emerged among gay activists. Frank Kameny, an astronomer who had been fired from his government job for being gay and who, since most work in his field required a security clearance, was thus virtually unemployable, led and typified the more militant approach. He peppered his writings and speeches from these years with references to the struggle for civil rights. The Negro, he wrote in 1964, "tried for 90 years to achieve his purposes by a program of information and education. His achievements in those 90 years, while by no means nil, were nothing compared to those of the past ten years, when he tried a vigorous civil liberties, social action approach." Holding up as an example the self-confidence exhibited by nonviolent demonstrators in the South, he told a gay audience that "we cannot ask for our rights from a position of inferiority, or from a position, shall I say, as less than *whole* human beings."[3]

Kameny amplified his confident assertion of self, which soon won him a bevy of allies in gay and lesbian organizations in the Northeast, through two forms of activist expression central to the spirit of the 1960s. One was a rebellion against authority. Whether it be Southern sheriffs enforcing segregation statutes, or university administrators cooperating with the draft during the Vietnam War, or city governments ignoring the needs of the poor, or psychoanalysts describing woman's allegedly passive nature, authority found itself challenged on every front in the 1960s. Increasingly, the targets of institutional power insisted on the right to define their own experience and claim fully the power to shape their lives. In the case of homosexuality, the church and the medical profession were the twin pillars of cultural power, stigmatizing gay men and lesbians by rendering their sexual desires immoral or pathological. Kameny roundly rejected the external authority of church and science. "I take the stand," he declared, "that not only is homosexuality . . . not immoral, but that homosexual acts engaged in by consenting adults are moral, in a positive and real sense, and are right, good, and desirable, both for the individual participants and for the society in which they live." As to the theorizing of medical scientists, Kameny's organization, the Mattachine Society of Washington, D.C., bluntly announced that "homosexuality is not a sickness, disturbance or pathology in any sense, but is merely a preference, orientation, or propensity, on par with, and not different in kind from, heterosexuality."[4]

The other activist form that Kameny appropriated was public protest. The civil rights movement and the antinuclear movement of the early 1960s had incorporated various forms of direct action into their repertoire of tactics. In doing so they won publicity, attracted new recruits, pressured the targets of their protests into making change or, by the resistance they provoked, aroused the supportive anger of their fellow citizens. But public protest by gay men and lesbians was no easy matter since it meant relinquishing the invisibility — the ability to pass — that protected individuals from sanctions. By the mid-1960s, protest had become so widespread in America — mostly around issues of racism, but increasingly about issues of war and peace as well — that some gay men and lesbians were willing to absorb the risk. In Washington, Kameny and others mounted picket lines outside the headquarters of the Civil Service Commission, the Pentagon, and the Department of State, all agencies implicated in the harassment and persecution of homosexuals. As the 1960s wore on, the impulse toward protest expanded, as did the targets of gay protesters, which included the police in Los Angeles, where several hundred gays rallied in the streets after a particularly violent police attack on a gay bar, and doctors known for their hostile views about gay life, when they spoke at a New York City medical school forum on homosexuality. In a number of cities, gay activists found themselves taking up the cry that African Americans had raised against police brutality, calling for civilian review boards and other forms of citizen control over police behavior.

Before the end of the decade, gay activists were also following the lead of other social movements of the left in the effort to create "alternative institutions" to replace what were seen as the corrupt oppressive institutions of liberal capitalism. In San Francisco and Los Angeles, the first gay newspapers were established. Designed to cover the news that the mainstream media ignored and to provide a different viewpoint on the stories that did appear, they especially exposed the police harassment that was endemic to gay life in that generation and pushed an ethic of gay pride. In 1968 Troy Perry convened the first meeting of what became the Metropolitan Community Church, a nonsectarian Christian congregation founded to allow lesbians and gay men to worship without censure. In New York City, Craig Rodwell opened the Oscar Wilde Memorial Bookshop, stocking his shelves with gay titles that most bookstores eschewed and that many gay men and lesbians would have been too scared to buy in a mainstream retail establishment; soon it became more than a bookstore, serving as an informal community center for the exchange of news and information about gay politics and the gay community.

The gay echo could be heard not only in the arenas of collective protest and community organizing, phenomena quintessentially associated with the sixties, but elsewhere as well. From the late 1950s through the mid-1960s the Supreme Court issued a series of decisions on the matter of censorship that dramatically expanded the range of expression protected by the First Amendment. In the course of the decade, writers and artists — and pornographers too — expanded the boundaries within which creators of literature, art, photography, theater, and film worked. The formal power of Victorian sensibilities, surviving even several decades into the spread of a modernist outlook in the arts, was finally toppled. In its place, Americans found themselves possessors of a much more substantial freedom, as creators and consumers of cultural products, than had previously been the case.

Manifestations of gay experience can be found coursing through the mid-century cultural revolution that we identify with the sixties: in the San Francisco trial of Allen Ginsberg's book of poems, *Howl,* and the boost it gave to Beat cultural dissent; in the ability of a writer like James Baldwin to put sexual issues front and center in his fictional depiction of the ravages of racial conflict in contemporary America; in the shifting content of the Broadway theater, as expressed in a hit musical like *Cabaret,* which was based on the stories of Christopher Isherwood, a gay writer, and that portrayed a range of sexualities; in the explosive growth of the paperback pulp novel, sold in drugstores across America, that offered romance and sexual adventure for a broad spectrum of erotic sensibilities. It can also be found in the writings of a new breed among social scientists who, in the 1960s, were breaking with the detached pose that had characterized much intellectual work during the Cold War. Sociologists like Howard Becker, Erving Goffman, Edwin Schur, and Martin Hoffman frequently drew on the example of gay life and gay oppression to illustrate a theoretical perspective preoccupied with enlarging the sphere of human freedom. Martin Hoffman used the historical example of religious freedom and the Constitution to urge "radical tolerance for homosexual object-choice" as a solution to the "problem" of homosexuality. Writing in the 100th anniversary issue of *The Nation,* in 1965, Becker used the courage of lesbian activists to make the point that sex ought to be "the politics of the sixties" and that sexual expression ought to be one of the "inalienable" rights guaranteed to Americans.[5]

Rather than identify the Stonewall Riots of June 1969 as the *birth* of gay liberation at the *end* of the 1960s, perhaps we would do better to see them for what they were: as symbolic of a shift that had been in the making for a number of years. Rather than containing homosexuality within a narrative structure of "rise and fall," perhaps we can use the eruption of a full-fledged gay freedom movement for a different interpretive purpose: as a sign of just how deeply the changes wrought by the sixties reached into the structures and assumptions of American life. As Charles Kaiser wrote of the 1960s in *The Gay Metropolis,* a history of gay male life since World War II: "Because everything was being questioned, for a moment anything could be imagined — even a world in which homosexuals would finally win a measure of equality."[6] By noticing the many forms that the "gay echo" took in the 1960s, by including it in our historical repertoire of what the sixties provoked, we can interpret the sixties not as an era that failed, not as a story of declension, but as a watershed decade out of which nothing in American life emerged unchanged.

Gay as Sensibility

I cringe a little when I look at that heading. The notion of a sensibility skirts the boundary of stereotyping. When applied to a social group, it smacks of the suggestion that there are some inherent characteristics that all members of a group share other than their oppression. In a gay context, the notion of sensibility also conjures up certain images and specific associations widely held in American culture — of camp and gender-bending, of the aesthete and the dandy; of the sensitive young man of artistic bent. But I mean gay sensibility in another way and am ascribing to it a content very different from what it usually has.

When I think about the sixties, especially about the sixties that have retained value and meaning for me across the decades, certain figures come into mind: James Baldwin, Allen Ginsberg, Bayard Rustin, Paul Goodman. None of them are the "top tier" names that we associate with the decade: Kennedy, King, Malcolm X, the Beatles, Dylan. Two of them, Rustin and Goodman, functioned far enough below the radar screen of history that one needs to be an afficionado of the sixties even to know who they were. Yet, as one scans the decade, it is remarkable how they, and their influence, keep surfacing.

In many ways, these men were dramatically different from one another. Ginsberg was a poet of the cultural fringe, an artistic rebel whose verse ran along the edges of madness and who incorporated into his literary output a mystical spirituality that crisscrossed the boundaries of religious traditions. Without attachment to institutions or organizations, he wandered the globe in the 1950s and 1960s, somehow managing to make appearances at what proved to be key moments in the unfolding of the sixties. By contrast, Baldwin won mainstream success and plaudits, even as he often cultivated in his writing the stance of outsider. Where Ginsberg employed the frenzy of insanity in his verse, Baldwin's prose, whether in his fiction or in the essays that reached a mass audience in the decade, had a razor-sharp realism, a lucidity that left little room for confusion or ambiguity. Moving back and forth in the sixties between the United States and Europe, he served almost as a roving conscience of the nation's racial crisis.

While Ginsberg and Baldwin moved primarily in the arena of literature (though heavily doused with social commentary), Rustin and Goodman operated, respectively, in the spheres of political activism and social criticism. In some ways, Rustin can be considered the "invisible hand" of sixties activism. A Gandhian radical who came of age in the 1930s, he was a stalwart of the post–World War II peace and civil rights movement. Rustin was especially known for his command of the tactics and strategy of protest and social change. He was a close adviser of Martin Luther King in the early stages of King's public career and played an important role in creating for King a national profile; he trained a large number of the key younger activists of the sixties; and he was the mastermind behind the historical March on Washington in 1963. A practical, hardnosed realist, he was always looking for the ways that progressive change, whether in the realm of international affairs or America's racial order, might be institutionalized and made permanent. While Goodman also cared about progressive social policy, he was more the utopian, imagining ideal systems. When he did address himself to what he called "practical proposals," he devoted little energy to detailing the political strategy of making them achievable. A philosopher by training, Goodman wrote prolifically, and his books and essays critiquing American education and examining the role of youth in modern society won him a wide and appreciative audience among the students who comprised the New Left of the 1960s.

To me, the differences among the four are of the formal variety, the kind that surface when one is pigeonholing an individual with a short tag line: poet, political organizer, philosopher. What they had in common ran much deeper.

One area of experience they shared was homosexual attraction and, to varying degrees, a *public* profile as gay or bisexual. In the early twenty-first century, this may not seem to be much to share or even especially significant. So many men have come out of the closet, and gay life is so visible, that we are more easily aware of the differences between them — of class, race, ethnicity, and political viewpoint. How much, after all, do a gay Republican and a queer nationalist, a gay union activist and a gay corporate executive, a gay rock star and a gay waiter, have in common? But in the 1950s and 1960s, secrecy and invisibility were core features of queer experience and, though there was a well-developed public discourse about homosexuality, most of it was condemnatory and written from the outside. A generation ago, then, gay was an even more powerful marker of identity than it is now, and few chose to have themselves marked in this way. To be public implied either great trouble or great integrity, or both.

Ginsberg embraced homosexual passion openly. For those in attendance, his 1955 public reading in San Francisco of *Howl*, a poem that described gay sexuality as joyous and holy, seemed to crystalize the literary and cultural movement known as Beat, itself a portent of the sixties. The *Howl* censorship trial in 1957 gave the slim book of poetry a wide audience and, as the media began to spotlight the Beat rebellion, Ginsberg became perhaps the most visible homosexual in America. Baldwin, too, could be considered openly gay by virtue of what he chose to write, though the codes of discretion observed in the fifties and sixties meant that one was generally not labeled gay unless one committed a misdeed or made a public declaration of identity. Nevertheless, the fact that Baldwin published a gay novel, *Giovanni's Room*, and peopled his bestseller of the early 1960s, *Another Country*, with gay characters, marked him in the eyes of the knowledgeable as queer.

Rustin's case was different from either Ginsberg's or Baldwin's in that he never chose to have his homosexuality be a matter of public record. Within his circle of friends and political associates, Rustin was quietly open about his sexual and emotional leanings as early as the 1940s, an unusual choice for a gay man to make in those years. But his sexuality also became a matter of public controversy on several occasions because of the trouble it brought his way.[7]

Goodman's situation was more complex, since he married twice and was the father of three children. A political and philosophical anarchist, he seemed to delight in injecting matters of sex into situations not typically defined as sexual. It was a propensity that in more than one case cost him a job, including a position at the experimental Black Mountain College in North Carolina. But Goodman was also bold enough to write openly about homosexuality. The subject appeared in *Growing Up Absurd*, his commentary about youth and education that was so influential among radical college students in the 1960s. It also surfaced in his poetry and fiction, which was heavily autobiographical.

As I suggested above, gay identity may not seem such an overriding commonality at the turn of the new millennium, all the hoopla about Ellen Degeneres coming out notwithstanding. But a generation ago, it was a big deal. Whether it happened by choice or imposition, assuming a public profile as a sexual *deviant*, as someone heavily stigmatized by the overwhelming weight of cultural opinion, meant taking on a characteristic of which one was always aware. It branded one's consciousness with a marker of difference, even if one had the independence of character to resist the negative definition that American society attached to it. It necessarily made one perpetually aware of separation, of division in the body of humanity, of marginalization and ostracism. Admittedly, Rustin and Baldwin as African Americans and Ginsberg and Goodman as Jews living in the wake of the Holocaust had other reasons to experience exclusion. Yet Jews and African Americans also had access to strong traditions of community that homosexuals in America did not.

As I think about these four men and try to make sense out of what they offered the United States in the sixties, the abiding perception of estrangement that America's sexual order forced on them leads me to highlight a second commonality among them. Each in his own way functioned as an apostle of hope. Each held out the conviction that the bitter conflicts and the cruel inequalities that caused deep rifts in American society could be overcome. Each believed in an ideal of community expansive enough to include everyone.

In the case of Bayard Rustin, this claim is easy to make. A Quaker by upbringing, in the early 1940s he abjured his involvement with the American Communist movement in part because he rejected the unscrupulousness of its methods — the willingness to rationalize any tactic or strategy if it seemed to advance "the final conflict" in the international war of the classes. Instead, he chose allegiance to a Gandhian philosophy of satyagraha — "truth-force" or "love-force" — with its commitment to active but nonviolent resistance to injustice. Throughout the 1940s and 1950s, in his pacifist activities and in his work to challenge American racism, Rustin faced personal danger again and again without deviating from his attachment to a respectful nonviolence designed to win over his opponent. In his many speeches in these decades, he reiterated his belief that the evil at the heart of war and racism was the sundering of human community, the shattering of a natural impulse toward love and fellowship.

For Rustin, whose sexuality and political radicalism together placed him at the fringe of American life in the Cold War decades, the March on Washington in August 1963 was a revelatory moment. It was not simply that the event's spirit and tone seemed to capture perfectly the sense of unity and community toward which he was always striving in his work. The support that the march won seemed to promise the mainstreaming of a social vision; the power that the march embodied suggested the political ability to implement the vision as well. And so Rustin, who had lived and worked on the margin for his entire adult life, devoted himself in the middle years of the 1960s — before the spirit of the decade had shifted from the "good sixties" to the "bad sixties" — to arguing for a shift "from protest to politics." He believed that the progressive forces in the United States had to find allies, work in coalition, and shift from a rigid outsider mentality as protesters to a more flexible ability to engage the political and economic system from the inside. He believed that the civil rights movement, the emerging white student movement, and the expanding peace movement could forge ties with the churches, organized labor, intellectuals, and the most socially conscious of American liberals. Together they could build a broad progressive alliance capable of becoming the working majority of the Democratic Party and of transforming the American political economy.

We can never know, of course, whether such a strategy, if initiated and pursued by the democratic left in the United States, might have worked in those years. We do know that it was embraced by very few. Major segments of the black freedom movement instead chose a more militant politics that polarized, that created lines of division, that despaired of winning over white America, and particularly white liberals, to their side. Major segments of the white student movement came to see liberalism as intrinsically compromised through its connection to an American capitalist world order. Major segments of the peace movement placed their opposition to American policy in Southeast Asia above their commitment to peace and reconciliation and built an antiwar movement that was at least as anti-American as it was antimilitarist, and that supported uncritically the militarism of the other side.

All these developments, central to how the sixties unfolded, signified in important ways a politics that intertwined rage and despair. And, to many of the actors in these dramas, Rustin's perspective seemed to be a politics of compromise and betrayal. But I wonder if it is not more accurate to see Rustin's efforts as a continuing commitment, under the changed conditions of the 1960s, to reach for unity by building a movement meant to embrace an ever larger part of the American nation. Rustin, in other words, was offering not crass compromise but wild hope, the hope that the vivid exposure of injustice and evil, combined with practical politics, might lead to renewal, to the restoration of community.

One could make a comparable claim for Baldwin in these years. Like many African American cultural figures in the twentieth century, Baldwin chose the existence of an expatriate in France as a way of escaping the grueling insistent cruelties of white America's racism. But as the civil rights movement became the most dynamic social and political force in the United States, Baldwin spent more time on this side of the Atlantic. He rallied other black artists, met with members of the Kennedy administration, and appeared at major public forums with political activists like Rustin. And, always, he wrote—both the fiction that was at the heart of his creativity as an artist but also substantial essays in which he commented on the state of America.

At first glance it might seem strange to label Baldwin a voice of hope in the sixties. To be white, as I am, and to read either *The Fire Next Time* or *Another Country*, his two widely read books of the first half of the 1960s, is inevitably to squirm. Whether as novelist or essayist, Baldwin was unflinching in his description of racism and its impact on African Americans and merciless in his indictment of whites. "This is the crime," he wrote in *The Fire Next Time*, "of which I accuse my country and my countrymen, and for which neither I nor time nor history will ever forgive them, that they have destroyed and are destroying hundreds of thousands of lives and do not know it and do not want to know it."[8] In *Another Country* he depicts various sexual couplings of blacks and whites mangling each other with the sharp edges of their society's racial history. He dressed down Robert Kennedy, the attorney general, for the inadequacies of the Justice Department's initiatives on race; he exploded with fury after the Birmingham church bombing that killed four young black girls.

But Baldwin, like Rustin, believed that redemption could only come if one looked injustice squarely in the face and named it. His critique was meant as a pathway to another place. "We can make America what America must become," he wrote at this time.[9] Choosing to close *Another Country* on a note of hope, he uses his gay characters to deliver the message. He ends with a young French gay man arriving in New York, embracing his new country and his male American lover.

As with Baldwin, one can find in both Ginsberg and Goodman this dual perspective: the naming of all that is wrong with modern America yet, still, a message of hope. Whether it be Ginsberg leading a gathering of hippies in a Buddhist chant in San Francisco's Golden Gate Park or Goodman determinedly producing one of his utopian essays, the two of them projected some measure of optimism about the ability of right-thinking Americans to chart a saner course for a nation that by the late 1960s did seem to be spinning out of control. Like Baldwin, too, their note of hope often times seemed attached to their experience of gay sexuality. In an essay Goodman published late in 1969, he explicitly addressed his gay identity and the politics of homosexuality. "In my observation and experience," he argued, "queer life has some remarkable political values. It can be profoundly democratizing, throwing together every class and group more than heterosexuality does. Its promiscuity can be a beautiful thing."[10] Frank in his criticism about the things that were not right with gay male life, he nonetheless saw it as a counter to the coldness and fragmentation that characterized contemporary America.

Now let me be clear, at least, about what I am *not* saying. I am not trying to claim that there is something about male homosexuality and gay life that inherently points gay men in the direction of community and makes them messengers of hope in a fractious society. I am not saying that this is even true of gay men as a group in this particular era of history. But imagine, for a minute, other groupings of key male activists or engaged cultural workers associated with the sixties. If I had chosen Stokely Carmichael, Norman Mailer, Malcolm X, and Jerry Rubin, would the themes of hope and community so readily emerge?

I am trying to point our attention to an opening, an unobserved window onto an understanding of the sixties. When we look at the careers of the four men I have highlighted, at the animating vision behind their work, we find something that stands outside an interpretation that emphasizes failure. Not, mind you, because they succeeded, or because their dreams of a new world were realized, but because they felt impelled to hold them out steadfastly to the rest of us, and to hold on to them for themselves in the years that followed. I think there is reason to believe that in the mid-twentieth century, the experience of gay oppression provided a particular angle of vision that brought certain themes, aspirations, and civic desires to the foreground. If we dig more deeply, what might emerge from excavating this territory? Can we learn something different about the sixties? Does it allow us more readily to imagine placing gay back into the sixties and seeing the sixties, accordingly, in new ways?

Gay as Harbinger

In questioning the persistence of a "rise-and-fall" interpretation of the 1960s, I am not offering in its place the inverse: a story of the great march forward of progressive social and economic change. Anyone who has lived through the past two decades knows that we are in the middle of an era of conservative ascendancy. In the realm of party politics, the Republicans have grown and moved to the right; the Democrats have shrunk and moved to the right. The changing tax structure and the balancing of the federal budget, the direction of social policy as evidenced by the debates over welfare, the growing disparities in income and wealth, the composition of the federal judiciary, particularly the Supreme Court, and the mass incarceration of young African American men are some of the more obvious indicators of the shift. And the conservative wave has not yet crested.

Even as we acknowledge this, we also cannot escape the fact that there are living legacies of the sixties. Without the civil rights and black power movements of those years, we would not as a society be debating today the merits of multiculturalism. Without the resurgence of feminism in the sixties, we would not today find women just about everywhere in public life. And without the broad cultural shifts that the era of the sixties induced, we would not be living today with something thoroughly new in the history of modern Western societies — a mass movement for freedom of homosexual expression.

Yet all of these legacies, and probably others we could name as well, are still being fought over. None are secure; none offer predictable futures. If we define the dynamic edge of the 1960s as those forces campaigning for a just and equitable society, it is difficult to identify what is permanent about the decade's achievements *and* how those achievements position the nation to move once again in those directions. What, in other words, can the outcome of the sixties tell us about what is to come and how it will materialize? What of the sixties still resides with us so that a peaceful world, a fair distribution of wealth, and a civic culture in which no social groups experience forced exclusion or subordination, come closer to realization?

Let me suggest that a productive approach to these questions, and to understanding post-sixties America as something other than the triumph of reaction at home and abroad, might come through a look at gay America in the past generation.

One way of seeing gay as a carrier of the era's legacy is simply acknowledging the history of the gay and lesbian movement since the end of the 1960s. By the 1970s, the black freedom struggle was in disarray, divided and wary about the future. Feminism retained a dynamic quality for much of the 1970s, but the growth of a vigorous antiabortion movement in the second half of the decade and the final defeat of the Equal Rights Amendment in

1982 put the women's movement on the defensive. By contrast, the gay and lesbian movement has over the past thirty years grown in size, extended its influence, and expanded its list of achievements. This has not happened at a steady pace; there have been reversals and setbacks along the way. But, overall, it is remarkable that, in the midst of a deepening conservative impulse in American political life, this movement for social justice has marched forward.

One can point to a number of concrete measures of change. Since the late 1960s, a majority of American states have repealed sodomy laws that were as old as the nation and that led to the arrest and conviction of large numbers of Americans every year. In a dozen states, and most of the nation's large cities, civil rights law has been expanded to ban discrimination on the basis of sexual orientation. The federal government, which prohibited through much of the Cold War the employment of gay men and lesbians in *any* government job, has gradually relaxed these restrictions until only military service remains inaccessible. The American Psychiatric Association has eliminated the classification of homosexuality as a disease, which for decades had not only served to stigmatize gay and lesbian relationships, but also led to the involuntary institutionalization of many.

At the level of social life and daily experience, it is not too much to say that, for millions of gay men and lesbians, the changes of the past three decades have been nothing short of revolutionary. The constant, incessant fear of discovery and punishment has abated. The sense of carrying a dreadful stigma has lifted. Instead of being weighed down by a terrible loneliness that the enforced secrecy and invisibility of a homophobic society had imposed, gays and lesbians have created vibrant communities with robust institutions. Whereas in the early 1960s one could, at best, hope to find some bars where homosexuals could meet, gay men and lesbians in the past generation have invested heavily in the construction of organizations and institutions to knit people together. There are churches and synagogues for expressions of religious faith. There are health clinics, youth organizations, family services, senior citizen groups, and twelve-step programs to care for people's physical and psychological well-being. There are community centers that house an endless array of activities and services. There are political action and advocacy organizations designed to express the collective voice of the community in public affairs. There are bowling and softball leagues, bridge tournaments, running clubs, and outdoors groups that make recreation a community-building experience. Bookstores, arts and film festivals, conferences for writers, and theater workshops foster cultural expression and intellectual life. Among gay men and lesbians the impulse toward community building, certainly one of the signature impulses of the 1960s, has been extraordinary. It may not be too much to claim that, in a generation in which jeremiads about the collapse of community in America are commonplace, many gay men and lesbians have become the repository of vital wisdom about valuing and maintaining a vigorous communal life.

As with community life, so too with citizen action and empowerment. In an era in which disgust with politics and citizen apathy are widespread, in which the only mobilizations seem to be the armies of Christian conservatives on the march, the gay and lesbian community has been an important counterpoint — even though its significance has been largely ignored by progressives in America. At the level of both local and national politics, the community has been in an almost constant state of political agitation over the past twenty years. Some of what it has done looks like the routine operation of "interest group" politics. Thus, there are now about three dozen state federations, none of which existed twenty-five years ago. They lobby, coordinate constituent visits to the legislature, conduct voter registration, and sometimes organize statewide mobilizations. But just as often the gay and lesbian movement has kept alive a tradition of direct action and community organizing that one associates with the best of the sixties. In 1987 and again in 1993, national marches on Washington brought out more people than any demonstration of the 1960s. Gays and lesbians organized a mass civil disobedience outside the Supreme Court in 1987, the largest ever mounted against that venerable institution. The direct action protests of AIDS activists in the late 1980s and early 1990s built on the tactics developed by civil rights and antiwar demonstrators of the 1960s and extended by the antinuclear agitators of the late 1970s. They adapted the techniques of nonviolent civil disobedience to an MTV, media-saturated generation, devising eye-catching and attention-grabbing forms of protest. As the millennium ended, groups like Digital Queers were pioneering ways of adapting cyberspace to the requirements of political organizing.

I know that, for some Americans, the above paragraphs about the flowering of a gay community and gay politics read like a litany of what's wrong with America. For political and religious conservatives the growth of the gay movement and the rise of visible gay communities are elements of moral decay, and they have no difficulty in saying so, as public statements by Trent Lott, the Senate majority leader, Gary Bauer, a former Reagan administration official who now leads the Family Research Council, and William Bennett, a conservative educator and best-selling author, make clear. And I suspect that many on the left, many liberals and progressives, also experience varying levels of discomfort at the spread of sexual identity politics. While they would not object to the existence of a gay movement, the steady injection of gay issues into public debate seems to them symptomatic of the collapse of the serious politics of the sixties, another instance of the twilight of common dreams. Instead of an insistent focus on matters like America's global economic imperialism, justice for African Americans and immigrants of color, economic democracy and the welfare state, politics has devolved into a concern with mere lifestyle issues, into trivial inessential topics like sexual freedom.

But even the ground on which an American progressive tradition has staked itself—democratic participation, expanded notions of equality, justice for all—offers a firm footing for gay agitation. If the essence of being gay or lesbian concerns the pursuit of love, affection, intimacy and passion, if it is about the building of close human relationships, then surely it is a good thing that police across the country no longer arrest tens of thousands of Americans every year for something as innocent as holding hands in a bar. Surely it is a good thing that when men and women have epithets thrown at them and a baseball bat swung in their direction, they feel entitled to expect that the police will apprehend the assailants rather than add to the pain of the assault. Surely it is a good thing that a group of citizens is not formally excluded from major segments of the labor market. Surely it is a good thing when they do not have to worry that the discovery of the most loving relationships in their lives could mean the loss of their livelihood.

There is yet a second, perhaps more important, way in which gay not only carries forward the legacy of the sixties but points us toward what a new progressive political vision might embody. Increasingly since the early 1970s, political conflict and social justice struggles have developed around matters that once were defined as existing within the realm of private or personal life. Increasingly, sexuality and the family have become the fulcrum not only of public discourse but of policy debates and policy making as well. The list of issues is a long one: abortion, contraception, and reproductive rights; sex education and teenage pregnancy; censorship of the arts and the internet; wife-battering, incest, and the abuse of children; no-fault divorce laws and single-parent families; rape and sexual harassment; AIDS funding and prevention strategies; and, of course, the panoply of issues connected to the gay movement. Without too much effort, most of us can probably also generate a list of headline-making sex scandals, paralleling each of these issues, that mesmerized the public for long stretches of time.

Interestingly, the shift of sexual and family-based matters from the realm of the private to the center of national politics has even reshaped how issues more typically associated with the quest for economic and social justice are debated. From the presidency of Ronald Reagan through the rewriting of federal welfare law in 1996, the suggestion of sexual immorality threaded its way through the public discourse about welfare. Nativist attacks on immigrants and the renewed call to restrict the number of foreigners admitted to the United States are often rife with allusions to the procreative excess of immigrant populations: their children allegedly will overrun the schools and drain the resources of other public services.

There are good reasons why, even as the remnants of the American left rail against NAFTA, the IMF, and the depredations of global capitalism, sex and the family agitate our body politic. The connections between macro-level world economics and the micro-reality of personal life are real and substantial. As the movement of global capital and the fluctuation of world currency markets make us subject to powers beyond individual control, the need for dignity, security, and freedom at the level of intimate relationships and the uses of the body have become more important than ever. Solutions to problems in these areas, of course, cannot be divorced from changes in the rules of international economics. But a politics of economic and social justice that doesn't attend openly to the felt insecurities and aspirations of people at the level of the intimate won't bring folks to the barricades either. The extension of long-standing traditions of democratic rights to incorporate the realm of the intimate and the reframing of long-standing battles for economic and social justice in ways that incorporate the sexual behavior of peoples seem to be a requisite for a next cycle of progressive politics and social change.

Embedded in the rise of a people who call themselves gay are some gripping questions about how capitalist societies have evolved in the twentieth century and how they might be reorganized in the twenty-first. What has made it possible for a group of people to coalesce who choose to live outside a reproductive family unit? What can this development tell us about the changing relationship of the family and the individual to economic life in an increasingly global capitalist order? What options for personal freedom *and* for new forms of community does it offer? How might "family" come to look differently and have new and expanded meanings? How might we want consciously to change the structure of economic life in order to encourage the range of options that people choose in pursuit of intimacy, family, and community? Are the present ways that capitalism orders life — the privatization of reproduction and childrearing; the demand that more and more adults be drawn into the labor market; the shrinking resources available to the nuclear family — the best way to do things?

When gay liberation and lesbian feminism emerged at the end of the 1960s, these were the kinds of questions they put on the table. As movements, they not only offered incisive critiques of the organization of the family, sexuality, and gender, but they also developed in their practice ways of living that looked beyond the Ozzie and Harriet version of private life. New forms of invented kinship, new ways of fostering community, even new forms of conceiving children and raising them, were bred into the bones of these young liberation movements. In the 1980s, the AIDS epidemic dramatized, for those Americans curious enough to notice, that gay America carried within it an ethic of family and community that was deep and broad. In death as well as in life it turned out that a people stereotyped for their isolation and loneliness were able to draw into their circle caring friends, lovers, former lovers, the friends of their former lovers — people, in other words, without the formal legalistic relation of family that normally defines the limits of our personal responsibility. The compassion-numbing conservatism of the country at the start of the George W. Bush presidency makes all this seem distant; even within the gay community, the public battle seems to have devolved into a quest for marriage. But this should not obscure for us that out of the sixties emerged a movement that took the decade's ideals, applied them to the realm of the intimate, and over the past generation struggled against great odds to realize new meanings for human freedom and social justice.

*   *   *

In September 1997, in Washington, D.C., the National Gay and Lesbian Task Force held its annual Honoring Our Allies reception. As the name implies, the event is designed to acknowledge that gays and lesbians are not fighting for their rights alone and without help. That year, the honorees included Coretta Scott King, the widow of the slain civil rights leader, and John Sweeney, who had recently been elected president of the AFL-CIO; Senator Edward Kennedy presented the award to Mrs. King. The evening brought together sixty years of the American progressive tradition: the labor movement, which defined the militant social justice politics of the Depression decade; the civil rights movement, which propelled progressive politics forward in the 1960s; and the liberal wing of the Democratic party, which has been the electoral force that has institutionalized elements of a progressive vision of economic and social life in America. And the instigator of the evening was the movement that, in this current conservative era, has tried to keep alive and extend a progressive American tradition.

It will be at least a while yet before a new progressive politics asserts itself as a dynamic shaping force in American society. But when it happens, as it certainly will, this even newer left will inevitably draw on its sense of history and the relevance of historical traditions that preceded it. It will be stronger if it is able to look to a sixties, so emblematic of protest and political passion, in which gay is thoroughly integral, and if it acknowledges a more recent past in which gay has carried legacies from the sixties forward, along the way enriching our sense of what freedom and social justice might mean.

3

Still Radical After All These Years: Remembering *Out of the Closets*

It pleases me, on many counts, to see a twentieth anniversary edition of *Out of the Closets: Voices of Gay Liberation* brought into print. As a historian, I hear in these documents the distinctive voices of a particular era. As a teacher of twentieth-century U.S. history, I will now more easily be able to introduce my students to these essential threads in the fabric of those times. As an activist, I know that these articles and essays continue to speak to the aspirations of lesbians and gay men struggling for freedom. And, as a gay man, I can only say that *Out of the Closets* is like a special friend who touched my life profoundly and then disappeared for a long time. It's nice to have her back.

For the reader encountering *Out of the Closets* for the very first time, it may be difficult to appreciate what an extraordinary impact it had when it was originally published in 1972. Today, students on many college campuses can take queer studies courses. There are offerings in departments of English, communications, history, sociology, political science, philosophy, anthropology, art history, and many more. In a number of cities, bookstores are doing a thriving business by specializing in material on lesbian, gay, bisexual, and transgendered topics; many other retail outlets have gay sections. There are newspapers and magazines galore, published by and for the queer community. University presses are editing special series on lesbian and gay studies while some commercial publishers are competing fiercely to acquire

This essay originally appeared as the foreword to the twentieth anniversary edition of *Out of the Closets: Voices of Gay Liberation*, edited by Karla Jay and Allen Young (New York: NYU Press, 1992), xi–xxix. My thanks to both of them for the opportunity to revisit the literature of the early gay liberation movement and comment on its historical significance.

fiction, memoirs, social science, and literary studies that deal with the experience of sexual minorities.

It wasn't always so. *Out of the Closets* was one of a spate of books published
in the early 1970s. Publishers in those days were scrambling over each other
to get access to manuscripts that represented the latest political fever. (I
know I'm being a little unfair with this characterization. Publishing was
affected by the radicalism of the 1960s, and many trade houses had socially
conscious editors who saw their efforts to get these books out as a form of
political activism.) Many texts of the Black Power movement made it into
print in the late 1960s, as did groundbreaking works by radical feminist
writers like Kate Millett, Robin Morgan, Shulamith Firestone, and Ger-
maine Greer. When gay liberation came along, it too generated a vibrant
political literature. Dennis Altman's *Homosexual: Oppression and Liberation,*
Sidney Abbott and Barbara Love's *Sappho Was a Right-On Woman,* and
Donn Teal's *The Gay Militants* were among a smattering of books that saw
the light of day as part of this first wave of post-Stonewall writing. The
"boomlet" didn't last long, however, and it would be a number of years
before the stream of lesbian and gay books flowed with the speed of the early
1970s. But that only made books such as *Out of the Closets* all the more
precious. I cherished my copy.

*   *   *

I can date with fair precision my initial encounter with *Out of the Closets.* In
the early spring of 1973 I made my first venture into the world of gay
liberation. Before that, over a period of several years, I was engaged in my
own process of "coming out" — at least in the sense those words carried
before gay liberation transformed the meaning of the phrase. In the sixties,
coming out signified an acceptance of one's homosexuality and a willingness
to acknowledge it to other gay men and lesbians.

That much I had done. After first discovering as a high school student a
world of gay male sex in the subways of New York, and then finding a street
cruising scene, I had finally come to the point of realizing that each sexual
experience with a man would not be my last. This is who I was, I decided,
and though it wouldn't make my life easy, I had better come to terms with
it. In college, I began telling my closest friends that I was gay. (Actually,
homosexual was the word I used then.) I met a small circle of other gay
undergraduates in the dorms at Columbia. When I tricked, I began giving

my real name and phone number to my partner. During my last two years of college, I had a lover, a man ten years older and far more knowledgeable about gay life. He introduced me to the world of Greenwich Village, and I realized that our numbers were much greater than my random encounters had led me to believe. I also read as much as I could in those pre–gay liberation days. I consumed Andre Gide and Oscar Wilde and James Baldwin and Tennessee Williams (the kind of books and plays that some of the articles in *Out of the Closets* talk about). I saw a performance of *The Boys in the Band* and, though gay liberationists would attack the play as self-hating and oppressive, to me it was sweet as nectar.

I first heard about Stonewall from a distance. I was traveling in Europe with my lover Billy during the summer of 1969 and, that August in Paris, I picked up a copy of the *Village Voice* in which the Stonewall Riots were described. We knew this was important, but also didn't quite know what to make of it. That fall back in New York, gay liberation was in the air. There was a student group on my campus, but it felt too close to home for me to participate. One evening in the spring of 1970, I ventured alone (no gay friend would accompany me) to a church in the Chelsea section of Manhattan, where the Gay Activists Alliance held its meetings. I remember it as a stormy, animated gathering, and I didn't follow much of the proceedings. But, more to the point, no one spoke to me, a newcomer, and I was too tense and shy to initiate a conversation, so I never went back. That June, I heard about the upcoming march to commemorate the first anniversary of the Stonewall Riots. I wanted to go, and talked to my new lover and his friends about doing it together. Their response was so negative — the idea of fags marching put them in stitches — that I dropped the idea.

But for someone of my generation and experience living in New York City, gay liberation was inescapable. I had been involved in the antiwar movement and thought of myself as "radical." I was a soft-core hippie: I had long hair, wore sandals, dropped acid, lived in a group household, and had imbibed the ideas of sexual freedom that were rife in the counterculture. Many of my women friends and acquaintances had been struck by the new wave of feminism, and were talking about gender and sex roles all the time. My life was becoming more densely gay. I lived with my lover, we had lots of gay friends, and we and our friends were all tricking a lot. Inevitably, gay men finally were drawn into my world who had some involvement in the gay movement. The ripples from Stonewall were simply uncontainable.

When one of those acquaintances, Bert Hansen, invited me to a meeting of other university-affiliated gay people, I jumped at the chance. That Saturday gathering in March 1973 changed my life. It wasn't exactly a consciousness-raising group, but it certainly raised mine. I had never experienced anything quite so thrilling before. I was a second-year graduate student, approaching the point when I would have to choose a topic for my dissertation, and here were other graduate students, professors, and writers, talking about possibilities that I had never dreamed of. A blending of what I then thought of as my personal life with my inchoate professional identity had begun.

Over the next weeks and months that group continued to meet, growing by leaps and bounds. We transformed ourselves into the Gay Academic Union (GAU), one of whose goals was to foster scholarship on the lesbian and gay experience. It was a heady time. Many of the men and women I met in those years, like Betty Powell and Ginny Apuzzo, went on to become leaders of national significance in the movement. Others, like Martin Duberman, Joan Nestle, Jonathan Katz, and Julia Penelope, became key figures in the emerging field of lesbian and gay studies.

At this distance of almost two decades, two things about the early GAU remain most vivid. First, we argued passionately about everything. The intensity of feeling that characterize many of the documents in *Out of the Closets* was expressed among us. Whether we had been gay for a generation already or were just coming into "the life," we were discovering, even inventing, our identities, and especially as gay or lesbian political beings. We fought over bisexuality, over feminism, over the name and purpose of the organization, over how to draw more lesbians into the group, and over how, in the meantime, we could create a structure that would give lesbians an equal voice even if their numbers in GAU were smaller. Second, we had meetings, seemingly all the time. There were general meetings, conference committee meetings, men's caucus meetings, public forum meetings, consciousness-raising group meetings, study group meetings, newsletter committee meetings, and meetings to thrash through the problems caused at other meetings. I'd never been to so many meetings in my life. And, since quite a number of them were held at the large Morningside Heights apartment that I shared with several other men, my life for a while seemed very much like what John Knoebel describes in "Somewhere in the Right Direction," his essay in *Out of the Closets*.

It was through one set of these meetings—a GAU study group that formed in the summer of 1973 — that I encountered this collection by Karla Jay and Allen Young. Though I had read a good bit of homosexual-identified literature, I still hadn't probed any of the writings of gay liberation. I can no longer remember whether we read *Out of the Closets* together that year, but I do know that it was one of a small stack of books that I acquired at the Oscar Wilde Memorial Bookshop on Christopher Street and that I proceeded to devour.

These voices of gay liberation captured me, heart and soul. I recognized the writers as comrades. While GAU was the organizational context in which I first came to the gay movement, it was a motley collection of people. We were united by the fact of our gayness and by our institutional connection to higher education. Beyond that, our commonality dissolved. Our political views stretched across the spectrum from conservative to radical; some of us were "straight" in our values; others of us had been deeply affected by the counterculture, the New Left, and feminism. By contrast, the activists represented in *Out of the Closets* seemed like "my people." They were of my generation. They spoke in the radical accents that excited me. To them, gay liberation was about revolutionary transformation, about a society without exploitation and oppression, without the inequalities and injustices that many young men and women of my age cohort were fighting against.

As I read these essays, I felt as if I were making a whole new host of friends. I was awed by the audacity of Martha Shelley's angry polemics. I chuckled at the images Gary Alinder evoked of gender-bending gay radicals disrupting a panel of psychiatrists. I was struck by the raw power of "The Woman-Identified Woman." Reading the achingly personal testimony of Konstantin Berlandt, Mike Silverstein, John Knoebel, and some of the other gay male contributors, I tapped into reservoirs of old pain from my own years of struggling to come and accept myself. This book was a cathartic experience.

* * *

Even though I suspect that *Out of the Closets* can still speak in a direct and immediate way to readers today, it is also a historical document. I want to place it in its context and suggest some of the features that mark it as the product of a particular moment in time.

Every social movement, every people, creates a mythology. For gay men and for lesbians, Stonewall is a central piece of ours. Many of the essays in

Out of the Closets refer to the Stonewall Riots, that glorious moment when the patrons of a New York City gay bar fought the police. Out of that riot came the New York Gay Liberation Front (GLF), whose members contributed mightily to the radical stream of words that the movement produced. New York GLF also became the prototype for scores, even hundreds, of other groups that formed across the country in the next two or so years. A radical mass movement was born.

But major social insurgencies do not spring into existence with the wave of a fairy godmother's magic wand. They have roots and sources. They are the product of complex currents of social change, often traveling underground, often invisible or seemingly negligible; they come to our attention only at the moment when they have gathered enough force to burst through natural barriers or when several streams have flowed together to create a mighty river. Stonewall was that moment. But what had come before?

For almost twenty years prior to Stonewall, a small collection of gay men and lesbians was fashioning a politics in what many of them referred to as the homophile movement. Like today's lesbian and gay movement with its roots in the radicalism of the Stonewall generation, the homophile movement also had a radical beginning. The handful of gay men who formed the Mattachine Society in Los Angeles in 1950 and thus launched a history of political struggle that continues to this day were either members of the Communist Party or what were then called fellow-travelers. Also like the post-Stonewall movement, radicalism did not remain the dominant tendency for long. This was, after all, the McCarthy era, and in those days ordinary gay men and lesbians were as suspicious of leftists as were most Americans. But the movement they began survived the perils of that era and through the fifties and sixties it grew steadily, even if slowly. Through organizations like the Mattachine Society, the Daughters of Bilitis, ONE, Inc., the Society for Individual Rights, the Janus Society, and others, a hardy band of men and women tried as best they could to challenge society's hostility to homosexuality and the caste-like status into which lesbians and gay men were thrust.

It would be foolish to claim that homophile activists met with resounding success. Nonetheless, by the time of Stonewall they had achieved some important, though limited, victories. The Supreme Court had affirmed the right of a homophile publication, *ONE Magazine,* to use the mail: gay or lesbian was not, in other words, automatically to be judged "obscene." The first employment-discrimination cases had been won in federal court. In a number of states, courts had issued rulings providing gay bars with some measure of protection from the arbitrary closings initiated by state liquor commissions. In New York and San Francisco, police harassment had been somewhat contained. Homophile activists had initiated a dialogue with religious leaders from a number of Protestant denominations and with members of the scientific community. (To the extent that some doctors and mental health professionals were publishing research in those years affirming our sexuality, they depended on homophile organizations for obtaining subjects.) The ACLU had been enlisted in the cause of lesbian and gay rights. Activists were picketing and demonstrating in public and receiving media visibility because of it. Some fifty homophile groups existed, and they were no longer confined to California and the Northeast. Less tangibly, activists were responsible for spreading the idea that homosexuals were not isolated freaks or pathological individuals, but members of a mistreated minority group who deserved respect and dignity. This idea had not exactly won mass acceptance, not even within the gay subculture, but it was there to be discovered, in a way that had not been true a generation earlier.

None of this is the stuff of revolutionary transformation, but we shouldn't dismiss it. Homophile activists had opened up a social, cultural, and political space that was new. The Stonewall generation would make that space wider.

Another current of change involved alterations in the broad pattern of the nation's sexual mores and behavior. We often speak glibly of American "puritanism," or of our "Victorian" morality. But the fact is that neither of those two labels accurately describes the sexual world of the mid-twentieth century. By the post–World War II era, much had changed. Contraception had been incorporated into the habits of most married couples; young people of every class and race had created a vibrant sexual culture that strained at the limits that their elders tried to enforce. The Kinsey reports on male and female sexual behavior had exploded the myth of American sexual innocence, demonstrating the wide gulf that existed between dominant public norms and the everyday behavior of millions.

During the 1960s the pace of change seemed to accelerate. In 1960, the Food and Drug Administration approved the marketing of oral contraceptives. The pill was something of a symbolic marker in the history of sexuality. This seemingly magic contraceptive was heralded as promising sure-fire protection against pregnancy; significantly, few warnings were raised about what this might mean for "traditional" morality. Under Chief Justice Earl

Warren, the Supreme Court was handing down a number of rulings that dramatically narrowed the scope of federal and state obscenity statutes. The effects were felt almost immediately. In literature, the press, the movies, and television, sex was more overtly represented. Helen Gurley Brown's *Sex and the Single Girl* was a bestseller for months. *Playboy* was the publishing success story of the 1960s. Much of this new frankness in sexuality was crassly commercial and exploitative, and it was heavily gendered, as women's liberationists were soon to point out. But it also legitimated sexual expression apart from procreative intent.

Although the so-called sexual revolution of the 1960s was flagrantly heterosexual in its overt character, it also had a subversive impact on prohibitions against homosexuality. With millions of American women using the pill, how could one reasonably justify heterosexuality in terms of procreation? How, indeed, could one revert to a defense of it in terms of the natural, when modern technology was obstructing the natural outcome of heterosexual intercourse? The emphasis on individual sexual pleasure as a positive good, as one of the rewards of a prosperous postindustrial society, made the mores of the gay subculture less at odds with American life. Indeed, one can imagine some gay men and lesbians in the bar world seeing themselves as explorers of a new frontier.

This is not to suggest that change in the sexual culture of American society would have led to the evaporation of prohibitions against homosexuality. Only an organized movement would be able to accomplish that. But by the late 1960s, a space had opened in which one could argue that gay was good, too. (In fact, the homophile movement had adopted "Gay is good" as a slogan in 1968.) Some of the ideological props that held gay oppression in place were beginning to wobble.

Last, but by no means least, there was the radicalism of the 1960s. By 1969, millions of ordinary Americans, and especially the young, were in rebellion against the order of things. The civil rights movement had demonstrated that the traditionally powerless and oppressed could shake a nation. The black power movement that succeeded it offered a model of an oppressed group that took the social markers of oppression and transformed them into symbols of pride and self-affirmation. The white student movement was challenging the authority of campus administrators. A powerful antiwar movement was in open revolt against its national government. A new generation of young feminists was articulating a political language of gender and sexuality. The counterculture, that diffuse impulse among the young, was breaking with the materialism of American society and pushing toward new vistas of sexual freedom. Each of these movements spoke in some way to the situation of gay men and lesbians. Of equal importance, many young lesbians and gays were cutting their political teeth in one or the other of these radical movements.

Put all these currents of change together and the gay liberation movement seems like an event waiting to happen. One can see the effects of the homophile movement, the changes in American sexual values, and the radicalism of the sixties coming together on Christopher Street the night of the riot. The homophile movement in New York City had succeeded three years earlier in winning for gay bars a reprieve from harassment by the State Liquor Authority as well as in convincing the liberal Lindsay administration to rein in the city police. When the cops raided the Stonewall they were crossing a boundary that had come to seem secure. The Stonewall itself reflected the sexual flavor of the late 1960s. Unlike the staid, secretive bars of earlier years, where patrons behaved themselves in order not to provoke arrest, Stonewall was located at one of the busiest intersections in Greenwich Village and was a dance bar. (On one of my two forays to the Stonewall, I remember two young Latino men wearing G-strings and dancing atop the bar or on tables.) As for the riot that ensued, what could be more natural? By 1969, riots were commonplace events, especially when the young (and some of these were young men of color whose home communities were permeated by radical politics) and the police came face to face.

Of the various forces for change that I have described, the radical movements of the 1960s most directly shaped the new gay liberation movement that erupted after Stonewall. The connections are many. The group that formed in New York City a few weeks later chose a name — the Gay Liberation Front — meant to resonate with the National Liberation Front in Vietnam: how better to express one's political orientation? Most of the men and women who affiliated with New York GLF and its sibling groups elsewhere had been involved with one or more of the protest movements of the decade. Many of the actions that gay liberation groups initially took were "solidarity" demonstrations — appearing, for instance, with a gay liberation banner at an antiwar demonstration or at a rally in support of the Black Panther

Party. And, gay liberation could sweep across the country as fast as it did (its rate of growth was phenomenal) because the dense networks that existed among young radicals made it easy to spread the word.

* * *

As I reread *Out of the Closets* now, decades after its contents were initially written, what most stands out — and what is most distinctive about this brand of gay and lesbian writing — is its profound familial relationship to the radicalism of the sixties. The men and women who penned these words and whose stories fill these pages saw themselves as radical through and through. They brought that perspective, that sense that American society had to change from top to bottom in order to end oppression, to all of their work and to every aspect of their lives. I want to look a little more closely at four elements of that radicalism in order to flesh out the implications: (1) gay liberationists claimed a revolutionary political identity; (2) they saw the battle against sexism as the very heart of their struggle; (3) they broke decisively with hegemonic conceptions of homosexuality and of sexual identity more generally; and (4) they politicized everything, including sexual behavior and sexual relationships.

Revolution! So much has happened since young radicals in America mouthed those words with purposeful intent. After twelve years of Ronald Reagan and George Bush, after the patriotic orgy of flag-waving that accompanied the war in the Persian Gulf, after the collapse of Communism and the triumph of market values globally, after the crushing disappointment of the Clinton presidency, and in the midst of George Bush: The Sequel, the call for revolution may, today, sound like a quaint fiction or a faint echo from a distant world. The fact that a revolution, whatever that might mean, did not occur makes the claim suspect. Even many of the people who were calling for revolution a generation ago have disavowed those sentiments or have argued that the call for it was a political miscalculation, even a grand illusion.

The failure of a revolution to materialize should not cause us to dismiss the seriousness with which it was pursued or the depth of political conviction that made many subscribe to it. The intractability of racism; the obscene materialism in the midst of poverty; a brutal, destructive, and unconscionable war fought against peasants devastated by colonial exploitation; the indignity and inhumanity with which women in the United States were treated; the surveillance, the sabotage, and the violence directed at American citizens by agencies of our own government: all this and more gave many idealistic young Americans good reason to call for revolution.

I would argue that the revolutionary aspirations of these young lesbian and gay radicals are directly responsible for their signal achievement: their willingness to burst out of the closet and to come out in a public, uncompromising way. For all the change that had occurred before Stonewall, the prohibitions against homosexuality were still so deeply embedded in Western culture and the punishments attached to exposure remained so great that few gay men and lesbians were willing to affiliate with the homophile movement. The enticements of the closet were more alluring than the benefits of activism. But, because this cohort of gays and lesbians were committed to revolution, because they had broken with the values of American society and scorned the rewards that success in America offered, they were virtually immune to the penalties that kept homosexuals in line. What could happen to them? Rejection by the military? Exclusion from a civil service job? Arrest by the police? These were threats without power.

The commitment to, and belief in, revolution also accounts, I think, for the intensity of their involvement in this new movement. Reading between the lines of many of the essays in *Out of the Closets*, one gets a sense of young women and men whose every breath was filled with political activism. They met, and wrote, and demonstrated, and organized, and traveled around the country spreading the word. They engaged in fierce struggle with other radicals of the left—with organizers of the Venceremos Brigades to Cuba, with the Black Panther Party and its supporters, with radical heterosexual feminists in the women's liberation movement. Their revolutionary ambitions made them willing to do daring things—to confront the police directly, for instance, when they raided bars or harassed street transvestites, and to take to the streets when necessary. Because revolution was a full-time job, these gay liberationists were able to have an impact out of proportion to their numbers. They did enough so that a larger, vibrant movement would continue even after it became painfully clear that a revolution was not on the horizon.

Revolutionaries need ideology, a set of beliefs that explain the world in which they live, the injustices they are fighting against, and the goal toward which they are heading. Gay liberationists had no readily available, preexisting body of political writing from which they could draw, ready-made, an analysis of their situation. They had to invent one. Again and again, in their articles, their manifestos, and their political fliers, these pioneering radicals returned to the same point: sexism.

It comes as no surprise that the lesbians represented in *Out of the Closets* focused on sexism as the root cause of their oppression. Its impact on their lives was profound and pervasive. But what did surprise me when I returned to the volume was the regularity with which gay male radicals made the same claim.

Any full chronicle of the movement in these years would have to acknowledge the conflicts that erupted between women and men over male chauvinism and sexist behavior. A new understanding of gender relations was being born and, in the process, men would be called on the carpet to account for the way they treated women and for the unarticulated assumptions about gender that shaped their everyday actions. When the anger of lesbians ("A lesbian is the rage of all women condensed to the point of explosion" is the way the classic essay, "The Woman-Identified Woman," opens) who were beginning to see the many forms of sexism all around them collided with the ingrained habits of gay men socialized into dominance, the simplest interactions became a minefield.

Nonetheless, many of the men in the gay liberation movement were elaborating a *political* critique of sexism and male supremacy. Along with lesbian-feminist writers, they traced gay oppression back to the nuclear family. The family was the place where gender norms were learned and enforced. It was the main site of women's oppression and the institution in which children were first socialized into rigid, gender-dichotomized sex roles. Heterosexuality was a linchpin of the nuclear family ideal. Because lesbians and gay men deviated from these roles, they were the targets of brutal, systematic oppression.

To me, the striking feature of this analysis, as the male writers in *Out of the Closets* presented it, is that sexism was being identified as the primary cause of gay male oppression. It wasn't simply a question of sexism being one more form of injustice to combat, or of being opposed to sexism because it oppressed their lesbian sisters. Rather, these men grasped that the system of sex roles itself led to gay oppression. Gay men were mistreated, devalued, and despised because they were not "real men." Real men were, by definition, heterosexual. And so, gay liberation became a struggle not simply to win acceptance for a class of people, homosexuals, but to topple the gendered foundations of American society.

A third critical element of the anthology is the radical reconceptualization of sexual identity contained in many of the essays. At the simplest level, gay liberationists inverted the terms in which homosexuality was understood. Instead of being sick, sinful, or criminal, gay was now defined as good. Instead of seeing their sexuality as something to be ashamed of, these lesbians and gay men proclaimed their identity loudly and proudly. Instead of mimicking the gender conventions of society, they played with them, as the image of a bearded Konstantin Berlandt running around in a red dress at the American Psychiatric Association convention vividly suggests. But a more profound rethinking of human sexuality is to be found in this volume. The sentence that for me best encapsulates it comes from Martha Shelley's essay, "Gay Is Good": "We will never go straight until you go gay."

At first glance, the line reads as just one more example of the uncompromising, militant stance these radicals took. Since there wasn't a chance in hell that the straight oppressor was about to experience a sexual conversion, Shelley's rhetorical challenge is merely stating the obvious: gay is who we are, and we aren't about to change. (Or, as Queer Nation members have put it twenty years later, "We're here; we're queer; get used to it.")

But challenges can also be accepted and therein lies the true radicalism of her line. It implies that the categories of homosexual and heterosexual are not immutable, not fixed, not given. Even as lesbian and gay radicals were laying claim to their sexuality, they were also questioning the categories themselves. "Homo" and "hetero" were no more natural than were masculinity and femininity. An exploitative society channeled human sexuality into these narrow, separate streams. Without the oppression, without the hierarchies of patriarchal capitalism, the very concept of sexual orientation would disappear. Human beings would be free to love and express themselves sensually without regard to the gender of a potential partner. Or, as Allen Young framed it in "Out of the Closets, Into the Streets": "Gay, in its most farreaching sense, means not homosexual, but sexually free. . . . in a free society everyone will be gay." Long before queer theorists informed us in the 1990s that sexual and gender identities were not laws of nature, the young radicals of the late 1960s were making those claims.

With such a thoroughing critique of gender and sexuality, and in an environment in which feminism was asserting that "the personal is political," it is no wonder that these post-Stonewall radicals also cast a critical gaze on sexual behavior itself, their own and others. This is most evident in the section of *Out of the Closets* on sex and roles, but it can be found elsewhere as well. Nothing remained immune from political scrutiny.

This critique took many forms. Because so many gay liberationists were young and did not have strong roots in the traditional subculture, and because many of them had absorbed New Left and counterculture ideals about community and human relationships, they looked askance at what they saw in the pre-Stonewall gay world. Criticism was aimed at "bar dykes" for their butch-femme role-playing: roles seemed to be pathetic imitations of conventional heterosexuality. Radicals condemned the men who cruised public toilets, the parks, and other urban spaces looking for anonymous sex: such behavior only reinforced a tendency to objectify and dehumanize one another. Institutions such as the bars were seen as the site of gay oppression: lesbian and gay radicals would sometimes "liberate" a bar, bringing their own positive "vibes" into the Mafia-owned space.

Gay liberationists also looked inward and subjected themselves to merciless probing. How had they internalized oppressive patterns of sexual behavior and interaction? Did they choose partners because they were "turned on" by mere physical appearance? Were they using others for their own gratification, physical or emotional? Were they as guilty as the oppressor?

Out of this process of self-examination, a process facilitated by participation in consciousness-raising groups, came the outlines of a liberated sexuality. It would be sensual rather than genital. It would be egalitarian and mutual rather than hierarchical and ego-centered. And it would not be possessive, jealous, and clinging. The new world of gay liberation would be born not only in the streets, but in the bedroom as well.

*   *   *

By the time *Out of the Closets* was published in 1972, the particular brand of radical politics represented in it was already in eclipse. The gay and lesbian movement was fanning out in many different political directions. What happened? What became of the perspectives that I've just described? And what was the lasting legacy of the Stonewall generation of radical liberationists?

Calls for revolution faded. As the political climate grew more conservative and government repression of dissenters increased, and as economic problems multiplied in the 1970s, the larger sea of radicalism in which gay liberation was swimming began to shrink. It became harder and harder to hang on to revolutionary dreams. The plausibility of revolutionary change and the credibility of those who clamored for it evaporated. Moreover, the very success of gay liberation worked against the continuing dominance of radical visions. As gay and lesbian liberationists came out of the closet, their example proved infectious to many other men and women who were not embedded in the radical politics of the 1960s. For many of these new recruits, acceptance on equal terms into the mainstream of American society replaced revolution as a political goal.

Also, gay liberation was born at the moment when issues of identity were moving to the forefront of social consciousness. While identity politics — whether based on race, ethnicity, gender, or sexuality — succeeded in mobilizing large numbers of Americans to struggle for social change, it also pulled those forces in separate directions. Early gay liberation was a special, even if brief, time when men and women, whites and people of color were engaged in struggle together — against an oppressive society and with each other — for the purpose of revolutionary change. But the sharpened awareness of how one's many layers of identity targeted an individual for mistreatment unleashed explosive emotions. Unity and cooperation could not be maintained in the face of this pressing need to explore and understand the implications of identity-based politics.

These young revolutionaries also compromised their effectiveness because of their failure to formulate strategies for change. It was one thing to argue that only a revolution would end gay oppression or that sexism was so deeply planted in American society that pulling up the roots would require everything else to crumble. But how was one to do that? What did it mean to destroy the nuclear family and smash sex roles? What were the steps that would get us from here to there? And what improvements — or reforms — could be achieved in the meantime to keep hopes alive, to make life better, and to smooth the path to more far-reaching alterations in the structure of power? These were questions for which no fully convincing answers were provided, although some theorists, such as Rita Mae Brown and Carl Wittman, made stabs at it. Short on strategy and long on political rhetoric, radical gay liberation proved frustrating for the less revolutionary-minded, and the more pragmatic, activist.

The result was that as the 1970s wore on, the gay and lesbian movement began to travel along many different paths. One of these might be labeled a gay rights movement. Composed mostly of white middle-class gay men, though with some lesbians and people of color as well, this reform-oriented politics focused on gay issues only, and largely abandoned the broad analysis of oppression that animated gay liberation. These activists, many of whom were quite militant in the tactics they espoused, sought entry into the system on terms of equality. What they lacked in vision was somewhat counterbalanced by their practical, hardnosed strategy. They were willing to work for passage of municipal gay rights legislation, to campaign for repeal of sodomy statutes, to enter into dialogue with the churches and the medical profession, and to negotiate with the media in order to achieve concrete though limited gains.

Another major political tendency of the 1970s was the emergence of a separate lesbian-feminist movement. These activists maintained an allegiance to the goal of radical social transformation. In their writing, they deepened the analysis of the interconnections between sexism and heterosexism. They devoted a great deal of energy to creating lesbian-feminist institutions so that a community could take shape and a culture be born in the midst of the patriarchy. They succeeded in building a home base from which lesbian feminists could venture into other social struggles. Yet, whereas their vision remained broad, lesbian feminists proved unable to fashion a political agenda that was distinctive: virtually all their goals were either about gender (in other words, feminist) or about sexual identity (in other words, gay). As time went on, this separate movement became more insular, more inward looking. It became utopian.

Gay rights and lesbian separatism do not exhaust the political options of the 1970s. People of color organized in small collectives, slowly creating networks of activists and organizations whose influence would be asserted in the 1980s. Some gay men maintained an allegiance to the radicalism of gay liberation. Many politicized lesbians chose to work within the feminist movement, some within the radical wing of feminism and others within reform feminism. Out of all these experiences would emerge lessons and options that would surface and be more widely picked up as the movement became larger in the 1980s and 1990s.

The analysis and understanding of sexism also went through changes. Although lesbian feminists held fast to the conviction that sexism was a central defining feature of their oppression, by the 1980s the analysis of many of them, particularly among lesbians of color and white lesbians with a commitment to antiracist work, broadened to encompass issues of race and class. Rather than look for the "primary" oppression, lesbian activists began seeing oppression as a many-headed monster, all forms of which had to be attacked.

For gay men, the post–gay liberation years have proved more ambiguous. On one side, it seems to me that far more gay men, at least within activist organizations, have absorbed a rudimentary feminist analysis of sexism. At a personal level, more of us have modified our patterns of behavior and have discarded many sexist assumptions about women so that our interactions with lesbians are less offensive to them. But, politically, the understanding of sexism seems to have narrowed. Unlike the gay men in *Out of the Closets,* who saw sexism as the root of gay male oppression, now sexism is perceived as being about "them." One opposes it because it hurts lesbians, or women in general, not because it is a defining element in the subordination of gay men as well.

The revisioning of sexual identity has certainly proved to be a casualty of the waning of radical gay liberation. By the mid-1970s, phrases like "sexual orientation" and the "gay minority" had entered the lexicon of the movement. The ideas that human sexuality was malleable and that the categories of homosexual and heterosexual were aspects of socialization in an oppressive society seemed to lose their appeal. Especially in the 1990s, research claiming a biological basis for homosexuality captured headlines. Over time, gay and lesbian reverted to their pre-Stonewall formulation: these were fixed identities, determined early in life (perhaps, even from birth), but natural, good, and healthy rather than unnatural, bad, and sick.

A number of reasons account for this slippage. For one, the notion of malleability seemed counterintuitive to most gay men and lesbians. For many, our sexual identity was so much a part of us, with roots that stretched so far back in time, that it made no sense to argue that sexual identity was in some sense contingent. Then, too, the suggestion of malleability seemed to play into the hands of our opponents. If identity was fluid, then maybe homosexuality was changeable. If it was changeable, then it was also willful. Isn't this precisely what homophobic doctors and fundamentalist Christians were arguing? Thus, it became easier to fall back on the view that gay men and lesbians had no choice. This is who we are and the issue was acceptance.

Concepts of sexual orientation also meshed with the reform brand of political action that evolved in the 1970s, 1980s, and 1990s. It was easier to argue before a city council for civil rights for a fixed social minority than for a capacity inherent in everyone. It was easier to argue that religious groups should accept the gay and lesbian members in their midst than that they should approve polymorphous perversity. And, it was easier to demand that the medical profession eliminate homosexual orientation from its list of mental diseases than that they endorse a sexual philosophy of "anything goes." A reform politics won institutional changes and improvements in the quality of life, but at the price of losing a more thoroughgoing critique of human sexuality.

Finally, the politics of sex has changed dramatically since early gay liberation. In their efforts to scrutinize the ways that oppression shaped gay and lesbian sexuality, these radicals too often sound moralistic and condescending. In attacking roles, anonymous sex, objectification, and bar culture, they ended up constructing a *prescriptive* sexual politics. They did this in the name of liberation, to be sure. But in passing judgment on their own and others' sex lives, they teetered on the edge of becoming a new vice squad.

The notion of a "politically correct" sexuality would wreak havoc on lesbian-feminist communities by the early 1980s. Debates about pornography, butch-femme roles, sado-masochism, and other issues provoked searing community splits. Out of this came in the 1980s a more fluid discussion of lesbian sexuality. Among gay men, the burgeoning of a visible commercialized urban sexual subculture in the 1970s virtually buried the gay liberation critique. Gay liberation transmuted into a movement for sexual freedom; exploring new frontiers of sexual pleasure, beyond the boundaries of what middle-class America approved, became a central element of gay male life. Critiques of our sexual culture came not in the form of political tracts, but in literature. Novels such as *Dancer from the Dance,* by Andrew Holleran, and *Faggots,* by Larry Kramer, come to mind.

I mourn the loss of this aspect of radical gay liberation even as I recognize its flaws. The prescriptiveness was of no value. There was also a naïveté about the dynamics of sexual desire; change was assumed to be easier than it was. Yet, in reacting against that, it often seems as if we have given up any possibility of thinking critically about sexuality. Our sexual politics often reduces to a campaign against prohibitions. Perhaps this is for the best. In a culture in which sexuality has come to define the truth about the self and in which sexual desire appears coterminous with who we are, perhaps it is too divisive, too volatile, to subject something so personal to political scrutiny.

*   *   *

So, the phase of the gay and lesbian emancipation movement that the documents in *Out of the Closets* represent passed from the scene. The revolution did not come. Does that mean it failed? Is radical gay liberation just a historical curiosity from an age of political excess?

Hardly. The legacies of that era and that politics are very much with us, and the achievements are profound. The Stonewall generation invented a new language and style of homosexuality. While some of the particulars are lost, the accents on pride, self-affirmation, and determined self-assertion are alive and well. The terms in which gay and lesbian issues are debated and understood were forever changed by these bold radicals.

Radical gay liberation also unleashed a mania for organization. At the time of Stonewall, there were about fifty homophile organizations in the United States; by the end of 1973, more than a thousand lesbian and gay groups existed. This impulse to create organizations and institutions able to knit a community together and to deepen a sense of collectivity was a product of the Stonewall generation. All the gains we have made since then are dependent on that impulse staying alive and maturing.

Finally, as the phrase "out of the closets" so aptly reminds us, it was the radicals of the Stonewall era who modeled for the rest of us "coming out." By coming out of the closet and by holding this out as both goal and tactic for the movement, they found the way to create an evergrowing army of recruits to the banner of lesbian and gay freedom. This, I believe, more than anything else marked Stonewall as a turning point not only in *our* history as a community, but in Western history itself. The Stonewall generation initiated a move toward the mass public affirmation of homosexual desire, certainly an arrestingly new direction in the culture of Western societies. Is this, perhaps, the portent of more thoroughgoing change that may someday warrant the term "revolutionary"?

But now that *Out of the Closets* is back in print, you, the contemporary reader, are better placed to judge for yourself the significance of that era.

4

A Meaning for All Those Words: Sex, Politics, History and Larry Kramer

Between the early 1980s and the early 1990s, Larry Kramer arguably had achieved a higher level of visibility and public influence than anyone else in the United States associated with the gay and lesbian freedom struggle. I want to place Kramer's feat in historical context, and connect his career and his influence to the larger pattern of change that the gay and lesbian movement, the evolution of public queer communities, and the AIDS epidemic have provoked in American life. On the face of it, the task seems fairly straightforward, not unlike what any biographical profile by a historian should do.

In Kramer's case, the assignment is perhaps somewhat more complicated, since his influence lies, as does his work, at the juncture of culture and politics. Think for a moment about what he is best known for. He wrote *Faggots*, a novel that received wide attention as a commentary on gay male sexual culture in the 1970s; *The Normal Heart*, a play that, through its many productions, brought the politics of AIDS to a national audience; and essays, such as "1,112 and Counting," whose polemical power galvanized the outrage of the gay and lesbian community into political action. Kramer was one of the founders of the Gay Men's Health Crisis in New York City, the first — and still the largest — AIDS service organization in the United States. His speech at the New York Lesbian and Gay Community Center in March 1987 provoked the founding of ACT UP, an organization that changed the face of AIDS activism and initiated the most vibrant, media-savvy brand of direct

This essay originally appeared in *We Must Love One Another or Die: The Life and Legacies of Larry Kramer,* edited by Lawrence D. Mass (London: Cassell, 1997), pp. 73–85. My thanks to Larry Mass for soliciting the piece and for his editorial advice and assistance.

action politics in this country since the late 1960s.[1] Add to this his op-ed columns in places such as the *New York Times,* interviews in the *Washington Post* and elsewhere, and appearances on television talk shows, and it is not unreasonable to claim for him a unique level of recognition.[2]

What have I left out? Just the fact that Kramer is as passionately loved by his supporters in the queer world and as deeply reviled by his antagonists in the same world as it is humanly possible to be; that the split between passionate love and deep antagonism can often be found in the very same individual; and that Kramer himself is capable of swinging between poles of self-praise and self-criticism that are as far apart from each other as are his most rabid loyalists and detractors.

As the passions he unleashes suggest, assessing Kramer's place in history requires more than totaling his accomplishments and measuring his output. His words and his actions touch some very deep places of pain in many of us, particularly among the white, urban gay men of the Stonewall generation whose experience he has commented on and whose tragedies he has chronicled. I may be a dispassionate historian of the gay and lesbian movement, but I am also a gay man whose life has intersected with Larry's and whose social and political worlds he has commented on. It would be foolish to claim that I can approach this essay only in the guise of the former role and not in the latter. In what follows, I am examining his work and the response to it in order to see what it can tell us about the larger context of historical change, but it is an analysis inevitably informed by my own experience.[3]

*   *   *

Like many others, I first encountered Larry long before I met him. The fall of 1978 brought into print two novels, *Faggots* and Andrew Holleran's *Dancer From the Dance,* that were immediately recognized as breakthrough books. Each of them was set in the urban sexual culture of middle-class white gay men that had taken shape above ground in the wake of Stonewall; each described that world from the inside, without reticence or apology; and each of them was widely reviewed, not only in the burgeoning gay press but in mainstream papers and magazines as well. Just as many of us were coming out proudly as individuals in the 1970s, as the decade drew to a close our collective world was now finding its chroniclers and bringing our experience out en masse.

Despite these commonalities, as works of fiction the two novels were dramatically different. Holleran's was lushly romantic, eliciting the longings for love and emotional attachment that surrounded the pursuit of sexual pleasure. Though it lacked the self-hatred endemic to much of the gay "problem" fiction of the previous generation, it nonetheless played on familiar tropes of desperate desire, unfulfilled longing, and doomed love that still circulated not only in the products of popular culture but in gay male life as well.[4] *Faggots* occupied another place entirely. Bitingly, viciously comic, it cast a satiric eye on the gay quest for love. None of the sexual institutions of the gay subculture were spared; no concessions were made to the libertarian principles of the so-called sexual revolution. Although the critique of a world in which physical attractiveness and orgasm counted for everything was fierce, the novel stood firm in the unspoken assumption that gay is good, even if the social world and sexual mores it sometimes produced were not. Fred Lemish, its erstwhile hero, was neither struggling to be heterosexual nor contemplating suicide.

Faggots and *Dancer* differed in another way as well: their reception. Holleran's novel attracted worlds of praise while Kramer's was savaged. Reviewing them together in the *New York Times*, John Lahr described *Dancer* as "superb." As for *Faggots*, Lahr called it "an embarrassing fiasco," containing "sentence for sentence, some of the worst writing I've encountered in a published manuscript." Martin Duberman, in *The New Republic*, described *Faggots* as "a foolish, even stupid book. . . . It has nothing of discernment to say about [the gay] scene nor, in place of insight, any compensating literary distinction." Duberman further damned it for "primitive moralizing." A reviewer in *Gay Community News* of Boston, one of the more radical of gay papers, called the novel, "appalling" and "offensive." The examples could be multiplied.[5]

I'm no literary critic. But I remember reading both novels soon after they were published and reacting differently from the reviews — and my friends. *Dancer* immediately drew me in. I could hardly put it down, yet I responded to it with anger. Despite its dreamlike quality, it evoked the emotional landscape of gay male life as I knew it with razor-sharp accuracy. But, to my mind, it also lacked any critical distance from that world. The absence of a view from the outside left no room for escape; the quest for love and attachment was doomed — as gay men had always been doomed — to failure. *Faggots* at least rebelled. I confess: I never finished it because it seemed like a one-line joke, but at least its one line was on target. Many of us did find ourselves enmeshed, more than we wanted to be, in a circle of sexual encounters that had no exit. Instead of "both sex and love," we were left with "either sex" — but no "or love"!

What raw nerve had *Faggots* touched? The venom in many of the reviews in the gay press had little to do with Larry's skill as a stylist. They were content focused and came with accusations of betrayal of the "lifestyle" (a word that came into vogue in the 70s) of a community that was just emerging into the open. It seemed not to be his particular critique of gay male sexuality that provoked outrage as much as the fact that there was any critique at all.

For many, *Faggots* would continue to shape their reaction to Larry. As the AIDS epidemic hit in the early 1980s, Larry's warnings — his jeremiads — would be filtered through ears that had already judged the speaker. Larry, a relative newcomer to gay politics, was typecast as antisexual, a Puritan or a Victorian depending on one's historical frame of reference, someone whose internalized homophobia ran so deep that his judgment was always suspect. Someone, in other words, who stood at odds with the gay liberation tradition. Interestingly, Larry himself accepted a piece of this characterization in that his own commentaries during the AIDS era often identified gay liberation with the sexual subculture of the meat rack at Fire Island, the baths, and the backroom bookstores and bars that proliferated in American cities in the 1970s.

Before I move on to Larry and AIDS, I want to jump this story backward in time and scrutinize the unexamined elision of gay liberation and the sexual scene of the seventies. Something, it seemed to me, happened on the road from Stonewall to AIDS, and it isn't often commented on.

* * *

Gay liberation, in its immediate post-Stonewall incarnation, has already had its share of chroniclers.[6] Those wild-eyed radicals who picked up the banner of the Stonewall riots exist more as myth — or nightmare — than as flesh-and-bones historical actors. Some cast them as authentic revolutionaries, who threw off generations of oppression and opened a brave new world of human freedom and justice. Others brand them as impractical extremists, utopian anarchists who mixed too many radical causes into an unstable brew.

Let's leave aside whether we agree with them or not, whether we approve of their politics or don't, whether we consider ourselves their political heirs or claim another ideological mantle. One thing *is* certain: they elaborated a critique not only of the mistreatment of homosexuals, but of human sexuality in a society they defined as exploitative, hierarchical, and oppressive.

To be more specific: they did not simply say that gay was good, that notions of homosexuality as sin, sickness, or crime were wrong. They claimed that the expression of sexuality in a capitalist and patriarchal society was inherently deformed. Patriarchy structured a system of gender roles that produced males and females whose erotic lives were misshapen. Capitalism played with human sexuality every which way: it channeled men and women into heterosexual roles to reproduce workers; it repressed as well as incited sexual desire; it demanded that we defer gratification until our desires exploded outward. Sexuality under capitalism became another kind of commodity, to be bought and sold, as objectified and alienated as were the products of our labor.[7]

This perspective often led gay liberationists, in the immediate aftermath of Stonewall, to be as critical of the gay subculture as they were of the heterosexual dictatorship. They dissented from the gender norms of American society and the way those norms shaped the eroticism of gay men. Male socialization placed a premium on dominance, aggression, coldness, and competitive success; it taught men to manipulate and use others as objects. Gay men were oppressed in large part because they failed to fill their role within the patriarchal nuclear family. Not fully male, they were drawn into the orbit of sexism, treated with the kind of contempt that women routinely received. At the same time, even as gay men were targeted for oppression, their socialization as men made them enact their own version of masculinist sexuality. Anonymous sex, the objectification of youth and beauty, and the endless tricking of the bar world all came under merciless attack. The heirs of Stonewall were as likely to "liberate" a gay bar — by disrupting the bar's grim cruising scene with a circle dance, for instance — as they were to "zap" a homophobic shrink. For them, the institutions of the gay subculture did not inspire reverence.

These radical gay liberationists also played with notions of sexual orientation. Even as they defiantly embraced a public gay identity, they treated both heterosexuality and homosexuality as suspect categories, the products of an oppressive society. Liberation meant the shattering of restrictive identities. How else is one to interpret the injunction of Carl Wittman, in *A Gay Manifesto*, to "free the homosexual in everyone."[8]

Less than a decade separates the stormy politics of radical gay liberation from the publication of novels like *Faggots* and *Dancer,* but their respective sexual worlds couldn't be more remote from one another.[9] By the end of the 1970s hardly a trace of the former's sexual critique of gay male life remained. Instead, the subculture they had once defined as flawed had emerged into view, bigger, grander, glossier than before. Ironically, an anticapitalist gay liberation movement had made this possible. By containing police harassment in major cities, gay liberation opened the door to legitimate investment in gay sex. Cleaner baths, palatial discos, a Fire Island summer undisturbed by intrusive cops: the sex scene these allowed had more allure than self-reflective ruminations about what our erotic lives would look like in a world without alienation, economic insecurity, or gendered oppression.

I am not sure why or how the transition happened. Some of it can be traced to who those Stonewall-era gay radicals were and how they offered their criticisms. Most were young, with roots not in the pre-Stonewall gay world but in the movements of the 1960s. In other words, even though they were gay, they were writing as outsiders. Their commentary on gay male sex life, moreover, arrived with a prescriptive edge. A heated moralism often shaped their words, as did a naïveté about how easily human sexual desire could be reshaped. They acted, in other words, as if a call to authenticity in human relationships (a New Left favorite), coupled with a bit of consciousness raising, was enough to rewrite the scripts of our eroticism.

But they also were no match for the force of a subculture rooted in both oppression *and* resistance. The gay world that predated them absorbed parts of their message — coming out and gay pride — while discarding others. Gay liberation served less to refashion the sexual ethics of gay male life than to allow the pre-Stonewall urban gay scene to grow larger, more secure, and more stable. It opened a path, in other words, not only for individuals, but for a whole social world to come out.

*   *   *

Oppression and resistance. We tend to see them as dichotomous concepts: there is oppression and there is resistance, and never the two shall meet.

I have come to believe that the line dividing them is not quite as sharp and clear as we would like to think, that there are times when acts of resistance can unwittingly reproduce, or at least give sustenance to, systems of oppression.

The best way I can find to explain what I mean is by playing with the concept of internalized oppression. Most of the time we use internalized oppression in a relatively flat, unnuanced way. Society has told us, monotonously and repetitively, that we are bad, evil, sick, perverted. When gays and lesbians act in ways that seem self-hating, we label it as internalized oppression, as mimicking the negative oppressive messages of the majority culture. When we speak or act in ways that assert gay is good, we are shedding these internalized attitudes.

But what if it's more complicated than the two poles of good and bad? For instance, the dominant culture also claims that we are different. When we proclaim our difference—even if we celebrate it—is this resistance, or does this simply recreate the conditions of our oppression? Gay and lesbian oppression also operates in ways designed to isolate and marginalize us from the rest of society. When we create vibrant, exciting—but thoroughly separate—social worlds, have we resisted our oppression or merely created a more comfortable zone of isolation and marginalization? An oppressive society has defined us only by our sexuality and defined our passions as uncontrollable. When we make our sexual desires the heart of our lives and our political movement, is this an act of resistance, or does it signify the acting out of the terms of oppression?

Let me push this further. What if the adaptations we've made to survive in a hostile world function as a tool of oppression, but one that we unwittingly wield? Battered as we have all been by a barrage of destructive lies, by a culture that once denied our existence and still denies our worth, we have understandably become distrustful, defiant, and defensive. For gay men, whose sexuality is so much the heart and soul of the hatred directly against us, is it any wonder that we are instinctively distrustful of any criticism of our sexual lives, that we defend ourselves against it, and that we defiantly assert our right to do whatever we please?

But when do these responses serve us well, and when do they fail us miserably? When do defensiveness, defiance, and distrust become modes of resistance, and when are they the kneejerk reactions of a people targeted for mistreatment? When, in other words, are they a form of useful skepticism wielded by us, and when are they the outcomes of a repertoire of responses severely constricted by oppression?

* * *

It matters very little whether reviewers react defensively to the fictional portrayal of gay life in *Faggots*. It matters a good deal more when one of the earliest, most public wake-up calls to AIDS elicits a similar response. Yet Larry's statements about AIDS have repeatedly evoked such angry, defensive denunciations.

Take one example, which Larry himself has commented on. In late August 1981, the same summer that the first cases of what became known as AIDS were reported in the press and soon after Kramer and others had begun meeting to plan a response, the *New York Native* published an appeal from Larry for funds. One sentence read: "It's easy to become frightened that one of the many things we've done or taken over the past years may be all that it takes for a cancer to grow from a tiny something-or-other that got in there who knows when from doing who knows what." The sentence seems innocent enough; in fact, it describes with perfect accuracy how many gay men, myself included, felt in the early stages of the epidemic, before anyone knew anything about retroviruses, antibodies, and modes of transmission. Fear was a chronic condition, fed by endless, futile speculation. Yet, for many, the sentence hit a sensitive nerve, prompting them to write back in anger. "Read anything by Kramer closely," Robert Chesley, a New York playwright, warned readers. "I think you'll find the subtext is always: the wages of gay sin are death."[10]

Or, consider this paragraph from a review of *Reports from the Holocaust,* Larry's collection of essays about AIDS, that Gregory Kolovakos published in *The Nation* in 1989[11]:

> Kramer equates sexual freedom with promiscuity and writes, "There's no question that the promiscuity of some gay men was unwittingly responsible for AIDS killing so many of us." There's the old wages-of-sin argument — those more sexually experimental killed "us." Sontag explicitly agrees with Kramer: "Promiscuous homosexual men practicing their vehement sexual customs . . . could be viewed as dedicated hedonists — though it's now clear that their behavior was no less suicidal" than that of addicts sharing needles. Are such pronouncements so distant from Falwell's statement about reaping "a harvest of corruption"?

Kolovakos asks the question rhetorically, intending "no" to be the only answer. Yet surely there is a world of difference between Larry's statement and Falwell's. And, isn't there something suspect about the way Kolovakos slides from "promiscuity" to "experimental"? For some gay men at some times, random, casual, indiscriminate sex (the dictionary definition of promiscuous) could be highly experimental. For other gay men at other times, there was nothing experimental about it. In fact, it was boringly, traditionally male, a textbook display of how male (hetero)sexuality has been described in the West for centuries.

The issue here is not whether Larry or his critics were "right." Rather, the reaction to Larry, from *Faggots* through AIDS, tells us something important about the dynamics of gay male sexual culture and sexual politics. To venture into this territory is like entering a minefield ready to detonate at any moment. Any word of criticism, or any suggestion of self-doubt that more is always better, or any hint of a reservation that sexual expression is always good, risks a barrage of verbal denunciation. I have no solutions as to how to clear the ground, but I know it doesn't serve us well when frank expressions of dismay or concern about our sexual lives set off such explosions.

* * *

Without AIDS, Larry would be one among many gay novelists and playwrights. Some of us would be moved by his work; others of us wouldn't; and most gay men would have no idea who he is.

AIDS gave Larry a national profile. Because AIDS appeared early in his social circles, he could be among the first to act. Because he was a writer with skills as a polemicist, he could give an articulate voice to emotions of anger, loss, and fear that circulated in the gay community. Because of the privilege that inhered in his class, his education, his race, and his gender, he expected to be heard. Because he was doing all this from New York, and not from Phoenix or Omaha or Cincinnati, he found a large audience.

The broad outline of Larry's career as an AIDS activist is easy to summarize. Late in the summer of 1981, after the first articles about a deadly immune deficiency among some gay men appeared in the *New York Times,* Larry was one of the conveners of a meeting that led to the formation of Gay Men's Health Crisis (GMHC). The organization grew and inspired others as cases of sick and dying men appeared in city after city. Larry became the earliest and most public polemicist about the epidemic, writing essays for the *New York Native* that were reprinted elsewhere. His writing raised consciousness, and also raised controversy.

Larry and GMHC parted angrily by 1983. Unencumbered by organizational ties, he continued to write essays and op-ed pieces, characterized by a willingness to attack anyone, friend or foe, who seemed to stand in the way of a no-holds-barred response to the epidemic. His play, *The Normal Heart*, premiered in New York City in 1985. A polemical piece in the tradition of the agit-prop theater of the 1930s, it was taken seriously by reviewers and became a favorite of local theater companies throughout the United States. Indeed, it would not be unreasonable to argue that *The Normal Heart*, more than any other single cultural product, spread the politics of AIDS to a mass audience.

Though never completely removed from AIDS political activism, Larry returned to it in a big way when his speech at the New York Community Center in March 1987 transformed simmering anger and frustration into a new form of direct action politics. ACT UP chapters spread rapidly. They could be found not only in New York, Los Angeles, and San Francisco, where one might expect them, but in places like Oklahoma City and Shreveport, Louisiana. ACT UP gave AIDS activism the hard, determined, driven edge that it needed. As with GMHC earlier, Larry eventually found himself at odds with the direction of ACT UP. He moved away from political action again, but continued to write — *Reports from the Holocaust, Just Say No, The Destiny of Me* — and to speak out against government policy and what he saw as the failure of gay, lesbian, and AIDS activism.

It's quite a résumé to ponder. What patterns of meaning can we extract from it?

The most obvious is the recurring oscillation between explosive bursts of energy mobilized toward making change and dramatic criticism of his peers leading to withdrawal from the fray. Larry himself has offered one interpretation of what might be called his "career development": "I wanted to be Moses, but I only could be Cassandra," he has the character, Ned Weeks, say in *The Destiny of Me*.

Let's leave Moses aside. But in reading *Reports from the Holocaust* I was struck by the aptness of the Cassandra analogy. Most of the essays in the volume were familiar to me; I had read them when they were first published in *The Native* and elsewhere. Reading them again, I remembered my original reaction to most of them: overblown, overstated, Larry the prophet of doom. And, I was shocked to realize that, in this encounter with them as historical documents, I found myself thinking: "Virtually everything that Larry said has turned out to be true; the worst case scenarios have become fact." Or, at least that was my reaction up to a point. The closer in time to the present an essay was, the less credible it seemed. What is this, if not the fate of Cassandra?

Beyond Larry's "predictive" powers, there is something else to be ana-lyzed in his AIDS career — the thread of acerbic criticism that runs through his words and deeds. The criticisms — indeed, if one is ever the object of them they look more like frontal assaults — are fairly indiscriminate in their targets: mayors, public health officials, Congress, presidents, drug com-panies, scientists; but also AIDS organizations, gay and lesbian organiza-tions, and the individual men and women who lead them.

I am especially interested in the way Larry has recurringly attacked those within the community and the movement. Sometimes the attacks are aimed at individuals; sometimes at an organization; and sometimes at the AIDS movement and the gay and lesbian movement as a whole. The themes are similar. A large collective "we" stand accused of failure. The movement and its members are second-rate, lacking power or afraid of it, unable to respond effectively to the challenges at hand.

If the measure of success is the end of the AIDS epidemic, then, of course, the criticisms are right on target. The epidemic is not over, the number of diagnoses continues to grow, and the deaths keep rising. But what are the assumptions behind that expectation? What baseline of political strength do we attribute to the gay and lesbian movement when we accuse it of failure? Underlying the negative assessment is a badly distorted view of the move-ment's history, and a confusion over the relationship between the gay and lesbian movement and the larger community of which it is a subset.

Just as Larry and others have tended to conflate the gay liberation impulse with the urban sexual culture that flourished in the 1970s, so the criticisms of the failure to respond adequately to AIDS conflate the collective political movement that developed in the 1970s with the much larger public commu-nity of urban gay men that coalesced during the same years. The two were not identical; in many ways they looked at one another with a mixture of wariness and resentment.

For those of us who were involved in the political world of gay and lesbian activism in the 1970s, the gains we had made were wondrous. Be-cause we all remembered vividly a time in our own lives when the isolation was impenetrable, the fear pervasive, and the hopelessness overwhelming, every bit of change seemed momentous. Every street demonstration, every column of media coverage, every conference filled to overflowing, every public hearing by a government body: all were historical, all seemed to be evidence of profound change. And they were. But they were also barely beginnings. "Been down so long it looks like up from here" went a Bob Dylan song of the 1960s. It captures a perspective that describes what happened politically in the 1970s more accurately than either the self-commendations of the time or the retrospective criticisms of Larry and others.

The fact is that were we to chart the trajectory of the gay and lesbian movement in terms of a human life cycle, we might say that the pre-Stonewall activism of the 1950s and 1960s represented birth and infancy; the decade after Stonewall was at best a childhood. Virtually all local lesbian and gay organizations in the 1970s were staffed by volunteers; they experienced an ebb and flow of effectiveness dependent on the volume of donated labor. Although organizations were popping up everywhere, only in the largest American cities and in some university towns was there anything like a sustained organizational presence. National organizations like Lambda Legal Defense and the National Gay Task Force had barely gotten off the ground. On the eve of the AIDS epidemic, New York City sustained fewer than a score of activists in full-time paying positions in the movement. Most of these jobs were to be found in national organizations based in the city, or in social service — not political — organizations, like Senior Action in a Gay Environment.

The real institutional gains of the 1970s — the repeal of many sodomy laws, the passage of municipal civil rights legislation, the removal of homosexuality from the medical profession's list of diseases, changes in federal employment policies, the curtailment of police harassment — had little to do with the strength of the movement. Rather, change was attributable to the weakness of traditional sources of institutional power in the wake of the upheavals of the 1960s. In other words, the relatively small amount of militancy we were able to muster in the 1970s went an unusually long way. To be sure, none of it would have happened without us. But the times were right for a small but determined holy band of warriors to achieve quite a lot.

By the time AIDS struck in the early 1980s, this favorable political environment was already history. A new conservative movement had reconstituted itself as a political force, in part by mobilizing against the gains of social movements based on racial, gender, and sexual identities. The free ride of the 1970s was over.

Framed in this way, the response to AIDS is nothing short of miraculous. Within a few short years, the community was able to build from the ground up an extraordinary network of service organizations that cared for many of the sick and educated the community: the only comparable organizational response I can think of is the creation of the Congress of Industrial Organizations in the 1930s among working people bombarded by the Depression. A relatively weak national organization like NGLTF was able to spark a large cooperative lobbying effort that penetrated the walls of Congress and shook funds loose for research, care, and prevention in the face of a Reagan administration that cared about nothing except large defense budgets and even larger tax cuts. AIDS pushed open doors for us that had been closed in the 1970s. Make no mistake: we were still only visitors. But a dialogue had begun.

In an ideal world, AIDS would never have happened. In an almost ideal world, a politically mature, organizationally stable, and collectively powerful gay movement would have orchestrated a response to AIDS in which everything that could be done was done. In the real world we inhabit, AIDS built a queer movement that didn't yet exist; it reconfigured our movement and our community in profound, irreversible ways.

Although an AIDS movement and a gay and lesbian movement are conceptually distinct, in practice the boundary proved porous. For instance, gays and lesbians of color by the end of the 1970s were creating their own autonomous organizations. Like their mostly white predecessors, these groups were volunteer based, with an unstable existence. AIDS created a material base of resources to push forward this organizing impulse: witness the importance of AIDS-related funding to organizations like LLEGÓ, the national Latino/a organization, and the national Black Lesbian and Gay Leadership Forum. In smaller cities and towns, gays and lesbians in the 1980s often established their first stable organizational presence through an AIDS-service group; political organizations were then a short step away. The massive 1987 March on Washington, whose energy flowed in part from the accumulated anger and frustration engendered by the epidemic, unleashed a major new round of grassroots gay, lesbian, and bisexual organizing around the country. And AIDS, by arousing from apathy an economically privileged segment of the community, tapped resources that have allowed us to make the transition from a movement of only volunteers to one with an ever-growing number of full-time paid workers.

Viewed from this angle, Larry's role in the history of AIDS and the gay movement can be defined more precisely — and modestly. As an activist, he was one of many. Though he was in the right place at the right time on a couple of occasions — for the founding of GMHC and ACT UP — it would be hard to claim that he was at the forefront of the steady, patient work that builds a social movement. But as a polemicist, as a wielder of words that can rouse and motivate, his role may be unparalleled.

It's a role that cuts two ways. For even as his words mobilized, his verbal attacks have also stung and have consequently limited the influence he has had on the shape and evolution of AIDS policy and the direction of the gay and lesbian movement. As a figure with cultural capital at his disposal, Larry has been able to mount a platform from which he can be heard. Yet, the stance that he has taken — the cultural critic as outsider — necessarily creates boundaries around this influence. Perhaps this tells us something about the state of the movement even after the enormous growth and institutionalization that had been achieved by the mid-1990s. The person associated with the movement who had as much visibility as anyone remained an outsider.

*   *   *

There is more that could be said, of course. Larry's political writings brim with specific criticisms of decisions that were made and actions taken — or not taken — in the fight against AIDS. But I have chosen to focus on two themes, gay male sexual culture and the trajectory of the gay movement, not only because Larry's work draws attention to them but because they seem to me of particular importance. Debates about gay male sexuality have continued to rage. From the mid- to late-1990s, for instance, a rise in HIV seroconversion rates among some cohorts of younger gay men and the reappearance of commercial sex businesses in a number of cities led to a round of bitter intramural polemics among some activists, journalists, and intellectuals.[12] Likewise, in our press, our books, and our everyday discussions among ourselves, we spin endless spirals of analysis about what the movement can or cannot do. Behind all these words lie implicit assumptions about the movement's past, from which we draw conclusions about the present and the future. Larry's are the words of only one of us, but they open a window from which we can view the past and thus better imagine — perhaps even influence — what is yet to come.

5

Cycles of Change, Questions of Strategy: The Gay and Lesbian Movement After Fifty Years

Fifty years have elapsed since Harry Hay, an American Communist living in southern California, entertained the guests at a gay party by spinning out a plan for an imaginary political organization of homosexuals. In the intervening half century, gay men and lesbians have taken Hay's idea and run with it. They have built thousands of organizations — local, statewide, and national — dedicated to the proposition that they deserve the same rights and ought to be treated with the same respect as other Americans.

Many of these organizations have been explicitly political. They work to influence the outcome of elections, affect the content of party platforms, lobby for or against the passage of new laws and the repeal of existing ones, reshape the interpretation of the law through litigation, negotiate with bureaucrats to change the policies of government agencies, and pressure public officials through noisy demonstrations. Many more of these organizations are not directly involved in the political process. Lesbians and gay men have created community centers, social service organizations, institutions

This essay originally appeared in *The Politics of Gay Rights,* edited by Craig Rimmerman, Kenneth Wald, and Clyde Wilcox (Chicago: University of Chicago Press, 2000), pp. 31–53. My thanks to Craig Rimmerman for approaching me to write the piece and to all three editors for their comments and help in making the argument stronger. A much earlier version was presented at the OutGiving Conference, sponsored by the Gill Foundation, in Aspen, Colorado, in May 1996. My thanks to Mickey McIntyre for inviting me to speak there and to other participants at the conference for their encouragement to develop the ideas further.

for religious worship, sports leagues, health clinics, newspapers, magazines, bookstores, and publishing companies. More social and cultural than political in their expressed missions, these organizations nonetheless feed into the stream of overt political activity. By fostering stronger community ties and a collective awareness of belonging to a minority group, these organizations constitute a foundation on which to build sustained political engagement. In other words, the relationship of the gay *movement* and the gay *community* is close and interdependent.

Over the course of five decades, the work of all of these organizations, along with the actions of individuals and the support of mainstream groups and institutions, has dramatically changed the place of gay men and lesbians in American politics, law, society, and culture. Enough has happened over a long enough time to make it possible to do more than simply describe change. Half a century of public engagement over the status of gays and lesbians offers the opportunity to observe cycles of activity, suggest patterns of change, and draw conclusions that go beyond single campaigns, particular issues, and discrete local studies.

In this chapter I do three things. First, I offer a brief overview of the history of the gay and lesbian movement in the United States, sketching with broad brush strokes the main contours of political activity and change. Second, I address the issue of the velocity and intensity of change by teasing out from the historical record some sense of cyclical patterns. Third, I turn to questions of strategy, not in relation to individual goals or issues but more broadly — to the underlying strategic assumptions that have guided much of the movement's work in different eras. I end by pointing to some of the implications this analysis may have for contemporary choices facing political activists.

A Historical Overview

POST–WORLD WAR II ORIGINS[1]

The gay movement was born from the tension created by a brief interlude of freedom quickly followed by intense repression. By disrupting typical patterns of heterosexual sociability, World War II dramatically accelerated the development of a shared group identity among lesbians and gay men. The increased sex segregation, the geographic mobility, and the temporary freedom from the constraints of family allowed large numbers of young men and women, in a concentrated period of time, to explore their sexual desires and discover communities of men and women like themselves. The effects can be seen in the immediate postwar years: a growth in the number of gay and lesbian bars; the appearance of a spate of novels with gay and lesbian themes; the release of the Kinsey study of male sexual behavior in 1948 and the attention its findings on homosexuality received; the courageous efforts of some veterans to challenge the discharges they received for homosexual conduct; and the publication in 1951 of *The Homosexual in America,* a plea for understanding and tolerance of an unrecognized minority group in America.[2]

But the postwar years also brought an intensely conservative reaction. Most often thought of as a political era of virulent anti-Communism at home, the broad phenomenon known as McCarthyism witnessed as well an attack on homosexuals at every level of government and in a wide array of institutions. The Senate investigated the employment of "sex perverts" by the government; the military conducted witch-hunts against gays and lesbians; the FBI began surveillance of the gay community; postal authorities opened the mail of suspected homosexuals. In cities around the country, police harassed and arrested lesbians and gay men, while the press reported the names of these targets of zealous law enforcement officials. Throughout the 1950s, hundreds of gays and lesbians daily experienced trouble with the police, other government agencies, or their employers.[3]

In this setting, Harry Hay and a few other leftist gay men formed a secret organization, the Mattachine Society, in Los Angeles in 1951, dedicated to "liberating one of our largest minorities from . . . persecution."[4] Although they envisioned a radical organization that would mobilize masses of homosexuals to make change, the conservative temper of the 1950s led the organization, and the inchoate movement it was launching, in a more moderate direction. The Mattachine Society, along with the Daughters of Bilitis (DOB), a lesbian organization formed in San Francisco in 1955, spoke in softer, gentler tones. Making a plea for tolerance, they focused on education and information. Each organization published a magazine, established chapters in several cities, held public forums, and made contact with sympathetic professionals in law, medicine, and religion. As a counterpoint, a small group of more defiant gays published a magazine, *ONE,* that offered a sassier, bolder and brasher voice — so much so that after the postal authorities confiscated copies of it as obscene, the editors of *ONE* challenged the action and won a Supreme Court ruling that protected their right to publish material about homosexuality. It was the only significant legal victory of the 1950s.

The accommodationist stance of the Mattachine and DOB was very much suited to the times. It allowed the groups to take root, thus beginning a tradition of formal lesbian and gay organization that remains continuous to the present day. But the approach of these first activists also did not promise much in the way of change.

Provoked by the heroism of the southern civil rights movement and the idealistic rhetoric of the Kennedy presidency, the temper of the country began to shift in the early 1960s. The changed mood affected the outlook of the gay movement. In the northeast, a group of newer recruits began to speak with greater self-assurance. For instance, activists such as Frank Kameny, Barbara Gittings, and Jack Nichols boldly rejected the dominant medical view of homosexuality as an illness and confidently asserted the inherent health and goodness of their sexual orientation. Through letter writing, meetings, public picketing, and court cases, they also directly challenged the discriminatory practices of the federal government, which banned the employment of lesbians and gay men in all federal jobs and denied them security clearances in the private sector. By the late sixties, they had won two key cases in federal court, which began the process of overturning the ban.

In San Francisco, meanwhile, a combination of police repression and political scandals was provoking greater militancy among activists there. In 1961, Jose Sarria, a drag performer in one of the city's gay bars, ran for the Board of Supervisors in response to the police attacks on the gay subculture. His campaign led to the birth of San Francisco's first gay community newspaper as well as the formation of a trade association among gay bar owners. Before long, activists were in dialogue with some of the city's liberal Protestant ministers, were meeting regularly with public officials, and were holding candidate nights during fall electoral campaigns.

By the late 1960s, gay and lesbian activists across the country were creating tighter networks among themselves. There were fledgling groups in as many as two dozen cities. Basic goals of sodomy law repeal and fair employment practices had won the endorsement of mainstream organizations like the American Civil Liberties Union, which, increasingly, was advocating for this still-small social movement. Court cases in a number of states had provided gay bars with some protection against harassment, while the Supreme

Court had further narrowed the applicability of obscenity statutes to homosexual material. Prodded by activists, dissenting voices within the medical
profession were beginning to challenge the reigning orthodoxy that viewed
homosexuality as disease.

FROM STONEWALL TO AIDS[5]

Even as these developments reoriented the focus of the gay movement away
from the cautious educational efforts of the 1950s toward a more active
engagement with law, politics, and public policy, the leading edge of social
protest in the United States had moved far beyond the liberal, though militant, reform efforts of most gay activists. Black Power, the New Left, the
antiwar movement, an emerging women's liberation movement, the youth
counterculture: together these were creating a profound generational divide
in which many adolescents and young adults broke sharply with mainstream
values. Espousing a rhetoric of revolution, radicals in a variety of movements
set themselves against not only the American government, but most forms of
institutional authority.

   The Stonewall Riots of June 1969—when the drag queens and other
patrons of the Stonewall Inn in Greenwich Village fought the police who
were raiding the bar—became the catalytic event that allowed young gay
men and lesbians to draw the connection between their own status as homosexuals and the larger political critique that the movements of the 1960s were
making about American society. Taking advantage of the extensive networks
of communication that radicals of the 1960s had built, they created a new
kind of gay and lesbian movement. Adopting organizational names such as
the Gay Liberation Front, Radicalesbians, and Third World Gay Revolution, these activists brought anger, militancy, and an anarchic kind of daring
to the goal of gay and lesbian freedom. They conducted sit-ins in the offices
of newspapers and magazines that purveyed demeaning images of homosexuals; they marched in the street to protest police harassment; they disrupted
the conventions of psychiatrists who proclaimed them to be sick; they occupied campus buildings to win concessions from university administrators.
Proclaiming the necessity of "coming out of the closet" as the first essential
step toward freedom, they acted on their beliefs by being as visible as they
could in every sphere of life. And, they produced a new kind of writing about
homosexuality, one that used the language of oppression, that analyzed

sexuality and gender roles as mechanisms of inequality, and that argued for the relationship between gay oppression and other forms of social injustice. The message of gay liberation and lesbian feminism proved infectious, and it spread very quickly. On the eve of Stonewall, almost twenty years after the founding of the Mattachine Society, there were perhaps fifty gay and lesbian social change organizations in the United States. By 1973, four years after Stonewall, there were more than 800. The impulse to work in an organized way for change spread quickly from large cities like New York, San Francisco, and Los Angeles, from liberal university communities like Berkeley, Madison, Ann Arbor, and Cambridge, to cities and towns in every region of the country.

The gay men and lesbians motivated by Stonewall and the protest movements of the 1960s left an important legacy, one in which the notions of coming out as the key to change and pride as a stance toward one's sexual identity were central. These characteristics were adopted by virtually all the individuals and groups comprising the post-Stonewall movement. But the radical sea that spawned gay liberation was already drying up by the early 1970s. As the decade wore on, most of the organizations campaigning for gay freedom eschewed revolutionary rhetoric and instead tended to adopt one of two approaches to social change: (1) the reform of laws, public policies, and institutional practices so that lesbians and gay men enjoyd fair and equal treatment; and (2) the building of institutions designed to create a strong, cohesive, and visible community. The two purposes, of course, were intimately related since a well-organized, articulate, and mobilized community has a greater ability to change laws and public policies. And, to describe many of these organizations as "reform-oriented" says little about the tactics they wielded, which ranged from drafting legislation, lobbying elected officials, and registering voters to picketing, marching, and civil disobedience.

For instance, Lambda Legal Defense and Education Fund, an "ACLU" for gays and lesbians, was founded in 1973 with the purpose of using litigation to make change. The National Gay Task Force, also founded in 1973, worked with federal bureaucrats to change policies in areas such as immigration and the issuance of security clearances, and also sought to mobilize gays and lesbians to run as delegates to the national conventions of the major political parties. Locally, an organization like the Gay Activist Alliance of

Washington, D.C., worked to change police practices and campaigned for gay-friendly candidates for office. Around the country, gays and lesbians created community centers; they published newspapers and opened book-stores; they formed bowling and softball leagues and attended services at gay churches and synagogues; they staffed their own health clinics. And they also began to form caucuses and mobilize within institutions such as religious denominations, colleges and universities, professional associations of various kinds, and labor unions.

Not surprisingly, the higher visibility, the more extensive level of organization, and the new language of pride and respect sparked a significant degree of change in the decade after Stonewall. By the early 1980s, roughly half the states had repealed their sodomy statutes; more than three dozen municipalities, including some of the nation's larger cities, had prohibited discrimination on the basis of sexual preference or orientation; and some political figures of national stature spoke out in favor of gay rights. Building on work that had started before Stonewall, activists succeeded in persuading the American Psychiatric Association in 1973 to eliminate homosexuality from its list of mental disorders; two years later, the federal Civil Service Commission dropped its blanket ban on the employment of lesbians and gay men. During the Carter presidency, a delegation of gay and lesbian leaders were invited to the White House to discuss their goals, and in 1980 the Democratic Party included a gay rights plank in its national platform. And, numbers of court cases had been won, which seemed definitively to establish that gay and lesbian organizations enjoyed the constitutional protections of the First Amendment.

Even as the gay and lesbian community grew more visible and became more densely organized, the almost utopian sense of optimism that followed in the wake of Stonewall was fading. By the early 1980s, the nation's politics and social climate were growing more conservative, as witnessed by the election of Ronald Reagan to the White House in 1980 and the Republican majority in the Senate. The further repeal of sodomy statutes virtually stopped in the 1980s, and the passage of civil rights protections for homosexuals slowed as well. At the same time that legislative advances became less common, a more aggressive opposition to the gay movement coalesced. First coming to national attention in 1977, through the campaign led by Anita Bryant to repeal gay rights legislation in Dade County, Florida, an antigay Christian conservatism mounted similar successful campaigns in a number of localities. In Congress, conservative Republicans proposed a Family Protection Act designed in part to fortify the legislative barriers against gay equality.

Coincident with the rise of these outside threats were the internal divisions that compromised the ability of activists to mobilize their constituents and have the movement speak with a unified voice. Since the early 1970s, male sexism had led many lesbians to organize separate groups for women; by the end of the 1970s, a similar process was underway among gay people of color antagonized by the persistence of white racism in the institutions of the gay community. Differences also regularly emerged between those who pursued mainstream methods of lobbying, education, and negotiation and those who urged more militant, confrontational tactics; between those whose work gave priority to opening up mainstream institutions to gays and lesbians and those who valued the building of almost "nationalist" communities; and between those who saw homophobia and gay oppression as self-contained issues needing political attention and those who saw gay freedom coming only through a broader multi-issue struggle for social justice.

In the short run, these conflicts variously bred anger, frustration, and the fracturing of a movement still too weak to achieve its full range of goals. In the longer run, the efforts to respond to them promised a more densely organized community, with the experience of employing a fuller range of tactics to make change, involving participants who reflected the broad demographics of American society. For beneath all the particular campaigns and conflicts there remained one overriding fact in the early 1980s: the vast majority of lesbians and gay men, more than a decade after Stonewall and a generation after the founding of the Mattachine Society, remained "in the closet." Many who were willing to socialize within gay and lesbian worlds nonetheless kept their identity a secret from outsiders. Many others even maintained a distance from the social institutions of the gay community.

AIDS AND ITS IMPACT[6]

The biggest challenge, perhaps because completely unexpected, soon became the source of renewed political momentum for the gay and lesbian movement. In 1981, the Centers for Disease Control first reported the mysterious outbreak of fatal illnesses among clusters of gay men in a few major urban areas. Soon labeled acquired immunodeficiency syndrome, it spread during the 1980s with alarming rapidity among gay and bisexual men. In contrast to some other recently identified medical conditions — Legionnaire's disease and toxic shock syndrome — the media gave AIDS little attention, and government, especially in Washington, was loathe to devote resources to combatting the epidemic. When combined with the antigay rhetoric that the epidemic spawned, AIDS initially highlighted the vulnerability and relative political weakness of the gay and lesbian community.

But AIDS also unleashed vitally new constructive energy. Within a few years, gays and lesbians had built a nationwide infrastructure of organizations that provided health care and social services, assisted in scientific research, spearheaded prevention campaigns, and engaged in spirited public advocacy to combat the epidemic and the discrimination entwined with it. The fight against AIDS had startling effects. It brought many more gays and lesbians out of the closet, as the life-and-death nature of the epidemic overcame the fear of coming out. It led to renewed cooperation among lesbians and gay men. It provided a more visible platform for lesbians and gays of color and resources for them to build organizations of their own to fight AIDS. Eventually, policymakers at every level of government and in a host of other mainstream institutions opened their doors to gay men and lesbians wearing the hat of AIDS activist. And, once opened, it became easier for activists to use this new access to address issues of homophobia and gay oppression.

The effects can be seen most clearly through two events in 1987: the national March on Washington to fight AIDS and promote equality for gays and lesbians and the birth of ACT UP. In 1979, activists had organized a first national march; the most generous estimates put the crowd at 100,000. Now, eight years and many deaths from AIDS later, well over half a million men and women assembled from around the country. The experience was so powerful for many that they returned home with a determination not only to halt the spread of AIDS but to live openly as gay or lesbian. For instance, in North Carolina, where I was living at the time, the year or so after the March on Washington witnessed the formation of activist organizations in several cities and legislative hearings in a number of locales. Meanwhile, a new militancy was spreading among AIDS activists, which found expression in the direct action group, ACT UP. In local communities and in Washington, D.C., members engaged in confrontational tactics in order to prod public officials to take more vigorous action against the epidemic.

Although the AIDS movement and the gay movement were not identical, the boundary between them has always been indistinct and permeable.

Thus, the activism that AIDS had engendered also translated by the late 1980s into a more dynamic movement for gay and lesbian liberation. Locally, for instance, the pause in the passage of municipal gay rights laws yielded to an upsurge in the number of cities adopting such measures. State legislatures joined the parade, too, as several of them extended legal protections based on sexual orientation, and many more enacted statutes punishing hate crimes against lesbians and gay men. At the national level, activists participated in two key coalitions that brought them historic legislative victories in 1990: passage of the Hate Crimes Statistics Act, which mandated that the FBI collect statistics on hate-motivated violence, including crimes based on sexual orientation; and the Americans with Disabilities Act, whose provisions banned discrimination against people infected with HIV, the virus that causes AIDS.

Other indicators of change were also emerging by the early 1990s. Mainstream news media were devoting more substantial coverage to the lesbian and gay community so that issues of sexual identity became woven into the fabric of what was deemed newsworthy. Out-of-the-closet candidates were running for political office and winning, while a few members of Congress who had been closeted were able to secure reelection after coming out. Campaigns to win legislative protection against discrimination were increasingly complemented by the efforts of employees in the workplace and through unions to secure on-the-job guarantees. Notions of equality expanded to encompass not just the rights of individuals, but also those of the family unit as gays and lesbians fought for domestic partnership recognition, legal marriage, and access to adoption. Finally, in 1992 a major political party for the first time nominated for president a candidate, Bill Clinton, who openly campaigned for the support of the gay community and promised to take action around issues important to this constituency. Within days of Clinton's inauguration, a gay issue — the military ban against homosexuals — moved to the front and center of national politics.

The 1992–93 political season also saw the opponents of gay rights coalesce into a more potent than ever political force. While the Democrats nominated Clinton, the Republican national convention of August 1992 witnessed virulent homophobic rhetoric and the incorporation of explicitly antigay planks into the party platform. That fall, in Colorado and Oregon, militant antagonists of the gay movement campaigned for voter approval of statewide ballot initiatives that would have repealed and prohibited legislative remedies against discrimination based on sexual orientation. Early in 1993, a bipartisan coalition in Congress quickly took the initiative on the military issue away from the president, and the gay community suffered a major defeat. By the mid-1990s, the Christian right had built a powerful network of organizations that made fomenting fear of homosexuals a central element of their strategy.

THE CURRENT MOMENT[7]

In the wake of the military debacle, leaders of the gay and lesbian movement were forced to pause and take stock. On the one hand, there was no question that the community's quest for equality now occupied a recognized place on the political agenda. Issues such as workplace equity, marriage and parenting rights, and the responsiveness of the public schools to its gay students and personnel remained prominently in the public eye, as they were debated in local communities and state legislatures across the country. Especially in the realm of popular culture, a new kind of plateau had been reached. Particularly on television, but in Hollywood as well, gays and lesbians were becoming a standard fixture. No longer framed as monsters, nor relegated to an occasional walk-on role, they were increasingly a regular part of the social landscape.

On the other hand, there was a fractiousness to the debate about homosexuality that highlighted the lack of social consensus and that often produced political stalemate, contradiction, or both. For instance, by the mid-1990s, state capitols had become the site of ongoing legislative debate on gay issues, but the measures that were introduced and passed were equally likely to be gay-friendly or gay-hostile. Or, take the question of same-sex marriage. By the late 1990s, activists had succeeded in injecting the issue into the everyday consciousness of the society, so that, to many Americans, it came to seem unexceptionable. But, at the same time, conservative opponents succeeded in building against gay marriage a legislative wall so sturdy that the likelihood of legal recognition had actually receded. Even at the level of the Supreme Court the absence of consensus was striking. In the historic *Romer v. Evans* decision in 1996, a majority of the court ruled that gay rights laws cannot be banned. "A state cannot so deem a class of people a stranger to its laws," wrote Justice Anthony Kennedy, in a strong enunciation of elemental principles of fairness.[8] Yet even as it issued this decision, the nation still lived with the consequences of a decision ten years earlier, in *Bowers v. Hardwick,* in which the

Court upheld the constitutionality of sodomy laws that, historically, have provided much of the justification for discrimination against gay people.

Without question, this overview has tended to flatten the story of the gay and lesbian movement. It offers a view of the forest and renders indistinct the wealth of detail and variety to be found in all the trees. It ignores, for instance, differences in regional experience; it gives scant attention to vigorous, often contentious, debates within the gay and lesbian community; it emphasizes general patterns at the expense of local particularity. But with these limitations recognized, the account I have offered does also provide a thumbnail sketch of the broad contours of change.

Cycles of Change

Students of American reform have long attempted to understand what provokes change in American politics, why some eras witness rapid mobilization of citizens and major alterations in policy, and what happens to social movements during "the doldrums," those periods of quiescence when a society does not seem responsive to agitation for change. One study of American politics has noted that change occurs "both incrementally and in bursts," leading the authors to conclude that a "punctuated equilibrium" best describes how new policy agendas get set and implemented. A study of feminism in the past generation has commented on the importance of understanding how social movements "endure," how there are periods when a movement seems to be "in abeyance," and other times when movements "change relatively rapidly."[9]

In looking at the history of the gay and lesbian movement over the past fifty years, it is abundantly clear that the velocity of change — within the movement and in the implementation of its goals — has not been steady. In fact, careful scrutiny suggests something very different. For the gay and lesbian movement, change has come in the form of alternating cycles of what we might colloquially describe as "leaping" and "creeping." Identifying these cycles, whose rhythms seem at first glance to be thoroughly unpredictable, can help us make sense of the course of the lesbian and gay movement. It may also contribute to a deeper appreciation of the processes of change in social movements more generally and in American politics as well.

The first leap forward came in the late 1940s and early 1950s and was marked by the appearance of the Kinsey studies of human sexuality, Donald

Webster Cory's manifesto for homosexual rights, and the founding of the Mattachine Society. An awareness of oppression had crystalized in the minds of a few, and some of them had resolved to do something about it in a collective and organized way. But it was almost as if the effort required to launch a movement exhausted all the available political opportunity. For well over a decade, a small core of brave people crept along one very small step at a time. They were floating the new idea that homosexuals were the targets of unjust treatment. They were standing up for themselves, initiating a social dialogue, and experimenting with different kinds of strategies, but they could not succeed at much more than that.

The second great leap forward came in the handful of years around the Stonewall Riot. Galvanized by the radical upheavals of the 1960s and further inspired by the image of rioting drag queens, a cohort of young adult gays and lesbians adopted a stance of confident, almost defiant pride toward their sexual identities. They adopted the imperative to come out as the key element in the new movement they were building. And, taking the need for militant political action as a given, they targeted the key institutions that seemed complicitous in the oppression of gays and lesbians. Since many forms of institutionalized authority in the United States were wobbling as a result of a decade of protest, these radicals were able to accomplish a lot in a short period of time.

But the revolution that gay liberationists and lesbian feminists saw on the horizon never arrived, and for the next long stretch of time, gay and lesbian activists once again crept along. Incorporating both pride and coming out into the core sense of what it meant to be gay, these activists formed organizations, built community institutions, persisted in their efforts to affect law, public policy, and mainstream institutions, and generally maintained a higher level of visibility than their pre-Stonewall predecessors. What they lacked, and what the previous leap forward had not yet provided, were two key ingredients for a successful social movement: a mass constituency and an organizational infrastructure capable of successfully mobilizing it.

Coming in the wake of the AIDS epidemic, the third leap forward was roughly bounded by the 1987 March on Washington and the debate over the military exclusion policy in 1993. Like gay liberation of the Stonewall era, activists in these years frequently used militant direct action tactics. But unlike the two earlier periods of leaping ahead, this one witnessed movement and community organizations sinking secure roots in every region of the country. The movement for gay and lesbian equality also shifted in these years from being a predominantly volunteer effort to one in which many organizations were able to hire paid staff. In other words, the resources of the movement expanded enormously in these years, and the results could be seen not only in an even higher level of visibility, but in the string of successes that were achieved at the local, state, and national level. Gay issues in this period became a permanent part of the world of politics and public policy, and gay people became a regularly visible part of American cultural and social life. But the failure to repeal the military ban in 1993 and the presence of an ever-stronger organized conservative force in American politics put the brakes on change before this leap could reach the longer range goal of forging a new majority consensus around the place of gays and lesbians in American society.

Something to notice about the periods of leaping ahead is that they cannot solely — or even primarily — be explained by the will, the grit, or the savvy of activists themselves. Rather, they are provoked by social or political turmoil that creates new openings for change or new motivations to act. The first leap forward occurred in the context of the intense social disruptions of World War II and the equally intense repression of the early Cold War. The second grew out of a decade of tumultuous political and cultural protest that threw into question many of the core beliefs of Americans. The third leap was a result of the sudden and rapid spread of a terrifying epidemic that made survival itself seem to be at stake. These upheavals admittedly did not in themselves lead to political gains for gay men and lesbians; the decisions of individuals to act were still necessary. But it is difficult to imagine these intense periods of concentrated progress occurring without some preceding dramatic circumstances. And, while it is probably true that societies can expect periods of disorder and disruption to recur, their timing and form are unpredictable.

A second thing to notice about these alternating cycles is that they seem to be characterized by different sorts of approaches to change. For instance, the moments of leaping seem tailored to radical visionaries willing to use bold, often militant, methods. By contrast, in the eras when a movement creeps along, militancy may work in very particular local circumstances, but as a general approach to making change the arts of dialogue and negotiation seem to dominate these times. Of course, some might claim that radical visions and militant tactics are themselves the causes of the shift from creeping to leaping. At some point the ideas and the model serve as inspiration for large numbers of people, who then initiate a period of dramatic forward movement. Or, alternately, some might argue that, if only the militants toned things down, the big gains made during an era of leaping might keep happening. But, as a description of *what* has happened, rather than as an explanation of *why* things happened, it does seem to be true that radical visions and militant action characterize the moments of leaping ahead, while dialogue, negotiation, and moderation describe the dominant approach during the longer periods of creeping along.

A final point to make about these alternating cycles of change is that each accomplishes something essential. It is easy to see this in relation to the periods in which a political movement leaps forward, but it might seem questionable about the far less dramatic eras of creeping along. Perhaps a climbing analogy will help: the eras of leaping are comparable to intense stretches of climbing upward to reach a new height; the eras of creeping represent the work of constructing a solid base camp so the *next* height can be scaled. In other words, what happens during the long stretches of incremental, almost imperceptible change, during which the landscape around us does not seem to vary, is critical for the future. The choices one makes during these periods will help shape how far ahead, and in what direction, a movement or a community is able to leap during the next period of tumultuous change. In the 1950s and 1960s, activists kept alive a young social movement: surely that is something worth achieving. For much of the 1970s and 1980s, another larger cohort of activists stayed out of the closet, built community institutions in which the message of gay liberation could be nurtured, and accumulated enough local victories to make change seem possible and desirable: certainly that, too, had value. In the movement's last leap forward, activists reached the goal of putting their issues on the table of mainstream politics and achieving sustained cultural visibility, a significant achievement. We are now in the middle of the next era of creeping along: what are its chief characteristics? What, in other words, are the current goals of the moment and what strategies have emerged to achieve them?

Goals and Strategies

Antigay ideologues often speak about "the gay agenda." In the way they use the phrase, a tone of menace often attaches to it, as if there is something self-evidently threatening or surreptitious about the notion itself. In fact, gay and lesbian Americans do have an agenda, although we might more profitably think of it as the set of goals toward which the gay movement is heading. Despite the wide diversity of the community, and the often fractious debates that occur within it, there has been over the past few decades an amazingly broad consensus about a core set of goals. It would be very hard to dispute the claim that the overwhelming majority of activists — and probably a large majority of gay men and lesbians — agree that the following set of goals are highly desirable: the repeal of sodomy statutes criminalizing homosexual behavior; the removal of the medical classification of homosexuality as a disease; the elimination of discriminatory provisions and practices at every level of government and in every institution of civil society; fair and accurate representation of gay life and gay issues in the media; due process of law, especially in relationship to the behavior of law enforcement personnel toward lesbians and gays; recognition of family relationships; and protection against hate-motivated violence.

"Broad consensus" does not, however, mean unanimity; it leaves room for wide disagreement about priorities and about the mechanisms to achieve these goals. Most gay conservatives, for instance, look askance at civil rights laws as a way of eliminating discrimination because they are philosophically opposed to the expansion of governmental powers, while many gays on the left have tended to underemphasize work to end the military ban. Political moderates and liberals see a single focus on gay issues as a sufficient way to go about eliminating homophobia, whereas gays and lesbians who define themselves as politically progressive emphasize the importance of linking the fight against homophobia and heterosexism to social movements fighting against racism, sexism, and economic injustice. There may be consensus that gay family relationships ought to be recognized, but for some this means the right to marry, and for others it means broadening our understanding of what constitutes a family.

If a goal describes a destination, strategy describes how we propose to arrive. Strategy can be simply described as the overall plan we have for moving toward goals beyond our immediate reach. Nations, corporations, sports teams, families and individuals: every unit of people from the smallest to the largest needs strategy. Strategies can be effective or ineffective (which we learn, unfortunately, only after the fact). They can be bold or cautious, simple or complex. They can have a shelf life of a week or a decade, depending on the goal.

Above all, strategy is something that every individual, group, or institution *always* has, whether articulated or not. When strategy is articulated, it has a better chance of proving effective because its articulation implies that some conscious assessment of conditions has occurred, that human intelligence has been applied to the goals at hand. But even when strategy is not articulated, it can be discerned through the patterns that emerge after examination of the actions that individuals or groups make.

Thinking about strategy for a social movement is trickier than studying it at the level of the organization or, even, the nation. Corporations have CEOs, nonprofits have executive directors, and both have boards of directors. Policies get set and then carried out. A democratic nation, like the United States, has citizens who elect executives and legislators who then propose, enact, and implement laws. Organizations and nations experience debate, factionalism, and dissension from within; they experience conflict, pressure, and opportunity from without. But they also have boundaries, lines of authority, policies, and procedures that make them definable units of analysis.

But social movements? A congeries of organizations and individuals, social movements lack boundaries, lines of authority, policies, and procedures. Membership in a movement can be declared at will; participants can be responsible to no one but themselves. The frequency with which individuals are described in the gay press as "self-appointed leaders" in itself suggests how anarchic the gay and lesbian movement is.

Under these circumstances, is it even possible to speak meaningfully of strategy for the gay and lesbian movement beyond analysis of particular goals and campaigns? I think it is, though its discovery will not come by finding the one key manifesto or the joint declaration issued by major organizational leaders. Paradoxically, despite the apparently radically democratic structure of the movement, one can discern in different periods a quite broad agreement about a core outlook that constitutes in effect a strategic approach to change. This core outlook, or underlying strategic assumption, is most clearly evident during the stretches of time in which the movement is creeping along. Almost by definition, the periods of leaping ahead are characterized by such an abundance of restless chaotic activity that strategy seems too structured a concept to have much meaning.

The core outlook, or strategic approach, of the period from the early 1950s through the mid-to-late 1960s is best encapsulated by the phrase "give us a hearing." The phrase has the tone of a pleading in that action depends on the cooperation of individuals and institutions that are neither gay nor gay-friendly, but it also has the structure of a command, which leaves room for more militant approaches to the issue at hand. Either way, as plea or command, the phrase reflects the dominant fact of political, social, and cultural life in the 1950s and 1960s. Gays and lesbians were not setting the terms in which their lives were discussed or understood. Laws, institutional policies, the shape of social life, and the cultural representation of love, romance, and sexual desire: all presumed heterosexuality as normative.

"Give us a hearing" also efficiently describes the chief methods by which activists hoped to achieve what was the key goal of the era: to break the consensus that viewed homosexuality as dangerous, deviant, and wrong. Before Stonewall, almost all the energy of the movement went toward two activities: publishing material that would offer a counter to hegemonic views of homosexuality, and making contact with professionals in law, government, medicine, and the church whose views they hoped to influence.

"Here we are" effectively captures the core outlook for the period of creeping along that stretched from the early 1970s through the mid- to late-1980s. It suggests both place ("here") and collectivity ("we"). It takes the form of a simple statement of fact. But try to imagine the inflection in the voice: there is an insistence in the tone that suggests a mix of defiance, determination, *and* a lurking uncertainty as to how secure the place and the collectivity actually are. The urge to transform that uncertainty into a clear statement of fact explains the dominant strategic impulse of this era: a dual commitment to coming out and building community.

Among activists, coming out of the closet became the gay equivalent to a biblical injunction. Those who remained in the closet had a shadow cast over their moral character. Their integrity was suspect, their courage lacking, their identity uncertain. Meanwhile, those who had come out possessed a compelling need to have others join them. While it was emotionally liberating to drop the pretense of heterosexuality and reveal the secret of one's sexual identity, safety — and future success — demanded that the number of open gays and lesbians grow.

Security also seemed to require that gays and lesbians work intentionally toward building the institutions that could weld all these disparate individuals into a visible, cohesive community. The greater part of what men and women who considered themselves part of the movement did in these decades was directed toward creating and sustaining a public community.

Whether they were socializing in or moving to urban neighborhoods perceived to be gay; expending a great number of volunteer hours staffing hot lines, health clinics, or rudimentary community centers; establishing small businesses like bookstores, publishing ventures, or vacation getaways; playing together in softball or bowling leagues or worshipping together in a church or synagogue: large numbers of lesbians and gay men in the seventies and eighties devoted themselves to the task of collective visibility through organizations and communities that held an aura of separatism, of incipient queer nationalism, to them.

The quest for visibility and community-building even drove the policy goals that were most avidly pursued from the early 1970s until AIDS seemed to overtake all other issues in the mid-1980s. The elimination of the disease classification of homosexuality, the repeal of sodomy statutes, the adoption of civil rights protections against discrimination, curtailing police harassment of gay meeting places and enlisting law enforcement in the effort to prevent violence against gays and lesbians: all these goals share a common insistence. "Leave us alone," they seem to imply. "Get out of our bedrooms and out of our psyches." "Put a stop to our mistreatment." If they were all achieved, the cost of coming out would be reduced dramatically. And they would make gay communities safer, thus accelerating the process of community building.

Coming out and community building have had enormous staying power as core strategic impulses. Both seem to speak directly to what is perhaps the defining feature of gay experience, the fact that almost all gay men and lesbians are neither raised in nor socialized at an early age into a gay community. The imprint of those critical years of isolation, especially when compounded by the historic invisibility of homosexuality in everyday social life and in popular culture, creates an insistent need for the alternative—for visibility and the connection that community provides. Hence, the great enthusiasm that greeted Ellen Degeneres's coming out in 1997 and the decision of some sectors of the movement to hold a great public rally in the nation's capital in 2000, despite the absence of a concrete political agenda that a rally might contribute toward advancing.

Yet even as coming out and community building remain powerful impulses, the current period of creeping along has seen a dramatic shift in the specific issues that are animating the gay community. Matters like civil rights protections and sodomy law repeal certainly remain on the agenda, but since the eruption of the debate over the military exclusion policy in 1993, the weight of gay and lesbian advocacy efforts have tilted toward a new cluster of issues: family, school, and work. The recognition of same-sex relationships either through domestic partnership arrangements, civil unions, or the legalization of same-sex marriage; the assertion of the right to parent, the quest for equitable adoption, foster care, and custody policies, and the need to have the law recognize that some children have two parents of the same gender; the proliferation of lesbian, gay, bisexual, and transgendered employee groups across the country and their efforts to achieve workplace equity; the local battles over school curricula, the rights of students to organize gay-straight alliance clubs, the need for gay-supportive counseling and other policies in order to make schools safe places for students of all sexual identities: these, more than the old staples of the 1970s, have become the key issues in the gay community since the early 1990s.

The importance of this shift has been masked by the fact that the issues can be seen simply as new planks added to an old political agenda. But in fact they are qualitatively different. Whereas the issues of the 1970s revolved around a demand to be left alone, those of the 1990s call for recognition and inclusion. Instead of a core outlook captured by the phrase "here we are," the agitation around family, school, and work puts forward a different demand: "we want in." If the former appears as a simple statement of fact that can be realized through visibility and the creation of public communities, the latter demands both action and response. It requires, for its realization, a strategy of winning allies, of building support outside the community from the people — heterosexuals — whose lives too will inevitably be changed by the full inclusion of homosexuals in the core institutions of American society. It also suggests the distance that the movement has traveled from the days over a generation ago when it would have been thrilled just to receive a hearing.

Implications and Conclusions

In this chapter I have attempted to identify temporal cycles of change in the history of the gay and lesbian movement. I have also sought to align the periods of incremental change (what I have described as creeping along) with unifying strategic impulses. Though this analysis by no means accounts for the full range of activity or the various crosscurrents that inevitably exist in any period of time, it does, I believe, provide a reasonably accurate overview of the movement's history and political evolution.

It also suggests that the current moment in which we find ourselves — that is, in a third era of creeping along — displays strategic incoherence. In previous periods, goals, methods, and strategic vision worked in tandem with one another. Today, the gay and lesbian movement still places high value on a strategic vision that emphasizes coming out and community building, but the actual goals toward which activism is directed — goals around family, school, and work encapsulated by the outlook "we want in" — will not best be served by primary emphasis on coming out and building community. Access to and equity within the key structures of American life will instead require that winning allies becomes a priority. Coming out, of course, is a necessary precondition for this, but coming out has been so absorbed into the value structure of contemporary gay life that it hardly needs to be the movement's main rallying cry. As for community building, it can in serious ways work counter to achieving success in these other areas. Community building easily becomes insular and separatist. It can unwittingly foster an isolation and marginalization that runs contrary to the imperative of political engagement, particularly of the sort that involves winning support from outside one's own community.

These comments are meant to be descriptive rather than prescriptive. That is, I am making no judgment on the suitability of the goals that seem to be animating large numbers of gay men and lesbians in recent years. But, to the degree that success in achieving these new issues matter to their advocates, they will be better served by adopting methods of organizing designed to attract supporters and build coalitions. Otherwise, when the next moment of dramatic opportunity arrives, the movement will find itself too poorly positioned for a great leap into the future.

6

Organizational Tales:
Interpreting the NGLTF Story

The history of the National Gay and Lesbian Task Force is important. No account of the changes in the laws and public policies that shape gay and lesbian life in the United States would be complete without attention to it. The task force played a critical role in the campaign to eliminate the sickness classification of homosexuality. It worked to lift the prohibition on federal civil service employment for gays and lesbians. It strove in the 1970s to make the Democratic Party responsive to the gay community. It took the lead in the 1980s in national organizing against homophobic violence. As AIDS began to devastate gay male communities, the task force shaped the first serious efforts in Washington to address the epidemic. It was a founding member of the Military Freedom Project, which prepared the ground for the gays-in-the-military debate of 1993. It has worked with the administrations of presidents from Carter to Clinton. Some of the most effective and dynamic leaders of the queer movement have made NGLTF their organizational home.

At the same time, the identity of the task force is elusive. Most lesbians and gay men are, admittedly, unaware of what any of their national organiza-

This essay first appeared in *Creating Change: Sexuality, Public Policy and Civil Rights*, edited by John D'Emilio, William B. Turner, and Urvashi Vaid (New York: St. Martin's Press, 2000), pp. 469–486. Thanks are due to my co-editors as well as to Jed Mattes, our agent, and Keith Kahla, our editor. Ruth Eisenberg, Nan Hunter, and Jim Oleson gave helpful readings of an early draft. Jason Gagnon provided research assistance. A grant from the Schlesinger Library of Radcliffe College let me examine the papers of Charlotte Bunch. To all the staff and board of NGLTF with whom I have worked, my deepest thanks for making my time there intensely passionate.

tions do. But, among the minority who do pay attention to such things, some groups are more readily described than others. Lambda Legal Defense and Education Fund, for instance, is easily perceived as an "ACLU" of the gay movement. It fights through the courts to win equality and justice on issues involving sexual orientation. The Human Rights Campaign is a national gay political action committee. It endorses candidates, works on congressional campaigns, and lobbies in Washington, D.C. Parents, Family, and Friends of Lesbians and Gays (PFLAG) provides support for straight family members, educates them, and mobilizes them as a force for change. But what exactly is a "task force"? What does it do and what does it stand for? What niche has it filled in an evolving gay, lesbian, bisexual, and transgender movement? How has it gone about its work? In what ways has it succeeded, and in what ways has it not?

Like the task force itself, the answers to these questions are both important and elusive. They are important because they can help elucidate one of the critical mechanisms through which change has occurred during the past generation. And they are elusive because very little serious sustained examination of gay and lesbian organizations has occurred.

For social movements that sustain themselves for any length of time, organizations are key to survival and effectiveness. An individual might lay claim to being a feminist or a gay liberationist by virtue of her beliefs, or how she conducts her life each day, or having marched on Washington. But what keeps a social movement chugging along are its organizations. They are the mediating institutions between the big cause and the individual. Through organizations, an amorphous entity called a "movement" is able to frame missions, define goals, develop strategies, implement campaigns, achieve objectives and, above all, mobilize lots of individuals to act. Organizations help set the direction of social movements. And, while individuals can and do shape an organization, organizations also set up constraints within which individuals work. Understanding organizations, then, is an essential element in any assessment of how a movement succeeds in creating change.[1]

All these issues — creating change, the dynamics of social movements, the role of organizations — are compelling to me. I study and teach about social movements. I have written extensively about the history of the gay and lesbian movement. I have been both the scholarly observer and the impassioned participant. I am especially drawn to understanding the role of

NGLTF because, for a dozen or so years, NGLTF was the primary place in which I expressed my activist impulses.

My own history has intersected with the history of the task force at a number of points. In 1973, as a newly minted gay activist in New York City, I remember the founding of what was then called the National Gay Task Force (NGTF). At the time, I saw it as one more sad indicator that the radicalism and militancy that drew me to gay liberation was dying. In 1976, when the Democratic Party held its national convention in New York, I was one of many thousands demonstrating noisily outside the convention. NGTF was inside the convention hall, working with a party that I saw as bankrupt and compromised. In the early 1980s, I found myself taking a second look at the task force after Ginny Apuzzo, an activist whom I knew and respected, became executive director. I did my first work for NGTF in 1983 when Apuzzo commissioned a report from me detailing the history and impact of federal antigay employment policies.

My involvement with the task force escalated dramatically toward the end of the 1980s. In 1987 I helped Sue Hyde, the director of NGLTF's Privacy Project, plan a "town meeting" on sex and politics to coincide with the national March on Washington. The event drew an overflow crowd of many hundreds. Moderating it, I found myself marveling that a seemingly mainstream organization devoted to legislation and lobbying would take on the issue of sex. In 1988, I joined the board of the organization, served as its co-chair for two years, and stayed on it for five years. They were five very intense years in the life of the queer movement in the United States. I left the board in the fall of 1993, but returned to the organization in 1995 for a two-year stint as a staff member, charged with launching a Policy Institute, or "think tank." After I left, I continued to work with the organization on discrete projects, such as its national policy roundtable. I think it safe to say that through my participation in NGLTF, I have learned more about social movements and their organizations than any amount of study alone could have provided.

This essay is motivated, at least in part, by an effort to make sense of my experience with the task force, particularly during the decade between 1988 and 1997 when it drew from me as much commitment as did either my academic career or my intimate relationships. NGLTF won me over because it seemed to be doing what social movement organizations rarely attempt.

It was combining outsider and insider stances into an elegantly choreo-graphed—and compellingly innovative—strategy for change. Not content with the constraints that the unwritten rules of inside-the-Beltway politics imposed, and unwilling to accept the marginality that often came with grassroots protest, NGLTF tried to play with both. It lobbied and it agitated. It negotiated and it mobilized. It supported breaking the law and changing the law. It tinkered with the system to effect small immediate changes, and it expressed a commitment to a more expansive vision of social justice.

Maintaining this stance was, and is, no easy matter. Many board and staff members, whether from temperament or political philosophy, inclined to-ward one direction or the other. But the years from the late 1980s into the early 1990s seemed especially conducive to this balancing effort. Through ACT UP and other local groups, there was a resurgence of direct action militancy, while in Washington, in some state capitals, and in many cities, the legislative process was newly hospitable to queer lobbying. These years, roughly extending from the 1987 March on Washington to the 1992 national elections, witnessed shifts as profound as those that came in the aftermath of the Stonewall uprising. And NGLTF's influence could be detected every-where.

For a brief season, the election of Clinton seemed to multiply the oppor-tunities for change. I say this not because of Clinton himself, since little in his previous career suggested any strong commitment to a progressive political agenda. Rather, Democratic control of both the White House and Congress ought to have shifted the political calculus just enough to make the victories of the previous few years pale in comparison to what might lie ahead.

It didn't happen. Rather than an opportunity, the "gay moment" of 1992–93 was a disaster for the task force. Instead of seizing the day, NGLTF almost imploded. During the next three years it shrunk precipitously in size, influence, and effectiveness. Why?

At the time, caught within the drama of the internal debates, I interpreted the near collapse of the task force as the result of poor political choices. The emotional intensity of Washington—and movement—politics in the face of the gays-in-the-military debate, the seductive accessibility of the new presi-dent, and the magnitude of the 1993 national march seemed to destabilize the precariously crafted balance of insider-outsider strategies. In the effort not to become, as the Human Rights Campaign appeared to be, a tool of an unreliable Democratic party, NGLTF moved far in the other direction. It saw itself only as oppositional, and it seemed to equate marginality and outsider status as values in themselves. In other words, I interpreted the travails of NGLTF through the very lens with which we participants framed, and debated, the story.

Now, a number of years and many hours of reflection later, I have come to see these events differently. They need, I believe, to be placed in the context of the organization's whole history. And they need to be understood not in the terms that participants used to debate political choices, but through the unarticulated fundament that lies at the core of NGLTF's organizational culture.

Though often a passionate advocate in many of the debates that shaped the organization's direction over a number of years, in the rest of this essay I will try to look at those debates, and the larger history of the organization, with some measure of detachment. I will provide an overview of the organization's history, detailing the key issues, people, and events that have comprised it. I will then suggest — and discard — a number of common ways of interpreting a social movement organization's history. I will pick up the concept of organizational culture, suggest how one might define this in relation to NGLTF, and detail the ways I think this can help us understand the history of the task force. Finally, I will suggest some lessons. Because I care so much about the organization, decoding the history of NGLTF is personally important to me. But I also think it is vital to raising the organization's effectiveness — and the efficacy of other organizations as well.

An Overview[2]

NGTF was founded in New York City in October 1973. In the four years that had elapsed since the Stonewall uprising in Greenwich Village, militant gay, lesbian, and transgender organizations had proliferated across the country, their numbers approaching a thousand. The gay liberation movement of those years, full of bravado and daring, was given to the dramatic gesture. Its hit-and-run tactics, its in-your-face rhetoric, succeeded in capturing media attention. The movement also won for itself an expanding body of recruits, especially among younger lesbians and gay men affected by the radical cultural politics associated with the sixties. But its style and methods were not particularly suited to the long, sustained march through institutions that the battle against homophobia, heterosexism, and gay oppression also required.

The key founders of the task force — Bruce Voeller, Nath Rockhill, Ron Gold, and Howard Brown among them — were New York City activists. Voeller, Rockhill, and Gold were all closely associated with the Gay Activists Alliance (GAA), one of the premier post-Stonewall organizations. They had grown tired of the GAA's chaotic style of operation in which every proposal could be debated endlessly and mass membership meetings seemed to stand in the way of the coordinated pursuit of long-term goals. Brown was a former health commissioner for the city of New York, a professionally successful gay man who had just come out on the front page of the *New York Times*.[3] He was looking for a vehicle to express his political commitments.

Voeller and the others saw the organization they were launching as a new departure.[4] Until the founding of the task force, volunteer energy had sustained the gay liberation movement, and almost all its work had been local in nature. The task force was conceived as a national organization, designed to work on issues beyond the reach of local groups, with a paid staff who would provide a measure of continuity and professionalism to the work of gay advocacy.

The task force came into being at a promising time for national gay advocacy efforts. Everything in America was up for grabs. An unpopular war was ending. The racial status quo had been shaken. Feminists were bringing a new brand of sexual and gender politics into everyday life. The conservative Nixon administration was unraveling in the wake of the Senate Watergate hearings. Everywhere, it seemed, traditional sources of power and privilege faced challenges. Could a national civil rights organization of lesbians and gay men capitalize on the moment and win concessions from a range of American institutions?

The early years of the task force fueled the optimistic sense that anything was possible. Despite its small size (a handful of staff members with an annual budget of a couple of hundred thousand dollars in its first years), it was able to nudge change forward in several critical areas. In December 1973, two months after NGTF was formed, the national board of the American Psychiatric Association voted to remove homosexuality from its list of mental disorders. When dissident psychiatrists insisted on an association-wide referendum, the task force worked with allies in the profession to win support for the change and defeat the referendum. Supporting the efforts of Frank Kameny, one of its board members, it pushed successfully to have the federal Civil Service Commission reverse, in 1975, the ban on the employment of lesbians and gay men in federal jobs. Other achievements included successful lobbying within the American Bar Association to put the organization on record in favor of sodomy law repeal (1974) and eliciting from the National Council of Churches a resolution condemning antigay discrimination (1975).

As the above examples suggest, NGTF cast its net widely. It saw change as coming not only through government, but through a range of institutions in American life. In 1975 Ginny Vida, its media director, coordinated one of the first national protests against the media, in response to a homophobic episode of *Marcus Welby, M.D.*, a popular television series of that era. The task force won a reversal of an Internal Revenue Service policy that denied tax-exempt status to organizations that argued that homosexuality was acceptable. It conducted the first national survey of major corporations to determine their hiring practices, and then began to advocate for explicit nondiscrimination policies. It worked with Bella Abzug and, later, with Ed Koch, members of the House of Representatives from New York City, to introduce a comprehensive gay rights bill into Congress.

Jean O'Leary, a founder of Lesbian Feminist Liberation in New York City, joined the staff in 1975 and became co-executive director the following year.[5] O'Leary brought a strong interest in party politics and in feminism to the organization. Focusing on the Democratic Party, which in these years seemed to offer the most likely opportunity for dialogue, she initiated a convention project in 1976. NGTF surveyed the party's candidates for the presidential nomination, organized constituent meetings in a number of districts, and maintained a communications center at the convention. Although the platform made no mention of gay and lesbian issues, O'Leary and the task force gathered signatures from 600 delegates in support of gay rights and sodomy law repeal.

O'Leary also worked closely with other female staff and board members (gender parity existed on the board almost from the beginning) to agitate within the women's movement for lesbian visibility and support for lesbian rights. Focusing attention on President Carter's International Women's Year's (IWY) activities, O'Leary managed to get herself appointed as the only openly lesbian delegate on the president's IWY commission. O'Leary and other task force women coordinated the passage of sexual preference resolutions at thirty state conferences and, at the national conference in Houston in 1977, won overwhelming support for lesbian rights. The Houston conference was a milestone in the effort to make equality for lesbians a key feature of mainstream feminist advocacy.

The late seventies saw both new opportunities and dramatic challenges. O'Leary's work within the Democratic Party had cracked open a door to the Carter administration. The task force was able to engineer a series of meetings with officials in executive agencies, initiating a dialogue about issues ranging from access to gay publications for inmates of federal prisons to the implementation of immigration and naturalization policy. At the same time, the gay movement encountered new resistance to its advocacy efforts in the form of an emerging New Right that deployed a rhetoric of family and morality to challenge both feminism and gay liberation. The first major battle came in 1977 in Dade County, Florida, where Anita Bryant, a popular singer, was spokeswoman for a campaign to repeal a gay rights ordinance. While the campaign brought sustained media attention to gay rights for the first time, it also was the opening battle in a continuing struggle that has stretched now for more than two decades. Voeller traveled to Florida frequently to help local activists craft a winning strategy. But in Dade County, as well as in Wichita, St. Paul, and Eugene, Oregon, in the following year, gay activists proved unable to prevent repeal of antidiscrimination ordinances.

Just when the shifting political winds began to constrict the opportunity structure for gay activists, NGTF experienced a turnover in leadership. Both Voeller and O'Leary, who had worked effectively together, left in 1979. As replacements, the board of directors chose Charles Brydon, a businessman who had built an organization of gay professionals in Seattle, and Lucia Valeska, a grassroots activist from New Mexico with long experience in the women's movement.[6] Very different from one another in temperament and political perspective, the two were a poor pair for jointly running an organization. Yet, the task force especially needed forceful leadership for the new decade. Reagan was about to enter the White House, and Republicans were winning control of the Senate for the first time in a generation. Powered by a newly mobilized fundamentalist constituency, the Republican Party was coming to dominate politics just as AIDS emerged in the lives of gay and bisexual men.

The few achievements of the task force during these years rested on decisions made earlier. In October 1979, the task force co-sponsored the first national conference of Third World gays and lesbians, which in turn helped spur autonomous organizing in the 1980s within people of color communities. It worked with other organizations to sustain a strong presence at the 1980 Democratic Convention, which saw the incorporation of some gay issues into the party's platform. The Fund for Human Dignity, a nonprofit educational arm of the organization, became fully operational. Mel Boozer was hired as a lobbyist, giving the New York-based organization a Washington presence for the first time.

But Brydon and Valeska were poorly suited to the new era. The differences between them meant that internal conflicts — between men and women, between proponents of more cautious approaches to change and more assertive ones — consumed much of the organization's energies. Instead of focusing attention outward on the increasingly well-organized opponents of the gay movement, the Task Force often found itself engaged in internecine quarrels with other gay organizations. Brydon and Valeska each committed a series of very public gaffes, which lowered the credibility of NGTF. By the early 1980s, the budget of the organization was shrinking, unable to keep pace with inflation. Important areas of work, like media advocacy, were dropped because of financial constraints. Brydon quit as codirector in 1981. The following year, Valeska was fired by the board of directors after a disastrous performance in Dallas at the first national forum on AIDS.

With the task force in disarray and close to collapse, the board hired Virginia Apuzzo to restore NGTF's credibility. Apuzzo possessed a number of strengths. She held the respect of both lesbians and gay men. She was a dynamic speaker who could rouse an audience to action. She combined a commitment to using conventional modes of politics with a visionary rhetoric of radical social change.

Apuzzo also displayed an uncanny knack for identifying cutting-edge issues. For instance, as gay men and lesbians became more visible in the 1970s, homophobic violence against them seemed to escalate. Police were often unsympathetic, blaming the victim rather than the perpetrator, and gays and lesbians were often reluctant to report crimes. In cities like New York and San Francisco, local antiviolence groups formed to address the issue. Apuzzo took a small volunteer-staffed initiative at NGTF and supported its development into a major national organizing effort. Under the direction of Kevin Berrill, the Anti-Violence Project provided technical assistance to local groups, coordinated the first national surveys of hate-based homophobic violence, and worked to put the issue on the radar screen of the

Justice Department and other law enforcement organizations. Years of patient coalition building eventually led to the inclusion of sexual orientation in federal legislation, the Hate Crimes Statistics Act of 1990. For many years, the task force's Anti-Violence Project stood as a model of the partnership that could develop between local and national advocacy efforts.[7]

Above all, Apuzzo focused the energy of NGTF on the AIDS crisis. When she took the job at the task force, AIDS was not yet a major story in the mainstream media or the gay press. The nationally reported case load was still below a thousand and, beyond a few big cities, the epidemic had hardly registered in the consciousness of the community. But Apuzzo sensed that a crisis of massive proportions was in the making, and its solution was beyond the capacity of local groups, like the Gay Men's Health Crisis in New York City, to solve. The AIDS crisis required resources that only the federal government was large enough to provide.

Apuzzo hired Jeff Levi, an activist in Washington, D.C., as a lobbyist to focus on AIDS. Together with Levi, a small number of other activists, and some friendly congressional staff, she began to craft a response that involved building key relationships within the federal government, mobilizing gay community organizations, and reaching out to likely coalition partners. At an early congressional hearing in Washington in 1983, Apuzzo wore a flaming red dress to dramatize her anger as she blasted the neglect and apathy of the Reagan administration. She found the money to help launch, with the support of other gay organizations, AIDS Action, which became the key lobbying organization in Washington. AIDS Action in turn, with Levi playing a critical role, formed the NORA coalition (National Organizations Responding to AIDS), which brought together a wide range of organizations whose work was affected by the AIDS epidemic. While the rewards of this work were great, the price was also high. It almost bankrupted the organization, weakening the organization's infrastructure.

After Apuzzo left the task force in 1985, the job of organizational rebuilding fell to Levi. The board approved the move of the organization's offices to Washington, in response to the increasing emphasis on work at the federal level. It also changed the name, to the National Gay and Lesbian Task Force, to make clear the commitment to gender parity and lesbian issues. Meanwhile, mounting frustration over AIDS and anger over the Hardwick decision of 1986, in which the Supreme Court sustained the constitutionality of

Georgia's sodomy statute, was enlarging the pool of gay men and lesbians willing to support the work of an organization like NGLTF.

Through the rest of the 1980s, Levi slowly added staff, augmenting the scope of the organization's work. Urvashi Vaid was hired as communications director and used the position to engage in an assertive brand of media advocacy. After Hardwick, Sue Hyde came on as director of a newly created Privacy Project, designed to work state-by-state for sodomy law repeal. Levi brought in Peri Jude Radecic, a lobbyist with the National Organization for Women, to handle the expanding volume of legislative- and executive-branch work in Washington. Ivy Young became the director of a new Families Project, providing resource for activists seeking to win domestic partnership benefits and to expand their right to parent. And Kevin Berrill continued his work on the issue of hate-motivated violence.

By the end of the 1980s, the task force occupied a unique niche in the gay and lesbian movement. It played an important role in Washington, D.C., where, along with the Human Rights Campaign Fund, it maintained a presence on Capitol Hill and worked with a broad range of federal agencies. But through its organizing projects, it increasingly saw its role as mobilizing the grassroots to make change. Radecic, for instance, not only lobbied members of Congress. She issued "report cards," grading them based on their votes on gay and AIDS issues, and then circulated the reports to local constituents as a way of holding legislators accountable. As organizations like ACT UP adopted direct action tactics as part of the practice of politics, the task force was able to walk a line that allowed it to lobby on the inside and support militancy on the outside.

When Urvashi Vaid succeeded Levi as executive director in 1989, she pushed the task force more strongly in the direction of movement-building.[8] The growing power of the religious-based New Right and the attacks on the gay community from politicians like Jesse Helms, William Dannemeyer, and Robert Dornan made it clear that a Washington-based politics alone would not succeed. Under Vaid, the task force devoted itself to strengthening the local infrastructure of the gay and lesbian movement. Creating Change, its annual conference, became the major site each year in which activists learned skills, shared strategies, and concocted joint organizing campaigns. Project directors at NGLTF spent much time on the road, working to strengthen local organizations and build statewide coalitions. At the same time, Vaid's tenure (1989–92) coincided with important legislative victories. Among them were the Hate Crimes Statistics Act, the Americans with Disabilities Act, the Ryan White Care Act, and important changes in immigration law.

The time between the summers of 1992 and 1993 was "the gay moment" in American national politics. Bill Clinton, the Democratic candidate, embraced the gay community as no other presidential nominee had done before. By contrast, the Republican convention in Houston witnessed an orgy of fiercely homophobic rhetoric and references to "culture wars." Early in 1993 the military exclusion policy became the subject of national debate. As hundreds of thousands marched in Washington for gay, lesbian, and bisexual rights, and as Clinton invited gay leaders to the White House, Congress was relentlessly moving toward support for the continued ban on gay, lesbian, and bisexual service members. For the gay community, the year was marked by a dizzying oscillation between exhilarating optimism and terrifying vulnerability. Many organizations, local and national, expanded dramatically during this period, as more gays and lesbians than ever before were motivated to support political mobilization. Despite the defeat over the military issue, organizations by and large emerged from this period larger, stronger, and better positioned to shape policy and public discourse.

But not the task force. The years from 1993 to 1997 were difficult ones for the organization. Leadership was unstable at a time of tremendous opportunity. Vaid's successor as executive director, Torie Osborn, stayed for only six months. The next two executive directors, Peri Jude Radecic and Melinda Paras, also had relatively brief tenures. They presided over a staff that was rent by internal debates over the direction the organization should take in this new era of national attention. Should the organization emphasize national work or focus on grassroots mobilization and movement-building? Should the task force work closely with the Clinton administration or position itself as a progressive opposition? Should it continue its issue-oriented projects or devote its resources to fighting and exposing an increasingly powerful religious right? Should its focus remain on gay issues, or should it work in coalition on a range of issues to build a strong progressive movement?

The effects of these divisions were debilitating, not strengthening. Appearing directionless and ineffective to many on the outside, the task force saw itself shrink precipitously. The opportunities for growth that the events of 1992–93 brought proved temporary for NGLTF, even as other movement organizations became permanently larger. Between 1994 and 1996, its budget shrunk by almost 50 percent, and its staff was cut in half. Organizing projects that had been very successful — like the antiviolence and campus projects — were terminated. The task force lost its leadership of issues that had long been associated with the organization. Its lobbying presence in Washington, formerly visible and effective, faded away. In the mid-1990s, it played no role of consequence in the negotiations over reauthorization of the Ryan White Care Act, the debates over the Defense of Marriage Act, or the lobbying for ENDA, the Employment Nondiscrimination Act.

However, even during this period of crisis, some important initiatives were taken. Under Melinda Paras, the board approved the creation of a policy institute, a combined "think tank" and research arm. Its mission was to produce fresh perspectives on critical issues, create academic-activist partnerships, and encourage innovative strategies for change. NGLTF also made the building of effective statewide federations a priority, as state legislatures in the 1990s became key arenas for the making of policy on gay, lesbian, bisexual, and, increasingly, transgender issues.

Under the leadership of Kerry Lobel, who became executive director at the end of 1996, the organization slowly began to grow again. Finances improved, and new staff were hired. Urvashi Vaid returned to the organization, this time as director of the policy institute. She initiated a national policy roundtable that brings together the leaders of more than three dozen key organizations and a religious roundtable that is welding activists in communities of faith into a more effective force for change. State organizing has continued, and in 1999 NGLTF led the planning for "Equality Begins at Home," the first-ever coordinated set of lobbying events, public rallies, and conferences in state capitals around the country. Whether this work is prelude to a new era of effective advocacy for NGLTF, or whether its historical era as a leading national organization has passed, remains to be seen.

Interpreting the Task Force Story

Much more could be written, of course. But even this brief overview suggests a few things. The task force has been involved in some of the key issues facing the gay and lesbian community since the mid-1970s. At particular moments, and on certain issues, it has played a key role in focusing attention, mobilizing support, and provoking policy change. But it also has a checkered organizational history. There have been periods when the task force was anything but effective, when it dropped the ball, when it became mired in internal squabbles, when it relinquished its leadership role to other organizations. What accounts for this oscillation between peaks and troughs of organizational effectiveness?

One way of interpreting the history of NGLTF is by looking at "leadership eras." Under Voeller and O'Leary, the task force accumulated a credible record as a national voice for gay and lesbian advocacy efforts. It compiled some important achievements and broke new ground. Under Brydon and Valeska it stumbled badly and accomplished little. Under the successive regimes of Apuzzo, Levi, and Vaid, it gathered a great deal of momentum, thrusting itself into important policy debates. It led nationally and worked closely with local grassroots activists to craft a variety of strategies for change. Under Osborn, Radecic, and Paras, NGLTF almost imploded and became increasingly marginal even as queer issues were agitating the body politic as never before. Under Lobel, the task force engaged in a process of rebuilding, of recouping lost ground and carving out a new niche for itself.

Another way of approaching the task force story is through the prism of politics, the series of conflicting perspectives variously thought of as left or right, liberationist or assimilationist, grassroots militancy or professional lobbying, multi-issue coalition building or single-issue identity politics. NGTF was founded specifically to free itself from the excessive democracy of local gay activist organizing, addressing national issues as a professionalized advocacy group. Lesbians brought more feminist styles of politics to the organization and, for a while in the 1970s, it blended a national lobbying perspective with efforts to mobilize local activists. Under Brydon and Valeska, these two perspectives clashed rather than cooperated. By the mid-1980s, a conscious effort was being made to keep both insider and outsider approaches to change in balance, so that both were in the task force tool kit of advocacy methods. Thus, NGLTF was willing to negotiate with the Food and Drug Administration over its approach to testing and approving AIDS drugs at the same time that it was actively supporting militant ACT UP demonstrations against the agency. It helped train local activists and build local organizations even as it worked for change inside the Beltway. In the 1990s, faced with the rise of an extremist right wing, the disarray of Democratic Party liberals, and the perception of betrayal by the Clinton administration that the military debate engendered, the tensions involved in this balance exploded. NGLTF headed in the direction of grassroots organizing rather than lobbying Congress or the executive branch. It self-consciously defined itself as "the queer voice of the progressive movement and the progressive voice of the queer movement," while it floundered over the effort to translate this perspective into an effective program and organizational mission. By the late 1990s it seemed to emerge from this turmoil. It reconstituted itself as an organization committed to progressive coalition building, even as much of its day-to-day work focused on issues of concern to gays, lesbians, bisexuals, and the transgendered.

Yet a third way of understanding the history of NGLTF is to place task force activities within the shifting social and political world of the last generation. How attentive has it been to the changing needs of the gay and lesbian community? Has it picked issues that mattered to its constituents? Has it read the political climate well enough to know where it could negotiate change and which victories were achievable? How has it responded to the falling fortunes of the Democratic Party and American liberalism in the 1980s and 1990s, and the simultaneous rise to political power of the Republican Party and a new American conservatism? Exploring questions such as these combine issues of leadership and political perspective with historical context to allow us to chart the varied fortunes of NGLTF over time.

Each one of these angles is useful. That the quality of leadership matters for an organization seems self-evident. The head of an organization sets a tone, shapes the environment in which staff works, and provides the public with a face, personality, and character. Other key staff can build — or destroy — credibility with the people whom they are trying to mobilize and the figures they are trying to influence by the skill and style they bring to their work. There is no single formula or profile for good leadership, but without effective leadership no organization will thrive and achieve significant goals. Leadership may not be the only thing that matters, but it is essential to an organization's welfare.

Similarly, the politics of an advocacy organization will shape its focus and position it in the world of public policy. A self-definition as liberal or conservative, reform oriented or radical, influences goals, tactics, the choice of coalition partners, and the target of one's activities. An organization's political orientation also will affect its relation to the kind of conflicts that an identity-based constituency confronts, such as the tension between a liberationist vision and assimilationist aspirations.

Finally, any incisive analysis of a movement organization will be attuned to the shifting historical context. The most compelling issues of one decade can fade away in the next, even if one's objectives have not been achieved. Successes open up new horizons. Generational shifts require rethinking one's goals as younger cohorts come of age with new expectations of how they would like the world to be. Meanwhile, a new balance of forces in national politics, changes in the cultural fabric, or shifts in economic or social life will often require a rethinking of strategy, tactics, and goals. Without the ability to grasp the significance of these trends, the most successful organization of one era will be dust in the next.

Let me propose, however, that even combining all three of these perspectives will leave the task force story indecipherable. For something else has been at play in the workings of NGLTF that has, as much as anything, shaped the contours of its history and molded its identity. The task force has a *culture* that drives it.

To describe this culture in a nutshell: NGLTF *exists to fill a void*. Its purpose from its inception has been to do what needs to be done, but what no one else is doing. This sense of purpose propels it forward, creating a sense of daring, innovation, and living on the edge. It also generates an atmosphere of missionary zeal and of sacrifice: the organization is there to serve selflessly the community's needs. Its periods of greatest achievement have come during those times when the void it chose to fill coincided with work that most needed doing and when the organization has been able to achieve consensus internally about what to do. But the imperative to innovate, to be on the edge, also has its drawbacks. It can lead to crisis and disarray as an organization tries to reinvent itself for the changing times. It prevents an organization from developing expertise and longevity in an area, as the work of one era comes to feel old and stale while the new always beckons alluringly. And it keeps the identity of the task force elusive precisely because its work keeps shifting. An organization always in search of the new, or always rushing to fill a void, will experience recurring difficulties. Supporters will peel away as the organization no longer speaks to them, and new supporters will always have to be found. Rather than build steadily, it will periodically have to start over again.

The need to fill a void animated the organization from its inception. No organization had national work as its mission when NGTF was founded in 1973. The absence of competitors and the sense of breaking new ground created an élan, a sense of excitement and achievement over virtually every initiative. But, in time, the thrill evaporated as the slow plodding work of extracting policy change from the federal bureaucracy moved to the foreground. The task force found itself paralyzed. Should it continue or abandon the work it had started in Washington? Or should it rush to fill a new void that had appeared—helping local organizations counteract a rising right-wing assault on gay rights legislation? Unable to stick with the old or embrace the new, the organization stumbled.

The solution came when the need to craft AIDS policy—a new, bigger, more menacing void—emerged in the 1980s. No movement organization was seizing the initiative in Washington where the federal government, for better or worse, held the future of the epidemic in its hands. Apuzzo's decision to embrace the issue, to rush to fill the gap, made a historic difference in the evolution of AIDS policy over the next several years. It also saved NGTF, restoring its sense of missionary fervor, creating an environment of desperate activity commensurate with the danger of AIDS.

By the late 1980s the task force had succeeded so well that it no longer was working alone. In Washington, the AIDS Action Council and the NORA Coalition were advocating for AIDS while in communities throughout the country ACT UP chapters were engaging in direct action protest, drawing major media attention to the issue. AIDS activism was still a life-and-death issue, but the field was now crowded. No longer did it satisfy the need to be on the frontier, or lean over the edge of the precipice, staring into the unknown and the uncharted.

Instead, AIDS had spawned something new. As the 1987 March on Washington revealed, a whole new generation of gays and lesbians had come out of the closet and were prepared to make of their identity a political statement. But the infrastructure to sustain local activism was still weak in much of the country. Toward the end of the decade NGLTF began reorienting itself away from AIDS work and toward nurturing grassroots activism. Partly it did this through its annual Creating Change conference, which not only taught skills but built desperately needed networks among activists. Partly it did this through emphasizing issue-oriented organizing projects. These projects—antiviolence, sodomy law repeal, families, and campus—provided local organizations with resources and technical assistance so that the generalized desire to do something could be more effectively translated into concrete action to change policy and institutions. NGLTF staff spent a lot of time on the road. Going to the "heartland" and aiding the building of a strong movement fed the need to be doing what no other national organization was doing in the way that, earlier, going to Washington had nourished the same impulse.

The powerful combination of AIDS, a proliferating grassroots movement, and a politically aggressive radical right together created the "gay moment" of 1992–93. Gay and lesbian issues received unprecedented national attention, posing both great dangers and great opportunities. The moment required leadership of the most flexible sort. It required imaginative strategizing. And it required skilled and determined mobilization. With a history of working in Washington, and with its ties to local activists around the country, NGLTF might have shaped a creative response that maximized the opportunities while containing the dangers. Instead, it found itself imploding.

This was the period of my own heaviest involvement with NGLTF. As I described at the start of this essay, what had won me over to the task force in the late 1980s was the profile of the organization at that precise point in its history. Insider and outsider perspectives were elegantly balanced within it. NGLTF seemed committed to doing what rarely happens within one movement organization. It was holding on to a full range of strategic and tactical options. It believed in working through the legislative process and with government bureaucrats to make change. It believed in the need to build a vibrant democratic social movement in which local people were empowered. It was willing to endorse direct action as a legitimate form of political activity. Then, in 1993, we seemed to be confronted with the rare political moment when such a broad conception of how to make change was most needed.

It surprised, puzzled, and disappointed me when the task force essentially abandoned its work of the previous decade. As a participant in these years, I saw the conflicts and debates that were erupting in NGLTF in political terms. They seemed to be variations of familiar political divisions that had often recurred in social movements. Should an organization work closely with those in power (in this case, the Clinton administration) to shape policy, or should it remain an independent voice? Can "the system" be trusted to reform itself, and can meaningful change be achieved through insider lobbying and negotiation with those in power? Or, must those with grievances always battle from the outside, building a power base that rests upon substantial grassroots mobilization? Were Democratic party liberals able to deliver the goods, or did a new progressive politics need to emerge, sufficiently robust to arouse Americans and to counteract an increasingly powerful extreme right wing?

These political issues had an internal analogue as the staff fought among itself about the nature of the organization's work culture. Was Torie Osborn, the new executive director, trying to create a hierarchical professionalized organization? Was she too attached to inside-the-Beltway conceptions of social change? Would big donors and high-priced fundraising events come to shape the organization's outlook?

To me, it seemed that the issues being debated, overtly and covertly, were creating a sense of mutually exclusive alternatives rather than building on what I saw as NGLTF's strength, namely, its ability to reconcile and synthesize approaches that often seem incompatible. It made no sense to me that one should have to choose between working with the national government and mobilizing the grassroots. This choice seemed especially destructive of the task force's progressive political goals since, if the organization abandoned Washington-based work, more conservative organizations like the Human Rights Campaign Fund were bound to dominate the scene and shape the agenda. Yet the organization seemed impervious to such arguments. Instead, over the next two years, NGLTF jettisoned significant policy work at the national level, allowing responsibility for it to devolve on other organizations. It also permitted its issue-oriented projects, which had given the task force its organic working connection with local activists, to atrophy and die. In its place, NGLTF devoted itself to "fighting the right." Its purpose became to expose the danger that the extreme right wing posed to democratic values and visions of social justice and to mobilize the grassroots to respond.

At the time, I thought that the wrong political perspective triumphed, that a poor strategic path had been chosen. Retrospectively, the debates seem less about the overt content and much more about something never clearly articulated. For the outcome revealed that, once again, the task force was shaping its program not in relation to a long-range vision of change, nor in terms of immediately realizable goals that might build the organization, but in order to fill a void. This time the void was combat against a more powerful, aggressive, and threatening right wing. Fighting the right not only was work that no other important queer organization was taking on, but it also fed the need to be on the edge, to be brave warriors, to exhibit the passion and fervor of missionaries. It certainly was more appealing than the humdrum tasks of moving the Washington bureaucracy during a friendly Democratic administration or of patiently following a few issues all the way to success.

"Fight the Right" proved a disaster as a program. For one, the task force was far too small an organization to have any noticeable impact on what the Right did. It also made the organization's program thoroughly reactive, completely dependent on what one's political opponents did rather than on what queer communities wanted or needed. Fighting the Right was able to offer very little in the way of tangible achievements that the organization could claim for itself or deliver to its constituency. It made many of the organization's partners angry because commitments to preexisting work, through mechanisms like the antiviolence project or the campus project, were dropped. Finally, it created within the organization a sense of embattlement, of being besieged by enemies, of daily being on the verge of armageddon.

In the wake of this disaster, the task force attempted to reinvent itself once more. Its new program and direction included several elements. It put resources into a Policy Institute, conceived as a combination research arm and think tank that produces high-quality innovative analysis of issues and fosters new strategic thinking. It worked to develop a strong infrastructure of state-level gay, lesbian, bisexual, and transgender organizations in order to facilitate legislative and policy change in state capitols across the country. It committed itself to coalition-building and multi-issue organizing, believing that justice is indivisible and that a quer policy agenda will move forward to the degree that the gay movement is aligned with a broad array of social movements. And it became a voice for inclusion, arguing that agendas must be developed that embrace the perspectives of bisexuals and the transgendered.

As at various other points in its history, NGLTF framed a program that can make a credible claim to representing a strategic perspective on how best to achieve significant change in the long run. Successes in each of the above areas would have a major impact on law, public policy, and the political climate. But, this program could just as easily be the latest in a long series that have all, I believe, been ultimately shaped by the unacknowledged culture of the organization: its need to fill a void, to do what no one else is seriously doing, to see itself as taking risks and living on the edge.

Conclusion

There is nothing wrong with an organization having as its central driving impulse the desire to fill a void. At different points in its history, NGLTF has been able to translate this impulse into effective work and impressive achievements. This has been most true in the earliest years of the organization, when it pioneered advocacy at the national level, and in its middle period, when it crafted a political response to AIDS and encouraged the revival of effective local activism.

But such an impulse, and the culture that surrounds it, is problematic when it goes unacknowledged. It is very hard on the people who work there, since the flip side of being pioneers who struggle on the edge is high, almost constant, stress. It is very hard on an organization's survival, too, since the expertise that brings accomplishment, name recognition, and fundraising capability is regularly discarded as one moves on to new challenges and new issues that appeal to a different constituency. Thus, it is not surprising that NGLTF has experienced recurring budgetary constraints, more so than many other national organizations. Finally, the compelling urge to rush toward where the void is has serious effects on the movement to which NGLTF is devoted. It has meant that the task force has periodically abandoned the constituents it has nurtured, ironically creating voids of its own as it leaves one arena of advocacy work to pursue something new and edgier.

In doing so, the task force unwittingly betrays the leadership role that it has, with justification, often claimed for itself. Periodically, its track record of success has brought it to a point where it could decisively affect the direction of the movement as a whole. Instead of embracing a higher level of influence and power, which accrued to it because of its effective work, it has backed away. In today's era when the mainstream of the gay movement seems to be accommodating to the conservative spirit of the times, steady reliable leadership from a progressive organization is more critical than ever. Wouldn't that be a void worth filling?

PART II *Interventions*

7

Why Is This Year Different
From Any Other?

Ever since the rhetorical onslaught from the Republican National Convention in Houston, my thoughts keep returning to a line from the celebration of Passover, the Jewish commemoration of the flight out of Egypt and slavery. A young child asks the question, "Why is this night different from all other nights?" And the question becomes an opportunity to tell stories of the past, to recall a moment when the tide of history changed for an oppressed people.

I write this article in the midst of the electoral season, not yet knowing what the results will be. But whatever the outcome, I am convinced that for us — lesbians, gay men, and bisexuals — this year is different from any other. The Republican National Convention, the referenda campaigns in Oregon and Colorado, the hyperactivity of God Squad demagogues like Pat Robertson and Lou Sheldon: all these have placed us close to the center of the nation's consciousness.

The voices of hate during this political season are loud and rabid. They can easily inspire fear and pessimism, panic and dread. But they can also alert us to our strength and lead us to renew our commitment and determination. For there are reasons why we are being targeted, and those reasons can tell

---

This essay was prepared for NGLTF's Creating Change conference, held on Veteran's Day weekend in 1992. Inaugurated in 1988, Creating Change had already become, by 1992, the premier annual gathering of gay, lesbian, and bisexual activists in the United States. I was on the board of directors then, and the staff asked me to prepare something, for distribution to all the conference registrants, that addressed the politics of the 1992 campaign season.

us much about what we have accomplished, about the current crisis in American society, and about the paths we need to pursue.

Our Accomplishments

Gay men and lesbians have been fighting for freedom for more than a generation. Starting in secret in the grim days of the Cold War, taking a few steps out of hiding in the more tolerant 1960s, the movement exploded on to the landscape with the Stonewall Riot in New York City in 1969. Since then we have grown as a movement in dramatic fashion, not always in a straight upward curve, not always without reversals, but in ways that mark the present as unmistakably different from the past. What have we accomplished in this last generation of activism?

ORGANIZATION AND COMMUNITY

We have achieved a miracle of organization. We have built out of nothing thousands of organizations. Gay Democratic and Republican clubs and gay political action committees (PACs) to give us a voice in the party system. National civil rights organizations to fight for equality in legislative halls and the courts. State coalitions to coordinate the energies of local activists. Direct action groups that raise the political heat through their willingness to dispense with "business as usual." Community centers that have become a hub of activity in many cities. Groups by and for the young and the elderly. Groups that span the range of our ethnic and racial diversity. Churches and synagogues where we can worship in peace and tranquility. Caucuses and professional associations in a wide array of occupation fields. Student groups, alumni groups, employee groups. Bowling and softball leagues, running and hiking clubs. A dense network of AIDS-service organizations that have mounted a dramatic, and unprecedented, response to a life-threatening public health menace.

These organizations span the nation. They may not be distributed evenly through the fifty states, but no part of the country remains beyond our organizational reach. And, in some places, the density of organization is awesome. In the mid-1970s *Gay Community News* of Boston could list *all* of the groups in New England on half a page. In recent years, the weekly event list in the Boston area alone filled the whole inside back page.

Organizational growth is not simply a matter of large numbers. In many cities and states, the quality and nature of our organizations have changed. They have become permanent institutions. No longer dependent on the shifting tides of a volunteer labor pool, many organizations now have permanent staff and revenue sources sufficient to pay them living salaries. Volunteerism is still (and always will be) essential to our movement's health, but the growth of a paid corps of organizers is profoundly important. It brings us continuity, accumulated experience, and the seasoning that comes with full-time activism.

Organizations are also the building blocks of community. They express our strength and they create ever stronger bonds between us. An organized community is a powerful community. An organized community is what brought 500,000 of us to Washington in October 1987. We went home to build even more organizations and accumulate the power that comes from them.

CULTURE AND VISIBILITY

No less impressive is the way we have carved out a place in the culture. One has to live in a cave in order *not* to notice that we exist, as individuals and as a community.

Much of this cultural shift is the result of our own hard work and creativity. There is a gay and lesbian renaissance alive in this land. The number of books pouring from our pens, or being pounded out at the keyboard, is extraordinary: serious fiction, detective novels, romances, plays, poetry, biography and autobiography, history, literary criticism, photography and the arts, social science, essays, and political commentary. On college campuses, faculty are writing gay, lesbian, and bisexual courses into the curriculum. The OutWrite Conference and the Gay Studies Conference each year attract close to 2,000 participants. We have a press of our own as well as performance artists, theater groups, and small presses who nurture our writers and artists.

In the past few years we have seen this cultural visibility spill out of our community and into the mainstream. Commercial publishers are actively courting gay and lesbian authors. The metropolitan press and the mass circulation weeklies are covering news about our community and our movement. Television and the movie industry have been slower to change, but even in these areas there are signs of change. The old complaint that we have been made invisible is no longer descriptive of the truth.

VICTORIES AGAINST OPPRESSION

Organization, community, culture, and visibility have translated into real, significant victories against the laws, public policies, and cultural practices that have oppressed us. Think for a minute about how deeply entrenched in Western culture the prohibitions and prejudices against homosexuality have been. In law, religion, and science, we inherited a tradition that stretches centuries back into the past. From that perspective, the victories we have already won are a profound testimonial to the effectiveness of our work.

The sodomy laws have been repealed in half the states. More than a hundred municipalities and counties have passed antidiscrimination statutes, including most of the largest American cities. The mental health profession has dropped homosexuality from its list of mental diseases. The federal Civil Service Commission has eliminated the ban on the employment of gays and lesbians. Many large corporations have adopted antidiscrimination employment policies. Within most religious groupings, gay and lesbian activists have provoked a vigorous debate about church teachings and ordination practices.

And the pace of change is accelerating. Since George Bush entered the White House, four states have enacted gay civil rights laws. Many states have passed hate crime legislation inclusive of sexual orientation. Our agenda has expanded to include family issues, and some corporations and municipalities have moved to provide partnership benefits. In the military, every week seems to bring another coming out saga, and support for the gay ban is eroding rapidly. Sacred cows like the Boy Scouts are having to deal with the consequences of their homophobia.

Yes, it is true that this is only a part of the task we have set for ourselves. But virtually all these changes have occurred in the short span of twenty years. Our power is growing, and with it our ability to dismantle the edifice of oppression.

THE TEXTURE OF EVERYDAY LIFE

In some ways the quality of our lives is both the most significant sign of change and the most difficult to grasp. It is significant because this is the goal of all our efforts, to make it possible for every one of us to live in dignity and peace, proud and free. It is difficult to measure because it can only be appreciated across the dimension of time. Change seems less dramatic when measured by the day, or the month, or the year, than it does across a decade or a generation. But from the longer view, from the experience, certainly, of the "over-forty" among us, the change has been profound.

Put most simply, we are able to live out our days differently than we did before Stonewall. Sometimes the markers of change are simple and undramatic. The hug of greeting on the street. The touch of two hands across a restaurant table. A same-sex couple applying for a car loan or mortgage or renting an apartment together. The configuration of family at Thanksgiving, Christmas, or Passover. Sometimes the changes are more striking. The lesbian couple deciding to birth and rear a child. The male couple insisting on a commitment ceremony in their local congregation. The soldier or scout leader demanding the right to defend their country or to lead the youth of the community.

Multiply these examples by all the individual incidences of them, add your own markers of change, and the bottom line is a new social tapestry. It is not simply that we are different among ourselves, that our community is open and visible. The whole society has changed. The business of daily life in America is different because we are there in an open and visible way.

The Present Crisis

So why, if all this good stuff is true, do we feel under siege?

One reason, of course, is the AIDS epidemic. The death toll and the infection figures are appalling. Despite the extraordinary effort we have mounted (and it is extraordinary), despite the money we've raised, the service organizations we've built, the endless volunteer hours, the care networks, the lobbying, and the disruptive action in the streets, we have not succeeded in eliciting the full-throttle national response we need. And, the sad fact is that even were we to get that response tomorrow, the numbers of dead and HIV-infected would continue to grow for several more years.

But we also feel under siege because we are being openly targeted — in Houston, Oregon, and Colorado. Our opponents are no longer the lunatic fringe. They are working at the center of the Republican Party. They have access to electronic media, they have tens of millions of fundamentalist Christians as their army, and their coffers seem full to overflowing.

As a community and a movement, we have been attacked before. In 1977, Anita Bryant was the public spokesperson for a "Save Our Children" crusade in Dade County, Florida. Through it, gay issues made front-page headlines across the nation for the first time. The success of the Dade County campaign to repeal a gay rights ordinance spawned others the following year: in Eugene, Oregon, Wichita, Kansas, and St. Paul, Minnesota, which we lost; in Seattle, which we won; and in California, where the statewide Briggs initiative would have mandated silence about our lives in the classroom. We won that battle, but the price was the assassination of Harvey Milk. In the early 1980s, we faced the threat of the Family Protection Act. During the past decade, we have been assaulted by the rhetoric and legislative maneuvering of members of Congress like Jesse Helms and William Dannemeyer. More recently, the battle over funding for the National Endowment for the Arts is another example of gay baiting.

Still, despite this history of attacks, we *know*, in our gut, that this time is different. This time, it is not a side show. This time, it has become the main event. This time, our community, our issues, our agenda, our deepest hopes and aspirations, are being laid before the nation — and not in the way we would choose. For the first time in our history, we have moved to the center of national political discourse. And we need to understand why.

One important reason, pure and simple, is that we *are* succeeding. If we were a small band of marginal folks hiding in the wilderness, no one would notice us. But because we have made change, and have the will and the resources to make more change, we have become a credible target. This is not the kind of recognition that we most want, but we should understand it for what it is: a tribute to our accomplishments.

But there are larger reasons why we have become the target of so much irrational hatred. Unlike our successes, these other reasons have very little to do with us directly, but we need to incorporate them into our strategic calculations.

The family values debate and the attacks on us can be likened to what some social scientists have labeled a "moral panic." Moral panics most commonly occur in times of serious stress in a society. And there can be no doubt that the United States is living through a period of grave crisis.

The crisis is international in scope. In the past three years, the Cold War has ended, Communism as an international movement has collapsed, and the Soviet Union has fractured. The structures and assumptions that organized the worldview of our national ruling group have disintegrated. The old enemy is gone, but the psychology that sustained Cold War politics remains behind.

In better times, the collapse of "the enemy" might provoke triumphant rejoicing. But it is difficult for the political and economic elite (whether they are conservatives, moderates, or liberals) of the United States to celebrate when they know that so much else is wrong. For it is not only the structure of international politics that has changed, but the structure of the international economy as well. In the generation after World War II, the United States was the preeminent economic power in the world. Its capital flowed into the war-torn nations of Europe, extracting profits that fueled prosperity at home, and into much of the Third World, where it found cheap and easy access to raw materials. All of that has changed in the past twenty years. Japan, Germany, and other nations of the Pacific Rim and of Western Europe have become fierce economic competitors. Oil-producing nations asserted control over their natural resources, and the result was skyrocketing energy costs in the United States. From being the world's biggest creditor nation, the United States became the largest debtor in the space of a few years.

Add to this the economic and social policies of the Reagan–Bush years. Resources were shifted from the public sector to the private. Defense spending, and the national debt payments that come from past defense spending, became the largest element in a budget that piled on more and more debt every year. Changes in tax policy and in government regulations of the economy shifted wealth upward. Huge fortunes were made in the 1980s, not through productive work, but through the magic of leveraged buyouts that created personal fortunes and corporate debt. And the debt is being paid for by lower wage rates for a labor force that has mostly lost the one resource it had — union representation. Family income has kept pace in these past twenty years only because more family members are working — for longer hours, and at low-paying jobs in the nonunionized service sector of the economy. Constraints on federal spending for social programs have shifted the burden to the states, and now the states are facing a fiscal crisis.

We see the results of this all around us: school systems that are in decay, basic services not being provided, a crisis in the delivery of health care, the ravages of drugs and crime in our cities, an increase in long-term unemployment, and a rise in the poverty rate.

What does this have to do with us? As our leaders stumble, as the crisis deepens, the tension and the stress rise. It is simpler to target us (and others) as the scapegoat for a deep-rooted national crisis than it is to articulate and pursue the hard political and economic choices that are necessary to turn the country around. The citizenry is in a panic, and some are leading a stampede in our direction.

Just as there is a crisis stemming from the largest structures of economic and political life, crisis stalks one of the smallest structures of social life, the family. Because of the way lesbians, gay men, and bisexuals have been oppressed, it is inevitable that our movement will raise issues of sex, intimacy, and family. In doing so, we have touched an open wound for many Americans.

In the past generation, feminism transformed the way we understand the family and sexuality. Through the efforts of women to understand their experience and articulate the ways they have been oppressed, the invisible has been made starkly clear. Family is a place of real needs — for caring, for nurturance, for intimacy and sociability. But it is also a place of victimization and abuse. We have learned, in painful and graphic detail, about the toll of domestic violence, about wife battering, about the physical abuse of children, and about incest. The figures are much, much higher than anyone would have dreamed a generation ago.

Many Americans — perhaps, even, most Americans — have been hurt badly in precisely the places where they expected to find love, intimacy, caring, and pleasure. These wounds have now been opened, and many are now responding like wild beasts who have been attacked. When they see us challenging certain norms of family life, pointing to mistreatment in our homes, and offering another vision of family, closeness, and sexual intimacy, they roar in pain and confusion. It is this pain, and this confusion, that can make millions of Americans enlist in a demagogic crusade against us.

So this year is different. Combine our successes with the deepening crisis in both the largest and most intimate spheres of national life, and it becomes possible to understand why we have moved to the center of national debate.

The Future

Vehement as the attacks on us are, resistant as some major institutions and power sites are to our agenda, the future rests in our hands. Adversity is not something new to us. In fact, almost all the gains we've made have come during an era of deepening conservative reaction. We will continue to move ahead, regardless of the election's outcome.

Most of the time, when we think about what needs to be done, we think in terms of competing political strategies. And there are many afloat in our communities. Some want us to throw in our lot with the Democratic Party. Others want us to concentrate our resources in state and national PACs so that elected officials are indebted to us. Some call for a solid gay voting bloc. Others want us to create so much disorder and disruption in the streets that the wheels of society will grind to a halt until our agenda is met. Some want us to build communities so strong that we are impregnable to attack. Some argue for coalitions of all the oppressed and disempowered, while others want to keep resolutely focused on gay issues only.

These debates over strategy will continue. Disagreement among ourselves is not a bad thing. It can be healthy and creative, and there are certainly enough activists among us so that a variety of strategies will be pursued.

But these are not the questions that are on my mind. When I think about this year, and the way that it is different, I find myself mulling over another set of issues. Issues not about what to do, but about how we think. Issues not about defining goals, but about how we work toward our goals. Issues that above all have to do with internalized oppression, with the way we have absorbed the negative, antisurvival messages of our culture, and how that internalization sabotages us. We know, from our past history of successes, that we can work hard enough, that we are smart enough, that we are determined enough to keep pushing forward. Yet I think we are all working at but a fraction of our capacities. Internalized oppression acts as a weight that slows us down, as an obstacle that trips us up. We need to fight our way clear of it.

LEADERSHIP

Leadership is a necessary thing. It is a potential that *everyone* has. Any collective enterprise needs it — *lots* of it. Leadership involves a decision to set things right in the world; it involves thinking about more than one's own narrow self-interest; it involves acting in a way that moves a group forward toward life-affirming goals. Our community has been fortunate in raising up a large number of hardworking, intelligent, and responsible individuals who have exercised leadership to the benefit of us all. And there is enough important work waiting to be done that we would all benefit from the appearance of many more of us willing to lead — willing, in other words, to take responsibility to see that our agenda moves forward.

But we also do something terrible to those of us brave enough and idealistic enough to lead. We savage them. We attack them. We subject them to public and private blood-curdling meanness.

Attacks on leadership are an elemental form of internalized oppression. When we abuse our leaders, we are treating another gay man or lesbian with the same level of contempt, disrespect, and hatred that confronts us on the outside. We are saying that they are untrustworthy, dishonest, irresponsible, immature, self-absorbed—all of the charges leveled against us as a group. Attacks on leadership are the purest form of self-hatred.

They also are destructive and counterproductive. I have never met anyone who has corrected a mistake or improved their performance because of an attack. Helpful criticism (and if it isn't helpful, what's the point?) can only work when it comes from a place of profound love, respect, and appreciation, and when the recipient knows that as well.

Think what a difference it would make if, as a community and as a movement, we "just said no" to attacks on leadership. Think about the difference it would make if we didn't keep losing valuable, talented activists because they couldn't take one more wounding confrontation. Think about how much more willing to lead each one of us would be if we knew that our turn to be roasted would not come. If the time that is currently spent on factionalism, on plotting and scheming, on protecting our backs from attack, and on recuperating from wounding battles could be devoted to constructive thinking and acting for political change, we would be unstoppable.

We must stop the attacks on leadership. We must stop doing to ourselves what our opponents are trying to do to us.

ALLIES

We need allies as much as we need leadership. To say this does not mean that we are weak, or ineffective, or incapable of waging a liberation struggle. It simply acknowledges what is true: that we are part of a much larger whole, and that if we are to succeed, the whole world around us must be willing to change as well.

To believe that we can do it alone is another form of internalized oppression. Believing that it is all up to us means that we have accepted the message that we are so separate, so isolated, so monstrous, so weird, that no one would bond with us, no one would walk with us side by side. Believing that we are alone concedes that we are so much the outsiders that the world does not belong to us. We need allies and we must recognize that need.

We already have allies — groups and individuals who have worked with us to achieve some of the victories we have already attained. Part of what makes this year different from others is that the opportunities for building alliances are greater than ever before. The way we have been scapegoated has made it clear to many Americans that the attacks on us are an entering wedge, that fanning homophobia is a tactic en route to a conservative social, political, and economic order. If we lose this election, many others will have lost too. And, perhaps for the first time, many others know it too.

Even as we build strong communities and organizations, we need to keep pushing ourselves outside of our community, beyond the comfort zone of what Urvashi Vaid has called "our lavender bubble." This will not always be easy, because it will often mean choosing to come face-to-face with homophobia. Building enduring alliances will require a flexibility and humility that is not easy to come by when we feel ourselves under the gun.

One way in which we need to be flexible is in what we expect from potential allies. Some heterosexuals have worked through enough of their homophobia that they are ready to embrace us. They love who we are, and they will move with us full steam ahead. Others will not. They will concede that discrimination and violence is wrong, but they will also have moral reservations about our sexuality. We need to be able to start from where the other person is, and build from that, rather than insist on complete acceptance of our lives and our agenda before we can move forward together.

We will also need to present ourselves to the world in more complex ways than many of us have been willing to accept. Ever since the beginning of our movement in the repressive climate of the McCarthy era, two warring definitions of who we are have competed for preeminence in our movement and in our communities. There are those who will go to the wall in defense of our "difference," who will say that the essence of who we are is different from the majority, and who will thrust that difference into the face of society. And there are those who plead for acceptance based on sameness, who will say that, really, we are just like everyone else and that's why we should be accepted.

This is not a productive debate. Both claims are true; neither one is fully credible by itself. To endlessly assert our sameness will only magnify our

134 THE WORLD TURNED

sense of alienation, because it denies the uniqueness of our experience. To relentlessly thrust difference in the faces of others will keep us forever apart. To say we are only the same is to ask nothing of the heterosexual world. To say we are only different is to build between us and the rest of the world a barrier that can never be surmounted.

We need to tolerate complexity in our community and in our relations with our allies. We need to acknowledge, share, and rejoice in what is unique to our experience, and we need to bond around our common humanness and aspirations. Differences in culture and social experience can be the ingredients that make us fascinating and interesting. Commonalities are the solid ground that allow others to appreciate our differences.

WINNING, LOSING, OR SOMETHING ELSE?

We live in a society that is organized around competition and scarcity. Life is a zero-sum game. If you win, I must lose. In the competition for resources, security, and power, enemies engage in mortal combat (this is not just a figure of speech), and only one side can survive. In this year of the family values debate, this in fact is how the opposition seems to be framing things. To listen to some of their rhetoric is to believe that only our annihilation would satisfy them.

It would be easy for us to go on the attack, to give as much as we get. It is understandable that we would jump to dehumanize our opponents, to paint them in as monstrous a light as they do us. But that's a setup. Take their bait and all we'd be doing is contributing to the degradation of public life in America, where the main goal often seems to be not to articulate what one stands for, but to attack, to discredit, to destroy, and to defeat. A zero-sum game.

They call us evil. If we respond in kind, we are only strengthening *their* way of looking at the world. What is happening in America is not a fight between good guys and bad guys but a battle between ideas, between organizing principles for our political and social life. When Pat Buchanan or Lou Sheldon is screaming in your face, it can be difficult to remember this, but in a real sense the bad guys are good guys too. They are operating from a position of deep pain; nothing else could explain the poisonous words that come from their mouths and their pens. They, too, must have a story to tell. It will be different from our stories of pain and oppression, but something must have happened to them to make hatred rest so easily on their shoulders.

"Victory" is not my goal. Success is. My victory requires your defeat. My success does not require any one else's failure. In this season of hatred, when we have seen how ugly the world can turn, I would like our goals to remain resolutely positive and life-enhancing. I would like us to know that we are united around something affirmative, something that builds rather than destroys, something that unites rather than divides, something that promises social peace rather than more political war. In this year of family values rhetoric, I would like us to know that since any boy or girl could turn out to be gay, we are committed to a world in which every child will flourish. If gay liberation means that to us, then this year will be different from any other year.

8

The Clinton Election: Historical

Perspectives on a Moment of Change

For the past several years, whenever I have spoken before movement and community audiences about our history, I have felt compelled to emphasize the enormity of our achievements: the organizations we've built; the visibility we've achieved; the communities we've created; the allies we've converted to our cause; the real victories we have won at the local, state, and even national level.

The reasons for this emphasis should be obvious. For most of the years since Stonewall and the birth of gay liberation, we have lived under a conservative Republican regime that, with its Christian fundamentalist allies, has relentlessly attacked us. In the late 1970s, we faced a series of repeal campaigns against gay rights legislation. In the 1980s, after the election of Reagan, we had to fight the Family Protection Act in Congress; contend with an increasingly conservative federal judiciary; try to outmaneuver the likes of Jesse Helms and William Dannemeyer in Congress; and, through all this, confront the devastatingly large toll of the AIDS epidemic. Throughout these years, we also had to suffer the blood-curdling rhetoric of hate that the

---

Each year elected and appointed officials who are gay, lesbian, bisexual, or transgendered meet in November, just after the election. In the 1980s, when these meetings started, a few dozen attended. Now, hundreds participate.

The 1992 conference was held in Chapel Hill, North Carolina. Joe Herzenberg, a member of the town council and at that time the only openly gay elected official in the South, invited me to give the keynote address. I prepared this talk a few weeks after I wrote the previous piece. The same issues were on my mind, but they are shaped differently here because of Clinton's election. My easy assumption that the military ban would be lifted is one small sign of the high — and unjustified — expectations that the election generated for many gay and lesbian activists.

Christo-fascist right wing spewed at us, until its culmination last August at the Republican National Convention in Houston. Is it any wonder that, as a historian, I have felt called on to accentuate the positive?

The election of Bill Clinton to the presidency has opened a window of opportunity. At the very least, it means that mean-spiritedness and hate-mongering has been banished from the nation's highest elective office. But it probably will mean a lot more. Already, Clinton has addressed the issue of the military's exclusion policy, and it will likely be abolished in the coming year. The appointments he will make in federal agencies will probably signal a new and unprecedented degree of bureaucratic openness to our issues. And, with a lesbian, gay, and bisexual March on Washington scheduled for next April, we can even expect there to be progress toward passage of federal gay rights legislation. The possibilities are enough to make us giddy with hope.

The momentary respite that the election results offer also allows me to shift my role as a community historian. It allows me to go beyond cheerleading. It finally feels safe enough to ask more complicated questions of our history and to raise thorny issues about our political direction as a movement. The issues I want to address—and I'm sure there are many other pressing ones—need airing because the new political era that we are entering offers not only opportunities, but also challenges as well.

What are the issues I want to discuss tonight? There are several: the attachment that our movement has to what I will call "outsider" status, our community's very ambivalent relationship to leadership, the much larger crisis in American life that shapes the framework in which we do our work, the serious limits of identity politics, and the need for us to have a visionary agenda that reaches beyond our own community's needs.

The Outsider Mentality

Virtually every movement for social change in this country's history—abolitionism, suffrage, the labor movement, civil rights—has experienced a tension between those who thought the system could correct itself and those who thought it was irredeemably corrupt, between those who wanted entry and those who resisted assimilation, between those who called themselves reformers and those who called themselves radicals or revolutionaries, between those who sought to work for change within the system and those who positioned themselves outside it. The moments of greatest change in the direction of equality and justice have come when these two sides have been able to work in tandem, when they have been able to play off each other in creative ways so that their respective strength was magnified rather than dissipated.

For most of our history since Stonewall, the gay and lesbian movement has operated from the stance of outsider. I don't mean to imply that our movement has been primarily a radical one, composed of activists who wanted to rebuild American society from the bottom up, but simply to say that most of the time, most of us have worked from the vantage point of outsider looking in. There are very clear historical reasons why this has been so, some of which have been chosen by us, and some of which have been imposed on us.

One obvious reason for our position as outsiders has been oppression. In the past, to the degree that we have been open and visible about our identity, we have been locked out of social roles that embody power. We have been shunted to the margin, kept apart, and punished for our selfhood. Another reason involves the heritage of the radicalism of the 1960s. Gay and lesbian liberation was born during a decade of revolt, when large numbers of the young, because of their encounters with war, racism, sexism, violence, and economic injustice, were in open rebellion. They did not seek entry into the corridors of power, but instead wanted to remake the world. Our movement's parentage guaranteed that it would cast a skeptical eye toward the structure of political, social, cultural, and economic institutions. The visionary writings of lesbian feminists and gay male radicals in the 1970s in part owed their power to the critical distance their authors maintained from society as it was.

But, even after the radicalism of the 1960s had faded away, we remained outsiders. Since the early 1970s, conservatism has been the dynamic edge of American politics. It has shaped the language and content of public debate. The right wing has been firmly in the saddle. Little wonder that we find ourselves on the outside looking in.

Finally, I believe we have remained attached to outsider status because of the workings of internalized oppression, because of the ways we have absorbed the hateful messages of the culture about who we are. These messages label us as weird, odd, abnormal, dangerous, marginal, and different. We have often managed to reshape these beliefs creatively, but at bottom we still play them out in ways that keep us apart, isolated, and on the outside. For many of us, acceptance and assimilation are the worst things imaginable. We are attached to outlaw status.

Outsider status, it should be said, is not necessarily a bad thing. The "system," the complex of relationships, structures, and institutions that shape power and the distribution of resources, seems to exist primarily to defend itself. One only has to look at the history of Congress over the past seventy-odd years to see what I mean. Except for a handful of years — during the Depression of the 1930s and in the wake of the civil rights movement in the 1960s — when social and economic justice issues had forced their way to the top of the national agenda, our national political leadership has rarely taken the lead on reform. Rather, the political system seems to swallow dissenters. It has developed an extraordinary ability to absorb the proponents of change into business as usual. The "system" exists primarily to defend itself.

On the other hand, permanent outsider status has very little to offer in the long run. It forces one into the perpetual role of protester, of reactive agent. Someone else always has the power; the best the outsider can seem to do is to make enough noise until those with power make some concessions. But the outsider, the protester, is not the one shaping the agenda.

An attachment to outsider status will not get us what we want and need. As outsiders, we will not be able to mobilize the nation's resources to fight AIDS, we will not win recognition of our family relationships, we will not achieve security against violence, and we will not be guaranteed basic civil rights and civil liberties.

The Clinton administration is going to offer our movement and our community an alternative to outsider status. Will we be ready to accept it? Will we be able to shape our roles as insiders? Will we be able to use the openness of the Clinton presidency to further an agenda for justice? Or will the allure of the system, the perks of power, swallow us up? Can we walk the corridors of power and still retain the animating vision of justice and decency that comes to us from having been cast as outsiders? It will be a very sad comment on the capacity of our society to remake itself if our only choices are powerlessness as the price of integrity, or the loss of integrity as the price of power.

Leadership

A discussion I have heard again and again runs something like this: "Where is our Martin Luther King, our Susan B. Anthony? Why haven't we produced leaders of great stature who can move our people forward toward freedom? Until we have such leaders, we will never get the attention that some of the great crusades in the past have captured."

The explanation that is usually offered for this state of affairs is that we have no leaders because we savagely attack those who dare to stick their head above the crowd. No other group, the argument goes, treats their leaders as badly as we do. Internalized homophobia is so great that we rip our leaders to shreds. No one survives long enough to reach national stature. No one wants the level of abuse they attract once they dare to assume the role of leader.

Our community does have a very puzzling relationship to leadership. We are decidedly ambivalent toward it. On one hand, we want leaders; and on the other, we do tear them down. The attacks on leadership must stop.

But it is simply not true that we lack charismatic national leaders because we, unique among oppressed groups, mistreat our own so badly. The history of other social movements, from the labor movement to the black civil rights movement to the women's movement, demonstrates that attacks on leadership are not a gay disease. Rather, in a hierarchical society, leaders seem naturally to draw out the deep-seated resentments that all of us harbor toward authority. Each of us has suffered enough from the arbitrary exercise of authority — by parents, teachers, bosses, and the like — that we seem to stand ever ready to attack anyone in authority if we think we can get away with it. Other movements have attacked their leaders, yet still have managed to produce men and women of national stature. So, why haven't we?

There are real historical reasons for this state of affairs. Fundamentally, the lack of leadership can be explained by our youth as a community and as a movement. Until the emergence of a lesbian and gay movement, we had few mechanisms to develop community leadership.

The contrast with the southern African American community is instructive. Even during the worst days of the Jim Crow system, when segregation and disfranchisement were enforced by waves of terrifying violence, southern blacks had a community structure that raised up leaders. Its churches, colleges, public schools, fraternal lodges, women's clubs, and small businesses pushed forward women and men who attained stature in the community on the basis of their skills, commitment, and accomplishments.

Until the 1970s, when gay liberation rallied around the slogan of coming out, we had no visible, recognizable community out of which to construct a network of leaders. One way of interpreting our whole post-Stonewall history is to see us as constructing a leadership ladder through community and institution building. Through our political groups, our service organizations, and our other community institutions, we are developing ways for people to accumulate skills, a reputation, a track record of commitment and achievement, and a constituency. We are providing training for leadership. This has been one of the great achievements of the past twenty years.

And, we are on the verge of seeing our efforts bear great fruit. Just as the Clinton victory will open opportunities for us to relinquish our attachment to outsider status, it is also likely that the Clinton administration will elevate some of our community members to more visible leadership. Are we ready for this? Will we be able to support those who are placed in strategic leadership roles? Or will we act out of petty resentments and attack them? Will our attachment to outsider status sabotage our opportunity to create a whole new level of lesbian and gay leadership? Or will our romance with marginality and isolation make these new opportunities too threatening?

The Current Crisis in American Life

However we resolve the issues of outsider status and our ambivalence about leadership, our movement and our community will be operating in the coming years within the very large constraints posed by the current crisis in American life.

The way we, as lesbians and gay men, experience the crisis most directly is through the demagogic politics of the right-wing God Squad. The stories coming out of Colorado and Oregon, where statewide antigay initiatives were on the ballot this fall, are scary. The leading edge of this authoritarian movement has all the characteristics of fascism. It also looks remarkably like what social scientists refer to as a "moral panic." Moral panics arise in times of great stress. And, make no mistake about it, we are in the midst of a crisis that reaches deeply into our economic, political, social, and cultural life.

Think about it: in the past few years the Cold War has ended. It should be a time of great rejoicing, but the celebration has been muted because so much else is wrong. The structure of international economic life has changed. The international power that the United States enjoyed in the generation after World War II has ended. With the rise of economic competitors in Western Europe and East Asia, we are no longer as easily able to extract ready profits from abroad to fill our pockets at home. The end of colonialism has brought a powerful surge of nationalism to the Third World, and many of these nations have seized control of the natural resources that American companies in the postwar era exploited with ease. Twelve years of Reagan–Bush economics has shifted wealth upward, burdened the nation with debt, and allowed the public infrastructure of institutions and services to wither. Unions are in decline, family income has stagnated, high wage jobs are shrinking in number. The schools are a mess, crime is out of control, and the health care system is a disaster. Not only the poor, whose numbers are expanding, but also working people and the middle class are living on the edge of disaster. No wonder large numbers of Americans are in a panic, and are scapegoating us for problems that we didn't cause and over which our opponents have no control.

What does this larger crisis have to do with the goals of gay and lesbian liberation? How will it affect our agenda during the Clinton presidency?

Some of what we want is cost-free: the repeal of sodomy laws, the elimination of the military exclusion policy, civil rights laws. But much of what we want will cost. The AIDS epidemic requires a coordinated national, state, and local response. Money is needed for treatment, for research, and for public health education to prevent the epidemic from spreading any further in this country or abroad. The demand for recognition of our family relationships will cost money in benefits that we currently don't receive and in tax deductions that we currently don't enjoy. Services for gay and lesbian youth, the development of lesbian and gay studies programs in our colleges and universities, and other such efforts that are part of our "gay agenda" require money. In the crisis environment in which we are living, even cost-free items like civil rights protections are read by our opponents as a call for "special privileges."

Receptive as the Clinton administration will be toward our community, the constraints that government faces in the coming years are enormous. How as a movement do we move forward with a progressive social and political agenda under these circumstances? I don't think we will succeed if we remain as attached to identity-based politics as we have been for the last generation.

The Limits of Identity Politics

For the past generation, a progressive agenda in this country has taken shape largely around identity politics. The modern origins of this form of politics can be found in the Black Power movement of the 1960s. The impulse was so startling and powerful that it proved contagious. In short order, women, gays, Chicanos, Native Americans, senior citizens, and people with disabilities took it up.

Identity politics has been tremendously important. Among the many things it has accomplished I would single out two as being especially important:

1. Socially and culturally, we have a much deeper and more sophisticated understanding of oppression than we have ever had before. This is of historic significance, and it is a necessary foundation for the building of a society in which all human beings are treated with respect. Identity politics is shifting the dominant paradigm in this country away from "the melting pot" and toward multiculturalism.

2. Politically and economically, identity politics has extended and codified the principle of equal rights and equality of opportunity. That codification is still not complete — as gay men, lesbians, and bisexuals know very well — but the structure of civil rights in this country is dramatically different than it was a generation ago.

But the benefits of identity politics — in every social movement that rests on this model — have not been equally distributed. In every case, the primary beneficiaries have been members of the middle class, those with access to education and training and privilege that have allowed them to take the most advantage of equal rights and equality of opportunity. Middle-class white women, middle-class African Americans, middle-class lesbians and gay men have gained the most from identity politics.

Identity politics does not offer a solution to the problems that tens of millions of Americans are facing today. In a class-stratified society, identity politics cannot provide access to sufficient economic resources to have a secure life. In fact, movements based on identity probably act as a barrier to solving class-based injustices because they place a premium on group loyalty across class lines. And, within those cross-class groups, it is the middle class that has set the group agenda and that has reaped the most benefits from the extension of civil rights protections. I know of no better recognition of the problems of a pure identity politics than the response of Toni Morrison, the distinguished African American novelist, to the Senate hearings to confirm Clarence Thomas as a Supreme Court Justice: "The time for undiscriminating racial unity has passed."

Moving beyond identity politics is a terrifying proposition. Each of you, as gay and lesbian public officials, achieved your position through a politics of identity. I have shaped my professional life during the past twenty years around my identity as a gay historian and writer. I am not saying that we should jettison our attachment to gay or lesbian politics. But I am suggesting that, somehow, we have to figure out how to hold on to the strengths that identity politics offers, while shedding its real and serious constraints.

The Need for an Inclusive Vision

I think the answer, or the way out, will come through the effort to construct an inclusive political agenda.

The issues of inclusion, diversity, and multiculturalism have been persistent ones in our movement and our communities during the past decade. Some real progress has been made, but most of it has come around an inclusionary politics defined by membership, representation, and accessibility: Is there gender parity on a board of directors? Is an organization's staff sufficiently multiracial and multiethnic? Are the voices of youth, or elders, or the disabled represented? But very little progress has been made in developing a political action agenda that is inclusive. This is the current challenge. To succeed at it will allow us to retain the best of identity politics while moving beyond its limits.

What would an inclusive political agenda mean? Let me give two examples:

1. The AIDS epidemic. We can frame this as a need for more money for education, for treatment, for social services, as a need for revising the procedures by which drugs are tested and approved. Or, we can place the AIDS epidemic in the context of an agenda that calls for universal access to health care, for a health care system organized in a way that meets the needs of everyone. The former is an approach to AIDS rooted in identity politics, in what we, as a community beleaguered by AIDS, need. The latter is an approach that meets the needs of people with AIDS, but places AIDS in a larger framework of social and economic justice.

2. Family issues. We can frame this as an issue of equal rights, of partnership benefits for gay and lesbian couples. Or, we can frame this in the context of a national family policy that supports the well-being of households and that promises security for every citizen. The former is a way for gays and lesbians to get our share. The latter is a way of obtaining security for ourselves by working for security and fairness for all.

An inclusive political vision, in short, is one in which our identity-based needs are met and our identity-based grievances are redressed because we are shaping a more humane society that values the life, dignity, and talents of everyone.

This is a tall order, and I won't pretend to know how to make it happen. But it won't ever happen unless we — or someone — decides to make it so. I would like to think that gay men and lesbians are particularly suited to lead the way toward an inclusive vision. After all, we contain among us members of every other group that has been systematically oppressed. The world is represented in our community. And, because we can never know which of the young ones around us will turn out to be gay, we have a special interest in seeing to it that all of the young in our society will get a fair shake. Any one of them might turn out someday to be a community member.

There are many other issues I could have discussed tonight. I chose the ones I did because I think they are especially relevant to you, as lesbian and gay public officials. You have had to come to terms with the legacy of our outsider status. By virtue of your public roles, you have become leaders of the community. As public officials, you have to deal every day with the constraints that the current crisis in American life imposes. You have both benefited from identity politics and have had to confront the limits of identity politics, if you have wanted to keep getting elected. And you are the ones who can take a leading role in shaping an inclusive political agenda.

It's important that you do it. Unless we move beyond each of these thorny issues toward an inclusive vision and a concrete agenda that incorporates such a vision, twenty years from now there will be more of you, more gay organizations, more civil rights legislation, and fewer sodomy laws, but we will still be living under a regime of homophobia and gay oppression. I don't think that's what we want to live with a generation from now.

9

Stonewall: Myth and Meaning

Growing up Catholic in New York City in the 1950s, I could never escape
the palpable presence of St. Patrick. His feast was a holiday in the city's
parochial schools, and one of the local television stations dropped its regular
programming to broadcast the St. Patrick's Day Parade along Fifth Avenue
in Manhattan. The day before, when school was in session, ethnic pride
burst forth as Irish American students and teachers sported various items of
green clothing. Even the local bakers cooperated in the celebration, with
cookies, cupcakes, and pastries of every sort sprouting green frosting.

As an Italian in an Irish parish and neighborhood, I experienced St. Patrick's Day as a hostile assault. My Irish friends suddenly metamorphosed
into marauding gangs attacking all the guineas and wops who, perversely
they felt, refused to wear green. My parents, aunts, and uncles grumbled at
home because their children *had* to march in the school's parade contingent
in the bitter late winter cold, while no comparable requirement was enforced
for Columbus Day, the closest Italian equivalent. I hated every minute of the
annual festivities and came to dread their yearly arrival.

My fifth grade instructor, Miss Schretlen, was the only non-Irish teacher
in our school, and she offered me an opportunity to bring the Irish down a

---

I wrote this piece for an anthology commemorating the twenty-fifth anniversary of the
Stonewall Riots that never appeared. The militancy of ACT UP still lingered and opportunities for mainstream advocacy were expanding. I was motivated by the way proponents of militancy often attacked those who embraced different tactics and used history
to justify their critique. I was also still living in North Carolina where, in the 1990s, it
took a great deal of courage simply to assemble publicly during Gay Pride Month. My
emphasis might change if I were writing now about the meanings of Stonewall. Moving
to Washington, and then Chicago, I have been surprised by how Stonewall celebrations
have been drained of political meaning. They have become an excuse for street parties,
filled with vendors. I like parties, but I wish these packed a political message.

notch. As St. Patrick's Day approached, she proposed a class debate on the question, "Did St. Patrick drive the snakes out of Ireland?" When she asked for volunteers, my hand shot up to present and defend the negative side of the proposition.

It was my first research project. For days beforehand, I foreswore after-school play and, instead, ensconced myself in the local public library. I read every encyclopedia I could find. I accumulated reams of evidence demonstrating that St. Patrick could not have accomplished this miraculous deed because, geologically, Ireland never had any snakes to be driven out! When the time for the debate arrived, I listened as my opponent simply repeated the tired old stories about St. Patrick's achievements. Then, I confidently addressed the class, presenting what I knew was an airtight case. When Miss Schretlen called for a vote, I lost by a two-to-one majority. All the Irish students voted their faith. The rest of the class, an outnumbered minority, voted for me. It was my first lesson in the power of symbol and myth.

Stonewall is our symbol of resistance, our myth of emancipation from oppression. As the years separating us from the riot grow, so does its power. In the biggest cities, the whole month of June has become a cornucopia of gay and lesbian delights, with theater productions, film festivals, political forums, museum exhibitions, and other events giving substance to our community's pride and strength and culminating in a massive outpouring on gay freedom day. In smaller cities, the ability to mount a march in honor of Stonewall figures as a metaphorical coming of age. Stonewall's power is so great that it resonates for gay men and lesbians around the world: The riot is commemorated on several continents. As the twenty-fifth anniversary approaches, there promises to be in New York the largest celebration of them all.

The story of Stonewall has been retold in print too many times to count.[1] Hardly a book about gay and lesbian life fails to make some mention of it, to describe in bareboned fashion what happened and what it was all about. A typical account goes something like this: Late on Friday evening, June 27, 1969, police came to raid the Stonewall Inn, a gay bar on Christopher Street in Greenwich Village. As they led patrons to the waiting vans, a crowd gathered. The patrons of the bar, many of whom were young, nonwhite, effeminate, and given to both camp and drag, began to resist and, with the support of the crowd, a full-scale riot developed. The following night, there was more street fighting in the Village. Thus was born a gay liberation movement.

No one but a fool would dispute the historical significance of the Stonewall riot. Yet, while its importance is not debatable, its meaning is most definitely up for grabs. As with all myths and symbols, we do more than retell and remember it. We *interpret* it. We extract lessons from the event and, in doing so, shape an understanding of the past and the present. Embedded in the story of Stonewall that writers narrate and political orators recount from their platforms are not only meanings that structure our sense of history, of how we came to be as a movement and as a community, but also theories of social change and strategies about how to end our oppression.

The lessons attributed to Stonewall are probably as numerous as the people for whom Stonewall is a symbol. But there are a few paradigmatic ones that recur endlessly. Like the snakes that St. Patrick drove out of Ireland, they figure prominently in our collective psyche:

— *Stonewall came out of the blue and started everything.* Before Stonewall there was naked oppression. After Stonewall, freedom beckoned.
— *Spontaneous riots and street action are the necessary keys to social change.* The raw anger erupting that night marks the path we need to follow.
— *The most oppressed will lead the way.* Because the young street people and the Puerto Rican drag queens who fought the police had nothing to lose, only they could take the risks that a freedom movement requires.

I mention these three because they are the ones I hear most often repeated and because they are almost completely untrue. They distort the past out of recognition, they elevate to preeminence an incomplete strategy for social change, and they become a weapon used within the community to discredit movement leaders. Each needs to be examined critically.

Stonewall Started Everything

Pure and simple, Stonewall did *not* start everything. For almost twenty years before, some gay men and lesbians were organizing for freedom. By 1969, when the Stonewall Riot occurred, their efforts had contributed to changing the context in which gays and lesbians lived. For instance, through sustained lobbying, activists had won the support of the American Civil Liberties Union for sodomy law repeal, equal employment policies, and due process. This meant help in court when someone challenged federal employment policies; it meant access to skilled lawyers who could command media attention when police victimized the community with bar raids and mass arrests. Activists had also opened a dialogue with liberal ministers in many Protestant denominations and were working with sympathetic mental health professionals to contest the disease classification of homosexuality.

Because of the courage of these activists, gay life was not as grim as it had been. Their willingness to publish gay and lesbian magazines had led the Supreme Court to declare in 1958 that homosexuality did not constitute obscenity. By the 1960s, images of gay life were beginning to proliferate in mainstream media and culture. The challenges of these early activists to law enforcement practices meant that, in some states, gay bars were less likely arbitrarily to be shut down by the state, and in cities like New York and San Francisco, police harassment had been somewhat curtailed.

By the late 1960s, a few thousand women and men were involved in movement organizations, and a few hundred could be said to have come out of the closet. Their actions were becoming more militant and visible. On the East Coast, activists picketed the White House, the Pentagon, the Civil Service Commission, and the State Department. On the West Coast, they held public press conferences against police brutality and distributed leaflets at the California State Fair. In Los Angeles, activists were speaking out boldly and holding street demonstrations against police raids on gay bars. The community's new sense of confidence was reflected in the founding of the Metropolitan Community Church and the launching of the *Advocate,* both of whose births preceded Stonewall. The San Francisco community had faced its major confrontation with the police more than five years before Stonewall. It emboldened and aroused the community, and by the late 1960s local politicians were soliciting the votes of homosexuals. In the months before Stonewall, gay activism in the Bay Area was taking a decidedly more militant, radical, and "post-Stonewall" turn.

We are also learning, from the work of historians, that all sorts of incidents of resistance occurred before Stonewall. Participants may not have interpreted their acts as "political," and most likely did not think of themselves as "activists." But their deeds did enter the collective memory, the group consciousness of the lesbian and gay world. Whether displayed through the tough fighting spirit of bar dykes, or the sassy tongue of a piss-elegant queen, resistance was a part of the everyday life of the pre-Stonewall generation.[2]

Stonewall, as I said, did not start everything. In fact, I think one can — and should — make the plausible argument that a street riot in New York could lead to the flowering of a gay liberation movement precisely because the soil had been fertilized and the seeds planted by the preceding generation. Had a riot such as Stonewall occurred ten years earlier, not much would have come of it, and we probably would not commemorate it. With riots as with so much of life, timing is everything.

Riots and Street Actions Are the Keys

Rioting and street demonstrations can be a lot of fun: I have participated in many in my decades as an activist. In certain circumstances, they have the power to galvanize people, crystallize sentiment, reveal discontent, and expose injustice. In other circumstances, they are a big dud. They can alienate outsiders, solidify the opposition, polarize a community, and mobilize the superior police power of the state. But in every case, a riot or a street action is nothing but an event—unless people choose to do something else after the rioting is over.

We already have other examples in our recent history of riots and street demonstrations. Some contributed to movement building; others led nowhere. The White Night riots in San Francisco in 1979 galvanized the community into further organizing and made it a more powerful force in the life and politics of San Francisco. Not long after that, gays in New York rioted for several nights to protest the making of the film *Cruising*. Not much came of it, and the New York movement in the early 1980s remained fractured and ineffective. In 1979, gay and lesbian activists called for a March on Washington; the turnout was not very large, and the results were disappointing. In 1987, a second march drew over half a million and led to an upsurge in grassroots organizing around the country. Many ACT UP chapters have used direct action and street activity to great effect; by contrast, many Queer Nation groups have employed similiar tactics, but have little to show for it.

Whether we realize it or not, the reason we commemorate Stonewall today is because, *after the rioting,* many gay men and lesbians chose to do something—organize. They moved from spontaneity to planned, intentional activity. Rather than wait for the police to come to them and provoke another outburst of anger, they formed organizations in order to engage in sustained activism. The first of the post-Stonewall groups in New York City was the Gay Liberation Front, an organization with a wide variety of members, but with a preponderance of people who identified with and were part of the radical movements of the 1960s. Around the country, GLFs formed, as did other kinds of gay, lesbian, and transgender organizations. The impetus for organizing often came from seeing a gay liberation banner or contingent at antiwar rallies and peace demonstrations. Other young radicals who were gay or lesbian returned from those events to form their own organizations.

In the first years after Stonewall, street demonstrations were a frequent and integral part of the gay liberation movement. The police and the media were often the targets. But these demonstrations required planning, discussion, and coordination: they didn't simply erupt spontaneously. Meanwhile, much of the work of gay liberation was far more mundane. Activists spoke in high school civics classes and college sociology courses. They formed caucuses in their professional associations and unions, and campaigned for visibility and job protection. They attended religious services as openly gay men and lesbians, met with ministers and priests and rabbis, and sought inclusion in these mainstream institutions. They lobbied for legislation, campaigned for progay candidates, and "zapped" homophobic ones. Some were part of the unspontaneous and unglamorous activity of litigation — filing suit in court to challenge discriminatory practices.

I am not privileging one form of activism over another. I do not believe marches are preferable to court cases, street riots preferable to testimony before a city council — or the reverse. The far-reaching revolutionary change that I yearn for will come about because we are flexible enough to use a broad spectrum of tactics and wise enough to develop a sound, long-range strategy. We will form organizations, support them, build them into powerful vehicles to advance our goals, and have the stamina to engage in the long march through institutions that liberation will require. When anger erupts into rioting, as it no doubt will again and again, we will know how to respond so that future Stonewalls likewise do not remain simply events, but become the building blocks of a just society.

The Most Oppressed Will Lead the Way

Of all the myths associated with Stonewall, this one packs the most polemical power when it is used. It has become a battering ram, wielded to attack the credibility, motivation, and worth of many movement leaders, to whom the phrases "self-appointed" or "self-proclaimed" are generally attached as modifiers. Especially since the early 1980s, as some of our community organizations have grown prosperous enough to pay middle-class salaries, the men and women who fill these slots have often faced criticism not because of what they believe or do, but because of who they are — the possessors of some of the privileges that an exploitative society parsimoniously dishes out.

"Privilege" is not, in itself, either a good or a bad thing. The problem with privilege — in income, education, housing, and the like — is not that some people have it, but that most don't. In a society stratified by gender, race, and class hierarchies, the material elements of a good life become accidents of birth or circumstance. The critical issue ought to be how one uses privilege: to perpetuate oppression and inequality or to challenge it. This is a political question, best answered by examining someone's words and deeds. Attacking leaders simply because of their identity, or simply because they occupy a prominent place in the organizational structure of the movement, makes no sense. It is destructive and harmful, an example of misplaced resentment.

The assumption that privilege makes one politically suspect or somehow inadequate as an agent of social change also threatens to obscure the truth at the heart of our movement: *All* homosexuals are oppressed; gay oppression is real and vicious. It isn't necessary to shed extra tears for the plight of prosperous white gay men in order to acknowledge that if one scratches below the surface of any gay life, one will find a bottomless well of pain whose source is oppression. And gays with privilege risk their status and expose themselves to penalties when they make the leap to activism.

To question the statement that "the most oppressed will lead the way" is *not* to argue for the inverse of that proposition. An authentic liberation movement must articulate the needs of everyone. The varied configurations of privilege and oppression that exist among us pose an enormous challenge in agenda setting. We will rise to that challenge only when the movement has incorporated the aspirations of the most oppressed. This is a political question whose answer is not perfectly correlated to identity. Oppression does not necessarily spawn political virtue or wisdom; privilege does not necessarily compromise integrity.

* * *

I marched in my first Stonewall Day parade in 1973. It was a gloriously bright day in New York. Like the buds that swell under the light of the spring sun, I could feel myself ready to burst with happiness as I strode through the streets of Manhattan, my arms linked with those of my friends. Years and years of gay freedom day marches have not diminished that feeling.

Stonewall will remain a symbol of prideful resistance as long as gay and lesbian oppression survives. Let's embrace the symbol and dispense with the myths.

10

Born Gay?

During the 1990s, the notion that homosexuality is biological, that lesbians and gay men are "born this way," has spread through American culture with amazing rapidity. It is espoused on the street, by Joe Gay and Jane Lesbian. Liberal heterosexual allies, from Al Gore to the anonymous editorial writers of the *New Yorker*, have taken it up. The view seems to have the support of the scientific establishment. The biological assumption is so widespread that the religious right has become obsessed with countering it, not only rhetorically but through counseling ministries designed to prove that gays can go straight.

As a historian, I am deeply skeptical of arguments rooted in biology and claims about fixed sexual orientation. The overwhelming weight of historical research into sexuality — and to this I could add the anthropological research as well — points to a picture of human sexual behavior far too complex and varied to be reducible to genes or endocrines or hormones. Even so, I'm not particularly interested in trying to counter the findings of scientists. In part, the reason is because I don't have the background to critique the scientific studies of the past few years. But mostly it is because my interest lies elsewhere. I'm fascinated by the rush, on the part of almost everyone except the most extremely homophobic elements of our society, to embrace the "born gay" view of sexual identity. In other words, I care less about whether or not

Versions of this essay were given as informal presentations at a board meeting of the National Gay and Lesbian Task Force, in 1993, and before the National Policy Round-table of the NGLTF Policy Institute, in 1998. My thanks to both audiences of activists for the lively discussions that ensued and that helped to sharpen my own thinking. Thanks also go to Pippa Holloway who compiled for me a bibliography of the scientific literature and discussions of it in the mass media.

it is true than in understanding why it is so damned attractive to so many different people.

I explore this phenomenon first by sketching out some recent history that will, I hope, place the current born-gay perspective in a broader context. Then I move on to outline a set of interlocking reasons why the perspective seems so compelling and, finally, suggest pitfalls or flaws in each of those reasons.

Some Recent History

In the literature produced by gay liberationists and lesbian feminists in the late 1960s and early 1970s, there is virtually a consensus that heterosexuality and homosexuality do not exist in nature, so to speak, but instead are products of culture. They are classifications of human beings that emanate from an oppressive society. They are artificial and deeply unnatural. Instead, these activist writers imagined sexuality as an unshaped potential. In the absence of oppression and social control, human sexuality would be polymorphous, a word meant to suggest that sexual desire was not fixed in its form or direction, but could flow any which way.

These notions were endlessly repeated. Here is one statement of it:

> Lesbianism, like male homosexuality, is a category of behavior possible only in a sexist society characterized by rigid sex roles and dominated by male supremacy. . . . In a society in which men do not oppress women, and sexual expression is allowed to follow feelings, the categories of homosexuality and heterosexuality would disappear.

Many other similar excerpts could be found.[1]

This viewpoint drew on both cultural theory from the 1960s as well as mainstream science. Radical intellectuals like Norman O. Brown, Herbert Marcuse, and Paul Goodman provided inspiration. But so did scientists like Alfred Kinsey, whose studies of sexual behavior emphasized endless variation in the patterns of human behavior, and anthropologists like Margaret Mead, whose best-selling books highlighted culture as a shaping force in the making of gender roles and sexual norms. Gay liberationists also drew on the vibrant writings of second-wave feminists who were challenging anything that smacked of biological determinism in the areas of gender and sexuality.

Out of this intellectual matrix came a formulation widely used in the 1970s but with almost no currency just a generation later: "sexual preference." As radical activists translated their theories into concepts that could be used to influence law and policy, they came up with the phrase. Today it is startling to the ear in the way it suggests "choice."

By the mid-1970s major change was underway, and we today are inheritors of it. As the radicalism of the first wave of gay liberation waned, shifts occurred not only in the tactics and goals and vision of the movement, but in its sexual theorizing as well. As the movement became institutionalized and more organizationally stable, as activists shifted from a rhetoric of revolution to pressing for steady incremental change in policy and institutions, the word "orientation" increasingly entered the movement vocabulary. For a while, there was a seesawing back and forth between preference and orientation; some used the terms interchangeably. The greatest resistance to orientation came from radical lesbian feminists who argued that lesbianism was an option that any woman might pursue in her resistance to male supremacy and patriarchy. But orientation, with its sense of placement, alignment, and clear directionality, gradually overwhelmed preference, with its suggestion of mere taste or fashion.

The concept of orientation came from the mental health professions. In the theorizing of the 1940s, 1950s, and 1960s, writers tended to look at orientation as something that got set relatively early in life, a result of experiences in infancy and early childhood. Many writers and practitioners, especially among American psychoanalysts, believed that, with work, sexual orientation could be reversed. Of course, they meant that it could, and should, be reversed in one direction only: homosexual orientation could be changed to heterosexual. But starting in the 1960s, gay activists appropriated the concept of orientation, inverted the meaning of homosexuality so that it became good rather than unfortunate, and argued — as a few liberal mental health professionals were already doing — that it was irreversible. Thus, while sexual orientation was not determined by biology, it was so deep that it might as well have been. And, since gay was good, there was no point in even trying to change it.

In the 1980s and 1990s conceptualizations continued to change, though this time in ways consistent with the direction charted by the proponents of orientation. Orientation remained in favor, especially in the writing of legislation and institutional policy, but it increasingly coexisted with "identity."

Postmodern theory notwithstanding, in common parlance identity suggests something even more solid than orientation. The directionality implied by orientation offered something more substantial than the taste implied by preference. But identity spoke to something deep inside the individual, something that went to the very core of who one was. And, simultaneous with the easy incorporation of "sexual identity" into the gay and lesbian lexicon came the release of a stream of scientific literature that seemed to substantiate the connotations of identity as reaching deep into the core of an individual. Studies about the hypothalamus, about identical twins, and the alleged gay gene all pointed to biology as somehow causal in the creation of homosexuals.

Some Reasons Why

The proclamations of some scientists are just one reason why biological explanations have appeal for gay people and their allies. There are many others. I want to try to distinguish five of them. Bear in mind, however, that the power of the born-gay framework comes from the ways that these different reasons reinforce one another, adding a persuasive punch to the explanation that seems thoroughly irrefutable and makes it appear almost self-evidently true.

REASON I: MOST OF US BELIEVE IT
The idea that we were born gay or lesbian corresponds to our deepest feelings, to the way we understand our own experience. Many of us have felt different for as far back as we can remember. There is hardly a time in our lives when we do not recall feeling special attractions for members of the same sex. The issue for us is not when we became gay or lesbian, but when we realized this was so, when we were finally able to put a name to the inclinations that we always had.

Despite my skepticism toward biological explanations, I am a very good illustration of this. I cannot remember not wanting to be with boys in a special way. I had a fascination for the male body from my earliest years. I have experiences that could be understood as sex play going way, way back. And, once puberty hit, there seemed to be no stopping me. Over the years, as I've told the short and the long versions of my coming out story to my gay friends, and heard theirs in turn, the truth of my identity seems incontrovertible. Who can argue with experience?

REASON 2: SCIENCE CURRENTLY SEEMS TO SUPPORT US

Science has lurked in the background of the why-are-we-gay routine for a long time. Remember that, as far back as the 1970s, activists appropriated psychological theories about fixed sexual orientation to refute claims that we could change. But psychological arguments have always been of mixed value since, however fixed sexual orientation might be, the mental health industry was still positing that there was a "before" way back in childhood.

In the 1990s, the ground shifted. In a short span of time, a number of independent inquiries into the biology of homosexuality appeared. In 1991, Simon LeVay released a research study in which he claimed a measurable difference in size between the hypothalamus of gay men and heterosexual men. Richard Pillard and J. Michael Bailey published results from their ongoing investigation of sexual orientation and identical twins, showing a large proportion of them to be gay. In 1993, Dean Hamer's study of genetic markers of homosexuality was published in the scientific press. And, since then, various studies have continued to be released, while scientists and journalists alike have rushed to produce popularized versions of these studies for a lay audience.[2]

Science wields a great deal of authority in American society. We attribute to scientists all sorts of power to solve a wide range of problems. Think, for instance, of how invested we are in the belief that science will devise the magic bullet for AIDS — either the vaccine to prevent it or the treatment to cure it. We attribute so much to science that these various scientific papers on homosexuality have received very wide play in the media. The week that LeVay's report on the hypothalamus was published in *Science*, Ted Koppel devoted a *Nightline* program to it. The *New York Times*, the *Washington Post*, and the *Los Angeles Times* all devoted front-page news stories to it. Halfway around the globe, Dean Hamer's study of the gay gene was written up on the front page of the *Canberra Times*.[3]

If scientists say it is so, it must be. How comforting that science supports the truth of our experience!

REASON 3: OUR OPPONENTS CLAIM THE OPPOSITE

While all sorts of Americans with all sorts of rationales have opposed the struggle for gay equality, the most rabid, organized, and aggressive opposition has been concentrated within conservative Christianity, particularly among the ranks of evangelical Protestants. They are having nothing of this born-gay routine. If we were born gay, it would be much harder to justify their hatred of us, since God does not make mistakes. To them, our loves and desires represent a perverse immoral *choice*. Their polemics bastardize our experience, distorting our lives beyond recognition. As the argument from biology has infiltrated our culture, their antagonism to it has grown. They have created counseling ministries designed to convert us to heterosexuality and thus prove the bankruptcy of scientific claims. We *know* we can't agree with them. Since any understanding of our sexual identities that smacks of choice risks comforting our enemy, we must be born this way.

REASON 4: "BORN GAY" HAS GREAT POLITICAL UTILITY
Phrased most simply, many of our allies, or would-be allies, love this idea. The people we are trying to convince to support our quest for justice and respect can take the argument from nature and run with it. Plus, Americans have a self-conception of fairness; it runs deep in our public rhetoric. What could be more unfair than to penalize someone for being true to nature's ways?

Put yourself in the shoes of activists in the mid-1970s who were trying to translate the raw energy of gay liberation and lesbian feminism into concrete institutional changes. Building on the model of civil rights laws, they decide to go to their city council to lobby for protections against discrimination. What do they ask for? Legislative protection for a capacity inherent in every-one? Or the addition of a phrase, "sexual orientation," that will protect a newly visible minority of people? Or, suppose you are opening a dialogue with representatives of liberal mainline religious bodies. Do you ask them to reconsider their teachings on sexual morality and endorse polymorphous perversity? Or do you persuade them that gay men and lesbians, a definable segment of humanity, are part of God's grand design? Or, you want the American Psychiatric Association to eliminate homosexuality from its list of mental disorders. Do you try to win their support for a sexual freedom platform? Or do you argue that this discrete group, men and women with a homosexual orientation, function well in society?

I am not accusing activists of being crassly expedient. It is much more complicated. These were men and women entering institutions, or worlds, each with its own set of discourses that construct its members's way of understanding social experience. Activists had to enter into dialogue; they were trying to communicate effectively. In doing so they were absorbed into the forms of understanding that already existed and tried to make themselves heard in these contexts. A good example was the work of gay and lesbian litigators. Because the courts, in ruling on civil rights issues, had set up immutability as one of the criteria that defines a group against whom discrimination is not justifiable, lawyers have tried to argue that sexual orientation, or identity, is a fixed unchanging characteristic. In other words, we are born gay.

REASON 5: THE EXTREME ALTERNATIVE IS TERRIFYING

The either/or framework that is so central to Western modes of thought — yes/no, stop/go, black/white, good/bad — makes it very hard to imagine ambiguity, fluidity, indeterminacy, or just plain old shades of gray. In this context, our conceptual options seem to be either that we are born gay and hence irrevocably are gay, or that we have free choice in this matter.

Even with the changes provoked by gay liberation and feminism in the past generation, being queer is a hard road to travel. Oppression is real. We get targeted with quite a lot of abuse. The emotional wounds go deep, and sometimes the physical ones do too. The idea that this struggle might have been unnecessary, that we could have spared ourselves all of this by choosing another sexual orientation, is acutely disturbing. "Born gay" closes this line of inquiry firmly. It spares us from the horrifying idea that our sufferings could end if only we exerted enough will or had made a different choice.

Some Problems with the Reasons Why

Alone, no single one of these reasons is persuasive enough to inspire conviction. Their power comes in the way that they work together, creating a package that makes the born-gay arguments of some scientists seem undeniable. But each one of these reasons why has weaknesses. These don't get nearly as much play as the reasons why, but they are out there lurking, ready to spring into action and undermine the solid structure of our convictions.

PROBLEM 1: NOT ALL OF US BELIEVE IT!

For many of us, perhaps even most of us, gay or lesbian seems to be who we are and who we always have been. But there is no unanimity on this point, and the apparent consensus can be upset at any moment by a contrary voice. For instance, a generation ago, many women very self-consciously *chose* to be lesbian as they encountered the ideas of radical feminism and decided to make women the center of their lives. They would hardly serve as poster girls for the born-gay argument. Or, think about the hoopla surrounding Ellen's coming out. Always in the background was the figure of Anne Heche, the pretty femme who was securely heterosexual until, wham, she fell in love with Ellen DeGeneres. In gay circles lots of us know men who led thoroughly heterosexual lives. They married and raised children, occasionally noticing an attraction to a male friend. Then, in middle age, something triggered a new sexual awareness, and they decided to come out. Born gay? I don't think so.

Besides all the exceptions that make biological explanations wobbly, there is also the discomforting fact that the stories we tell about our lives are — I hate to say it — suspect. As friendship circles form among young gay men, or when middle-aged gay couples begin to socialize together, inevitably they will spend an evening — or three or four — exchanging coming out stories. It is a long-standing bonding ritual among us. As we tell our tales, coming out becomes the destiny toward which all else in our lives was leading. We filter out our heterosexual impulses and experiences or we render them inauthentic. Since we are reciting our life stories from the vantage point of the present, and since they are being told in order to create a bond among individuals, of course we will shape them to achieve our main purpose — building ties of community among a group whose links are, frankly, tenuous. But these are retrospective reconstructions of our biographies. They eliminate the fluidity, the serendipity, the — yes — choice that went into creating our sexual selves. Do I mean choice in the way that we choose a flavor of ice cream for dessert? Of course not. But, our life stories, our experiences, do not provide a reliable body of evidence for claiming that we are born gay.

PROBLEM 2: SCIENCE IS A THIN REED!

The scientific fashion of the 1990s was to find biological explanations for the origins of homosexuality. Most of us aren't scientists and, as lay folk, we tend to bow to its authority. This is especially true when we are subject to little media blitzes that headline the research findings of experts. The problem is that science, especially with regard to homosexuality, has a way of changing its mind.

In the longer history of scientific research on sexuality, the most outstanding pattern is how core paradigms have oscillated from generation to generation. From the late nineteenth century through the 1920s, congenital explanations dominated scientific inquiry. "Contrary sexual instinct," said the scientists, was hereditary and inborn. But scientists were at a loss to prove these assertions and, as Freudian theory became more influential, environmental theories of origins took hold. The influence of these arguments from nurture peaked in the 1960s. Since the environmental explanations of this generation were closely associated with negative views of homosexuality, their influence has waned as the gay movement has grown. In the late 1970s, the pendulum began to swing back in the direction of nature, and the studies of the 1990s have made biology dominant. It is worth noting that recent biological, and more specifically genetic, theorizing is not confined to homosexuality. We are in an era when science interprets all sorts of social behavior as having biological roots, from a propensity to crime and violence to a predisposition to alcoholism. Could we simply be living in a time when the turn to science lets us, as a society, off the hook, absolving us from working toward solutions to social problems since they are, alas, rooted in nature? Could "born gay" be just one more bit of evidence of the conservatism of the present era?

Of course, one might counter that science isn't changing its mind. It is improving, advancing, moving us toward an ever more accurate picture of reality. That's what science claimed a hundred years ago when some practitioners argued that women's wombs would shrink if they received a college education, and others measured brain size to construct a racial hierarchy of intelligence.

More to the point, the science that our culture is relying on to prove that gay is a characteristic with us from birth is a thin reed. Of the thousands and thousands of studies published in scientific journals each year, why does the occasional study about the origins of homosexuality make its way into the news? When science does make advances, it is based on the slow meticulous building that occurs as study after study, experiment after experiment, adds to a point of view. Yet the studies on homosexuality have not been replicated. Even the twin studies, of which there have been more than one, are open to serious critique and contrary interpretations.

Despite its claims to objectivity, science does not stand apart from the society which produces it. This may not mean much if the topic is astronomy (although Galileo would have something to say about this), but it means almost everything when the topic is as contentious as same-sex love and desire. Just as I'm skeptical of the stories we tell about our lives, I'm dubious about the ability of science, uncontaminated by cultural preconceptions, to investigate an alleged biology of sexual identity. Until the forces that oppress people based on sexuality are lifted, the well of science is poisoned, its findings open to doubt.

PROBLEM 3: WHO IS SETTING OUR AGENDA ANYWAY?

Of course it drives us crazy when Jerry Falwell or Pat Robertson or Lou Sheldon or any other minister of the Christian Right tells us we are choosing sin. But we need to scrutinize very carefully any time we, as a movement or a community or an organization or an individual, find ourselves making decisions reactively. We cannot allow our opponents to shape our agenda, our self-conception, or how we choose to represent ourselves to the larger society. "They say choice so we say born this way" is not a smart approach.

PROBLEM 4: BEWARE OF ALLIES BEARING GIFTS!

Put me at the head of the line of those who advocate that allies are necessary if the gay and lesbian movement is to succeed in its goals. I believe that the goals of all identity groups targeted for oppression require us to work together, in coalition, in order to move forward, and that anyone, of whatever identity, can take a stand for justice. Nonetheless, the ease with which many liberal Americans have embraced the born-gay approach makes me very uneasy. It allowed them, too suddenly, to quell their moral reservations about our lives and push aside their personal squeamishness about what we do.

What will happen when the shallowness of the scientific evidence is exposed? How will allies react when our messy complicated life histories get a fuller airing? Will we slip back into the category of moral weaklings? Of sexual perverts? Of destroyers of the family?

In our rush to embrace biological explanations because of their political utility, let's not forget that an earlier generation of gay rights advocates, in Germany in the first part of the twentieth century, argued tirelessly for a congenital explanation of homosexuality. They believed it would promote tolerance. Their efforts came to naught after Hitler's rise to power when the Nazis decided that these congenital "defectives" ought to be eliminated for the sake of the master race.

Our alliances will be far more durable if they are grounded in arguments from justice rather than nature. The reason to support antidiscrimination laws, to counter homophobic speech and violence, to foster tolerance in the schools, to recognize our relationships, and to adopt many other planks of the notorious gay agenda is that what happens to gay men, lesbians, bisexuals, and transgendered people in this society is just not right. No one deserves to be treated the way we have been treated. No one should be the target of such hateful actions. It doesn't matter why we are gay. In a democratic society with notions of human rights and the dignity of the individual, oppression, mistreatment, and injustice are intolerable.

PROBLEM 5: WE'LL NEVER SUCCEED FROM
A POSITION OF WEAKNESS

Just as the born-gay argument lets our allies off the hook, so too with us. It allows us to sidestep our own internalized homophobia. We can feel good about ourselves because we bear no responsibility for our gayness; it's not our fault we were born this way.

But buried beneath our embrace of the biological is the uneasy—and unarticulated—feeling that, if we did have a choice, we might choose otherwise. This is not a secure foundation for a healthy self-respecting life, nor is it solid ground on which to build a freedom movement. Not only ought we be arguing for our rights from a standpoint of justice, but I would also like to know that we might embrace our sexual identity even if we discovered we had a choice of how to be. If there was a way to change us, would we rush to sign up? Or would we stare uncomprehendingly at the very idea?

*   *   *

The debate about the causes of homosexuality is bound to continue. As long as gay issues remain contentious, the search for explanations will carry on. And, among those explanations, the argument from biology is not likely to fade any time soon. Its appeal emanates from too many directions. But, I would hope that more of us become willing to step back from this framework, examine more thoroughly the hidden motivations behind its attractiveness, and at the very least opt for a skeptical agnosticism. As the authors of one study of the issue phrased it: "Why ask why?"

I I

What Does Gay Liberation Have to Do
with the War in Bosnia?

There's a hazard in agreeing to give a talk long before the event. Eight months ago, when I was invited to give this keynote, my work at the Policy Institute of NGLTF was channeling my thinking into particular grooves. I was working on a report, *Beyond the Beltway*, that analyzed the political shifts that had occurred since the so-called Gingrich Revolution of 1994. Congress, which had seen so many antigay battles erupt in the preceding few years — funding for the National Endowment for the Arts, issues about the sexual content of AIDS education materials, the gays-in-the-military debate — had become relatively quiet. But closer to all our homes, at the level of state politics, there seemed to be an explosion of gay-related legislation and citizen-sponsored initiatives. Some of the legislation was queer friendly, but much of it, and certainly all the ballot initiatives, seriously threatened the well-being of our communities.

At this same time, the Policy Institute was producing a series of papers called "linkages." We were responding to the way the extreme right in the United States was attacking not only the queer community, but other communities as well. So we released short analyses of issues like welfare reform, affirmative action, and immigration restriction, drawing connections

I gave this talk as the keynote address at a conference in Detroit, in February 1996, for activists from gay, lesbian, and bisexual organizations in Michigan, to focus on the issue of community building. It reflected my intensifying dissatisfaction with identity politics at a time when a broad-based conservatism was entrenching itself more deeply in Washington, even as I recognized the need for and value of identity-based communities and mobilizations. My thanks to Jan Stevenson for the invitation to speak at the conference.

between the needs and aspirations of our sexuality-based communities and those of racial, ethnic, and economically marginalized groups.

Put these two projects together, and what was uppermost in my mind was the way that the extreme right, based in the Republican Party, seemed to be picking off communities one by one. Hence my decision to tell the organizers of this conference on multicultural community building that my keynote would be called "Building Community, Building Alliances."

I am still thinking about such things. But I have also been reflecting on other topics as well. I have been noticing, for instance, how the right wing seems to have a broad comprehensive agenda, how they seem to be going after everything. They want power in the broadest and biggest sense of the word. The right talks often about "the gay agenda." But make no mistake: these religious conservatives have an agenda, too. They have an agenda for remaking America from top to bottom, for preserving and extending inequality and privilege—special rights in the truest sense of the word. The right thinks *big*, while progressive people these days—citizens and activists who truly care about injustice, who are motivated by deep commitments to compassion and generosity and fairness—often are preoccupied only with their one small corner of the universe.

So, as I've thought more about what I want to communicate to you today, a slogan and a question keep ringing through my mind.

The slogan comes from a bumper sticker produced by the environmental movement: "Think globally, act locally." It seems perfectly appropriate for today. This conference is filled with people who are the real experts in community building. You are doing the work locally every day in your neighborhood associations, civic groups, government agencies, and community centers. Is there some way, I've been wondering, that I—trained as a historian—could offer a bigger picture of the context in which you are doing your work?

Let me say at the outset that I think it is important that we always hold a big picture in view. Doing the nitty-gritty work of community building as openly gay, lesbian, and bisexual people, we can easily forget that the whole concept of visible, consciously self-identified gay communities is a revolutionary innovation. There is nothing like it in the previous history of this country, or in the history of the Western world over the past two millennia. A rupture with the past as profound as this must mean something worth keeping in mind!

Along with the slogan there is a recurring question: What does gay libera-tion have to do with the war in Bosnia? Now before I lose you with that one, I want you to think about the question for a minute. It's ambiguous. What it means depends very much on tone. For instance, said with a particular inflec-tion, it could mean "how absurd!" But spoken differently, it could also mean "Hmm? I wonder. Maybe there is some connection. What could it be?"

So, with our slogan and our question in mind, I want to talk to you today about two things: (1) Where do these precious communities that we work in and that we are building come from? What are the broad historical forces that have brought us to a point in time when same-sex desire is being pub-licly affirmed by masses of people? (2) Where do our politics come from? Why and how is it that we have come to develop in this last generation a community and a politics based on identity? And how appropriate is it for this moment in time?

Where Do Our Communities Come From?

For years I taught a U.S. history course called "Sexuality in Historical Per-spective." Somewhere around the third or fourth week of the course, after I had captured their interest through discussions of those wacky Puritans who executed the animals in bestiality cases, we would reach the place on the syllabus marked "the demographic revolution." The students would groan. But let me tell you about it.

In 1800, the average fertility rate for women of childbearing age in the United States was between seven and eight. High fertility was true across the board. It was true in New England, in the mid-Atlantic, and in the South. It was true for black women and white women, for immigrant and native-born, for free women and for the enslaved. Today, by contrast, the average fertility rate is slightly over two.

The decline has occurred steadily, but unevenly. It can be traced alongside the lines of change from a labor-intensive rural economy to an urban-based wage economy. Native-born white women in towns and cities were the first to experience the decline. Immigrants from peasant rural cultures in Europe, Latin America, and Asia had high fertility in the first generation but, if they settled in cities, the fertility of their daughters and granddaughters declined. In the post-Emancipation South, where a huge proportion of black and white families were sharecroppers or tenants or owners of small subsistence farms, fertility remained high well into the twentieth century. But, as migration to cities occurred—to the auto factories in Detroit, for example—fertility started to drop dramatically.

Think for a minute about what this might mean. What implications would such high fertility have for the roles of women in society? What possibilities would there be for a life outside the cycles of reproduction, childrearing, and family-based labor? There have always been individual women who found ways to cut their own path in life but, for the overwhelming majority, high fertility meant a life centered around the conjugal and parenting relationships.

Think, too, about what this might mean for the channeling and shaping of sexual desire. Particular men and women might experience all sorts of objects of desire, including someone of the same sex. But in some profound, seemingly natural way, sexual desire was being harnessed to a survival need to procreate. Survival required hard labor, and labor was organized either around family groups working together or around the forced labor of servants and slaves under the authority of a family patriarch.

Historians and anthropologists have found evidence of same-sex desire in virtually every culture and every era in which they have looked. And specifically, we know that same-sex desire floated in and through these family-centered procreating communities in seventeenth, eighteenth, and nineteenth-century North America. But what opportunity would one have had in this procreative world to take this desire and build a life out of it? What opportunities in the tightly knit farm villages of New England or on the plantations of the South? There wasn't what we might call a whole lot of "lifestyle choice" operating here.

In the course of the nineteenth and twentieth centuries, in the cracks of a new urbanized wage economy, we begin to see the emergence of communities of people drawn together by the commonality of same-sex love. Interestingly, and not surprisingly, these inchoate communities tended to be found along the outskirts of family life, in locations marked as in some way deviant, or where fictive family might form: in the boardinghouses that catered to the needs of young single working men and women, in the entertainment world of night clubs and the theater, among groups of self-conscious bohemians, in the red-light districts where female prostitutes gathered, in the maritime districts of port cities, in single-sex institutions like women's colleges. Between World War I and the 1960s, as historians like

Elizabeth Kennedy, Madeleine Davis, George Chauncey, Allan Berube, and Esther Newton have shown us, these communities grew, became denser and more complex, and offered a rich set of opportunities for sociability and connection. These communities developed and thrived even through the periods of intense persecution that erupted at different points over the past century or so. Today, it would not be inaccurate to claim that gay and lesbian communities are fixtures of the American social landscape.

Why should this history, which can be spun out over hundreds of pages of fascinating detail, matter to us? Why should you be thinking about this as you do the work of community building in Detroit and elsewhere? Because often, in the current political climate, we feel ourselves under attack. We feel as if the very survival of gay, lesbian, and bisexual people is in jeopardy. Well, as a historian, I want to assure you that, although we are under attack, our survival is not in jeopardy. Even though there are neo-Nazis who would like to annihilate us, extremist right-wing Christians who would force the schools to deny our existence, a reparative therapy movement eager to convert us, and Republican presidential candidates willing to pander to the basest fears, prejudice, and hatred: despite all this, our survival is not in question. As the configuration of politics continues to shift over the next years, we may find ourselves faced with heightened threats to our well-being and more resistance to our goals. But our *survival* is not in question.

We are here, as a community, as a people, as a collection of individuals who share something very important amid a lot of other differences, because of profound social and economic processes that reach deep into our history and have embedded us in the structure of contemporary society. As I said before, we are solidly rooted in the social landscape of the United States. So, while we act locally every day, keep remembering that our lives are part of a much bigger, broader story.

Where Do Our Politics Come From?

It's one thing to talk about how our communities have formed. It's another to think about how it has happened that our communities have become politicized. There was nothing inevitable or foreordained about that transition. Why is it that, on the basis of an identity rooted in our love for and attraction to members of the same sex, we have built a vibrant political movement? This question also has a historical answer.

Although the beginnings of a gay and lesbian politics in this country stretch back to the McCarthy era, and in some other countries reach even further back in time, most of us recognize, I think, that a qualitative shift occurred at the end of the 1960s, around the historical moment that we symbolically attach to the Stonewall Riots. The rebellion in Greenwich Village and the birth of gay liberation shortly afterward came near the end of what was by far the most economically expansive era in American history. The prosperity was unparalleled. Unlike the current expansion, during which inequalities of wealth are deepening, the economic growth of the post-World War II generation reached very deeply into the population. It also motivated an extension of the government's role in economic life that attended to at least some of the poor.

At the time, in the rhetorically frenzied context of the Cold War and rabid anti-Communism, this long economic expansion was heralded as the inevitable outcome of a beneficent American capitalism. With distance, we are now more easily able to see it as the product of something else, of a unique combination of very unusual circumstances: (1) a world war in which every other major industrialized economy was devastated, so that American goods and American capital could dominate a world market; (2) a world war that brought to the United States full employment and so much savings that it fueled the economy for years afterward; (3) a generous government social welfare program for able-bodied white men, called the GI Bill, that provided education, affordable housing and business loans to a generation of young men, resulting in mobility into the middle class; (4) a very high rate of unionization, which meant that many working-class jobs finally paid decent wages; and (5) a huge corporate welfare program called the defense budget that provided the difference between depression-era levels of unemployment and an almost full employment economy.

Why should this be of interest to us today? What are the lines of connection between the economic growth of the 1950s and 1960s and the politics of the lesbian, gay, and bisexual community? As prosperity became the norm, as it erased the memory of the depression and reached more deeply and broadly into American life, it shaped the national mood. Many boats were being lifted. Prosperity came to temper the anti-Communist hysteria of the McCarthy era. It built a material foundation for values of generosity, compassion, and fairness, and created openings for public policies that reflected those values. The Great Society programs of Lyndon Johnson are not easily explained without this floor of economic well-being. Prosperity also created a mood, a feeling that was expansive, one that allowed us to imagine the unimaginable. And one of those unimaginable visions was gay liberation.

But there was no straight line of inevitability that led from prosperity to gay liberation. Something else intervened to smooth the way, and that was the African American freedom struggle. The civil rights movement lighted the path that prosperity opened up. It's fair to say that it changed everything in the America of the 1960s. It juxtaposed vivid images of courage against a stark shocking background of hatred and brutality. It voiced its claims in a universalistic rhetoric of inclusion. It spoke from, and appealed to, conscience and moral values. It built a broad coalition committed to equality. This coalition was the political force that gave Lyndon Johnson the gumption to propose Great Society legislation that made war on poverty, that tried to extend opportunity to everyone, that attempted to distribute wealth to those who had been excluded from economic abundance.

The successes of these years were many. From the vantage point of today's conservative national politics, I look back on those years with envy. But the vision of a just society also collided with resistance to change.

By the mid-1960s, a Black Power movement had emerged. It was concerned with more than the formal structure of law and opportunity. It addressed the deep ways that racism infiltrated not only the law, but culture, social institutions, the practices of everyday life, even the psychology of oppressor and oppressed alike. While Black Power seemed to many whites to be born out of rage, hatred, frustration, and despair, it reflected the hopes of the era even more profoundly. After all, it is hard to feel angry or disappointed or betrayed — and then take action — unless one actually believes that real permanent change is possible.

The Black Power movement taught something new and powerful about oppression. Over the past generation, insights about the dynamics of oppression, about the many-tentacled reach of the monster, and about its appearance of intractability, have multiplied. They have allowed many of us — many of you — to develop a range of strategies and tactics for addressing oppression locally, nationally, even globally.

Black Power also marked the birth of identity politics in the United States. This birth wasn't widely heralded at the time. It took a number of years before the extent of this innovation and its significance for American society, politics, and culture emerged. But make no mistake about it. Identity politics proved contagious. With a very short time, vibrant movements among Chicanos, Native Americans, and Asian Americans had emerged. A women's liberation movement erupted as well. And, of course, the movement that brings us here today, gay and lesbian liberation.

Thirty years later, it's fair to say that we are still living through an era of identity politics. But the conditions that gave it birth — the prosperity, expansiveness, and hopefulness of the post–World War II generation — are gone. We are living through a time of cynicism, apathy, hopelessness, and distrust. The economic order has changed, not only in this country, but throughout the world. Increasingly, we hear talk of globalization, of a single economic world. And although our leaders speak of this in the language of utopians, the passions displayed in the recent fight over whether to approve the North American Free Trade Agreement suggest that not everyone is happy about this new world order. Even in the midst of an economic expansion, insecurity runs high. Living standards are going up for a few, while most working Americans are having to work harder to stay in place. The public sector is being starved in order to pay off past debts. Our schools and our health care system are in deep crisis. For many Americans and — thinking globally again — for a majority of human beings around the world, we are in the midst of a crisis of massive proportions.

The continuing power of identity politics is not unrelated to this sense of crisis. The desire to build a strong queer community, a vital African American or Chicano community, or an impassioned community of crusading evangelical Christians reflects the need to have an anchor when little else seems to be working.

So, if we ask the question again, "What does gay liberation have to do with the war in Bosnia?" maybe we have at least the makings of an intelligible answer. To my mind, the war in Bosnia is as clear and dramatic an example as one can find of identity politics gone amok. Here is identity shaped into a weapon, identity as a tool of hatred and division, identity as a road to destruction and holocaust.

As we explore at this conference the nuts and bolts of community building, and after we return home to do our work, I think we need to search our hearts, examine our values, and scrutinize our goals. Remember that all the social identities we construct are partial ones that never quite capture our fullness. Every one of us here, everyone we will ever encounter, represents an elaborate configuration of identities. Our loyalties, allegiances, and connections are multiple, and our work needs to be done with a recognition of these dense and intricate ties. Does our effort to build gay, lesbian, and bisexual communities represent a turning inward or a turning toward other communities and peoples? Does our effort to build these queer communities represent an effort to build a fortress against the world or an opportunity to build links with others? Does our desire to construct a strong community represent a desire to get more for *us* or to make the world better for everyone? Does our work betray a sense of chauvinistic superiority or a wish to create models that everyone can learn from? Our answers will tell us, I think, whether or not our work is worth doing.

12

Laying Claim to Family

The family has to a great extent lost its position as a conservative institution and has become a field for social change.
— William Graham Sumner "The Family and Social Change," 1909

Not too long ago, a discussion of lesbian and gay family issues would have seemed like an exercise in science fiction.

In the 1950s and 1960s, before Stonewall and the birth of gay liberation, stereotypes of lesbians and gay men had little resonance with ideas about family. The gay world was a hidden one, associated with urban vice, criminality, seedy Mafia-controlled bars, violence, and extortion. Homosexuality was variously viewed as a sin, a crime, or a disease. Individual lesbians and gays were portrayed as isolated, lonely, troubled, freakish, and without stable relationships. Oppressive stereotypes of the gay male child molester or of the lesbian "vampire" in search of new recruits fostered a view of them as a threat — a particularly dangerous threat — to the integrity of the family and the safety of children. Men or women who came out — or, in those times, were exposed as homosexuals — brought shame and disgrace to their family of origin and often found themselves expelled from its embrace.

Let's put aside the question of whether this was ever a fully accurate description of lesbian and gay life. Historians are discovering a much more complex and nuanced view of the gay world before Stonewall. Even under oppressive conditions, many gays and lesbians in the United States forged

This essay originated as a talk that I gave before campus and community audiences around the country between 1995 and 1997, when I was director of the Policy Institute of NGLTF. A somewhat different version of it was published as a Working Paper of the Policy Institute, under the title "Here to Stay." I especially want to thank Beth Barrett, Helen Gonzales, Kerry Lobel, and Melinda Paras for helpful discussions of these issues.

bonds of community and constructed their own forms of kinship. But, to the majority society, ideas of abnormality and of an almost natural exclusion from family life shaped popular belief.

In the three decades since Stonewall, lesbians and gay men have assumed a visible outspoken place in the public world. They have come out of the closet in large numbers. They have built a dense network of organizations and institutions, staggering in their breadth and depth. In every sphere of life, they have battered away at the laws, the public policies, the institutional structures, the social practices, and the cultural representations that have marked them as inferior and unworthy of full citizenship. Discussion, debate, and conflict over the place of lesbians and gay men in America have erupted in the military, communities of faith, workplaces, public school systems, government agencies, and legislatures. Lesbians, gays, and their allies continue to wage a sustained struggle for equality, fairness, and respect.

In important ways, we are winning this struggle. Yes, an extremist, fundamentalist Christian right wages rabid homophobic campaigns against us. But, despite their ballot initiatives, their hate-filled rhetoric, the hostile legislation in states dominated by a Republican party that is in turn beholden to its right wing, despite even the new level of institutional power that a not-at-all-compassionate Bush administration promises to wield on behalf of this politics, change for the better is happening all the time.

And change generates more change. In the first decade or two after the Stonewall Rebellion of 1969, many lesbians and gay men found themselves fighting simply for the right to be open about their loves and not be punished for it. The movement was filled with women and men who wanted the freedom to make choices about how they would shape their intimate, emotional, and sexual lives. They wanted to be able to do this without punishment from the state or penalty from an employer and without the threat of retaliatory violence.

As some of those battles were won in a few localities in the 1970s and 1980s, as lesbians and gay men created a space — physical, cultural, and emotional — in which it was possible to live as they chose, new issues emerged. Horizons expanded. A new set of questions could be asked. New options became visible, and new expectations were generated. Instead of simply fighting for the freedom to be gay or lesbian, it was possible to ask "how do I wish to live my life?" and "what kind of gay or lesbian life do I want to construct for myself?"

In searching for answers to these questions, lesbians and gay men all over the country, in large cities, suburbs, and small communities, find themselves developing, sometimes intentionally and sometimes not, a politics of family life. They are crafting a public policy agenda for their families and advocating for it. They are championing modes of living that are challenging and altering the fabric of American society.

These issues do not just affect the well-being of lesbians, gay men, and their family members. They ignite emotional flash points whose explosive power reverberates widely. Extremists of the right have used these issues to build a political movement that threatens core political freedoms and also endangers struggles for social and economic justice of every sort.

As lesbians and gay men have sought to lay claim to family, a range of issues have erupted in recent years.

Relationship Recognition

Except in Vermont, whose legislature passed a civil unions bill in 2000, same-sex relationships have no standing in law. Neither the rights nor the responsibilities that inhere in marriage extend to lesbian and gay relationships, whatever the length of time or depth of commitment. During the past decade or so, lesbians and gay men have fought to have their relationships recognized. In corporations as varied as General Motors, Citigroup, Philip Morris, Chevron, and Microsoft, gay, lesbian, and bisexual employee groups have successfully won the extension of spousal benefits to same-sex couples. In many universities and other nonprofit organizations, similar victories have accrued. Some local government units have done the same, as well as provide registries for same-sex couples. In a number of states, most notably Hawaii, Alaska, Vermont, and Massachusetts, gay and lesbian couples have filed suit to win the right to marry.

Simultaneously, even the barest prospect of "gay marriage" has spawned a vigorous counter assault. The fear that same-sex unions might become legal in Hawaii, Vermont, or elsewhere has led a large majority of state legislatures to launch a preemptive strike. They have enacted statutes to protect themselves from having to recognize same-sex marriages performed in other states. In 1996, Congress did the same when it passed the Defense of Marriage Act, which specified that, for the purpose of federal law, policies, and benefits, marriage shall only be considered the union of a man and a woman.

In other words, something of a legislative firewall is being constructed to create an impassable barrier between gays and lesbians on one side, and "family" on the other.

Parenting

Large numbers of men and women who formed heterosexual relationships and had children have later come out as lesbian or gay; estimates range from two to eight million. In the past, they were likely either to hide their identity or reluctantly give up access to their children. Increasingly, they are choosing to combine the identity of gay or lesbian with that of parent, and often they are able to work out equitable arrangements with their former spouses. More recently, women and men who already identify as lesbian or gay are choosing to become parents—through alternative insemination, adoption, or foster care. The quest for the right to become a parent, or to remain a parent, has placed lesbians and gay men in conflict with courts, legislatures, welfare agencies, and private adoption organizations.

Schools

As the number of children with openly gay or lesbian parents increases, and as the number of adolescents who come out while still in high school rises, an institution central to family life—the public school—has become the setting for a wide-ranging debate about homosexuality. Will the schools teach children to hate their parents? Will the children of gay and lesbian parents be subject to ridicule and ostracism? Will lesbian, gay, and bisexual adolescents be the target of harassment and violence? Will these adolescents have the right to form school clubs designed to support themselves and educate their peers? How will principals and school boards respond when a lesbian or gay teacher who had a commitment ceremony over the weekend comes to school on Monday morning wearing a wedding ring? In Utah in the mid-1990s, an effort by some high school students to form a gay-straight alliance led the legislature to ban *all* school clubs. Around the country, these gay-straight alliances are proliferating rapidly, forcing the issue on principals, school boards, and PTAs.

*   *   *

Each of these areas, as well as other emergent family-related issues, promises to become even more critical to the fight that lesbians and gay men are waging for justice and full participation in American life. This is so in part because the broad array of family issues speaks to the needs and aspirations of the lesbian and gay community.

These issues, and the changes they portend, are not just about lesbians and gay men. We may be the active agents placing our particular concerns on to the public agenda, but the issues exist in a much larger context of change. During the last quarter century, "family" has become a focus of national concern. The debate over family values, over the crisis of the traditional family, has been fierce, and the intensity of the debate ought to alert us to a basic truth: there is no agreement on how to interpret the history of the family in the United States or the current so-called crisis of the family. There is no agreement on what a traditional family looks like — what we mean by the word "traditional," how we make judgments about it, how we understand either the family's past or its present in American society. As the quotation at the start of this chapter suggests, for at least a century now, eminent social commentators have viewed the family not as a conservator of the past, but as an arena in which change gets enacted.

In the rest of this chapter, I offer an interpretation, a picture of the past and the present, to help us make sense of gay and lesbian family issues. First, I present the view of the family associated with the Christian Right, discuss where I think it comes from, and point out some flaws. Second, I put forward a different view of family history and family experience in order to provide a counter-tradition that we might draw on. Third, I propose some ways of looking at the so-called contemporary crisis of the family. Fourth, I suggest some reasons why family issues have emerged as compellingly important to the lesbian and gay community at this time in its history. Finally, I will raise some questions and do some speculating about the significance of these issues.

Family Politics: The View from the Right

From almost every quarter of American society comes a sense that the family, however it is defined, is in crisis. It is not surprising that concerns about family have such deep resonance among Americans, since there is hardly an area of domestic policy that does not, in some way, fall into the orbit of family. Jobs and wage levels, health care and education, sexual values and behavior all have complex connections to family life.

The understanding of the crisis varies. For some it is a question of stagnant wage levels, underfunded schools, the lack of affordable child care, the exorbitant cost of housing, and the absence of adequate health insurance. For others, the family crisis is about the large number of divorces, out-of-wedlock births, female-headed households, working mothers, and visible homosexuals.

One of the loudest voices in the contemporary debate about family has been the extremist Christian Right. They have created a broad array of organizations, such as the Christian Coalition, Focus on the Family, the Traditional Values Coalition, the Family Research Council, and Concerned Women of America, which have made the defense of traditional family the centerpiece of their rhetoric and political organizing. In the hands of the extreme Right, family serves as both a symbol and a weapon. As symbol, it harkens back to an imaginary past when everything was fine, good, and orderly. As weapon, it divides society into good people and bad, the moral and the immoral, the productive citizen and the social parasite.

Bashing gays, lesbians, bisexuals, and their families has become a key method through which the extremist Right builds its strength. Concerned Women of America launched a major fundraising campaign in response to the decision of the National Education Association to endorse Gay, Lesbian, and Bisexual History Month. In the mid-1990s, Lou Sheldon of the Traditional Values Coalition won a commitment from Newt Gingrich, the House Majority Leader, to hold congressional hearings on parenting, values, and the schools, and then milked those hearings for media attention. Right-wing Republican state legislators tap emotional flash points by introducing homophobic legislation that attacks the integrity of gay and lesbian family relationships.

At the same time, the family politics of the Christian Right and its Republican partners casts a wide net in its search for demons. It has used a rhetoric of traditional family values to condemn the immorality of single mothers and to build support for eviscerating the welfare system. It attacks government programs such as publicly funded day care and the working mothers who need it. The Right supports a "parental rights" movement that would undo a generation of feminist organizing around woman battering and child abuse by making it more difficult for the state to intervene when violence occurs within the home. It has campaigned for school vouchers as a back-door way of reversing school desegregation efforts.

A good deal of the emotional power of right-wing family politics comes from its appeal to "tradition," which it uses in two ways. It invokes the authority of two thousand years of Western Christianity to support its claims. And it evokes a nostalgic longing for an era when nuclear families were independent, self-contained, highly gendered, and models of a moral order that appeals to these conservative polemicists of family values.

Since few of us know very much about the history of Christianity, the appeal to Christian tradition is very effective. It is also deeply flawed. Consider this: for the first several centuries of the Christian Church, celibacy occupied the loftiest moral status. Heterosexual marriage was the option for the morally weak. The Christian Church thought so little of marriage that it did not elevate marriage to sacramental status until the thirteenth century. In other words, for more than half of Christian history, marriage for the majority of Christians was casual, suspect, and not highly valued.

The appeal to nostalgia draws on more recent experience. The Right elevates to traditional status a family experience that was typical, in the sense of statistically common, only for the generation who formed or were raised in families in the two decades after World War II. The nuclear family form that was celebrated through television, magazines, and the press had a particular profile. It had a working dad, a full-time homemaking mom, and children. It was white, owned a home, lived in the suburbs or in tree-lined small towns, and had an income that allowed for consumption and economic self-sufficiency. It took care of itself without the interference of others, particularly a meddling intrusive state. And it has been memorialized through forms of popular culture that recall it for us as "happy days."

Another Look at "Traditional American Families"

The right-wing vision of traditional American families is as far removed from the real historical experience of most Americans as is the Christian Right's view of religious history. For large numbers of Americans during the past three centuries, family has not been isolated, nuclear, and independent. Instead, families were deeply embedded in a web of community relationships. Americans have had expansive definitions of who constituted family. The "disruption" of the nuclear family structure has been commonplace. Consider the following examples:

— In colonial New England, white farm families hardly had an existence apart from the community. Notions of family autonomy and privacy were weak, and neighbors exercised the right to intrude in a family's affairs. They peered through the walls of cabins, or arrived in groups to accost members of neighboring families whose behavior they thought amiss. The intrusiveness of neighbors, magistrates, and ministers was commonplace. It meant that families were directly subject to community norms and to the interlocking authority of church and state, in matters large and small.

— Under slavery, African Americans had to struggle to maintain family ties in a system that denied them ownership of their bodies and disrupted their intimate familial relationships. Within the slave community, African Americans sustained an expansive definition of family and kin. Children had parents as well as a community of adults who cared for them, nurtured and taught them, and exercised discipline. Faced with racist violence, political exclusion, and continuing economic exploitation in the post-Emancipation South, African Americans maintained a broad system of kinship ties, which helped them survive oppression. Many adults beyond parents were stitched into the fabric of "family" and all that it meant.

— The waves of immigrants in the nineteenth and twentieth centuries who came from peasant cultures in Europe and Latin America brought strong kinship systems with them. Settling in cities, they extended their notion of family to include immigrants who came from the same town or province. Immigrants from Catholic cultures of the Mediterranean and Latin America made use of godmother and godfather relationships to increase the number of family ties. In urban immigrant neighborhoods, the street became an extension of the home, and adults watched over and attended to the children of "other" families.

What these and other historical experiences share is a *tradition* in which families were enmeshed in larger relations of community. Americans sustained social relations in which the boundary between family and community was very porous. They maintained cultural traditions in which they understood that families survived and were strong to the degree that they were not isolated, independent, and separate, but connected to others who are "like family."

This experience of family is a long distance from historical myths of the self-sufficient, sturdy, individualistic American family. And for a reason: families in the past experienced disruption all the time. It is not true, as conservative ideologues would have us believe, that families have only broken up since the "corrosive" influence of the 1960s — the sexual revolution, feminism, racial turmoil, and gay liberation. Families in earlier generations lived with upheaval as an essential part of their existence. For instance, life expectancy was much shorter, and many children could expect to lose one or both of their parents, making single-parent families commonplace. Women frequently died in childbirth. During the decades of industrialization, working-class men died on the job or were seriously injured at an alarming rate, with no workers' compensation or disability insurance. Many working-class occupations in the nineteenth century took men away from home for extended periods of time. In an era when strict divorce laws kept the official divorce rate low, many husbands simply deserted their wives and children.

In other words, extended family relationships and broad flexible understandings of kinship were necessary as insurance in a world that could not be controlled. And, in a contemporary world in which economic activity is organized around the earning power of the individual, dependable extended family ties are even more necessary for many Americans.

The Contemporary Crisis of the Family Revisited

With this angle of vision, the contemporary crisis of the family begins to look very different. Today's "crisis" has little to do with a collapse in moral values, or changing gender roles, or the creation of visible gay communities. Instead, it comes from elevating a particular and historically very unusual family form — the isolated suburban nuclear family of the post–World War II generation — into a norm, reading it backward so that it becomes tradition, and then adopting public policies that see other family forms as deviant and broken.

This model of the post–World War II nuclear family — lacking extended kinship ties, without deep connections to community forms of support — broke sharply with American experience of family and community. This model was viable in that generation, and it still resonates so powerfully for many Americans today, not because it represented the long historical experience of a majority of Americans, but because of a configuration of circumstances unique to that moment in time. Some of those circumstances were economic, some political, some cultural, and some demographic.

The quarter century after World War II was the most broadly prosperous in American history. Unlike the economic expansion of the 1990s, which concentrated wealth among the few, the prosperity of the 1950s and 1960s cut a wide swath across the population. It was a product of traumatic international events and conscious government policy. World War II had led to a huge expansion of the productive capacity of the United States at the same time that it devastated the economies of industrial competitors like Germany, Japan, France, and Italy. Enormous wartime savings fueled private consumption. The transition to a Cold War and a nuclear arms race meant that the federal government, for the first time in history, was continually pouring money into the economy. A GI Bill provided generous educational and homeownership benefits to large numbers of young, heterosexual, white working-class men, allowing them to aspire toward middle-class status. High rates of unionization meant that many blue-collar jobs in this era paid almost-middle-class wages.

These decades were unique in other ways that impinged on the experience and idea of family in the United States. The social legislation of the 1930s — retirement benefits through Social Security, unemployment compensation, disability insurance, assistance to families with dependent children — allowed many families successfully to weather crises of one sort or another. Federal housing policies privileged ownership of detached single family dwellings in racially homogeneous neighborhoods, leading to an accelerating suburbanization. The combination of extremely low rates of immigration, which were a product of the restrictive nativist legislation of the 1920s, and the mass migration of African Americans from the rural South to northern cities lifted many white ethnic families into the ranks of the prosperous working class, while cementing a tie between poverty, urban living, struggling families, and blackness. All these elements worked together to make a particular kind of nuclear family experience accessible to large numbers of white Americans.

Television dramatically intensified the sway of this particular family experience over the national consciousness. Here was a brand new technology broadcasting moving talking images into American homes. Recall some of the key family series for this first generation of television viewers: *Ozzie and Harriet, Father Knows Best, Leave It to Beaver, The Donna Reed Show.* Television reflected back to viewers a picture of what the ideal family should be. Fathers worked, and mothers stayed at home. Almost no other adults appear in the social world of these families. All problems, such as they were, reached resolution at the end of thirty minutes. Two generations, the young parents and the unusually large cohort of baby-boomer children they produced, had their understanding of what was normal and desirable shaped by the cultural products of this new technology. Together, these two generations were a majority of the American population during the years when a conservative family politics surfaced and grew.

Let's put this another way: a powerful emotional conviction about what constitutes a "traditional" family has been created out of what was essentially a particular, new, historically unique, and temporary experience. So, when someone like Helen Chenoweth, a right-wing Republican Congresswomen from Idaho, justifies her proposals for family policy with the statement "we want things to be the way they were," she is elevating nostalgia for her youth into a claim about a long historical tradition.

Looking back from the vantage point of the 1990s, it is easier to see what commentators of the time denied: that the prosperity of the post–World War II generation was not a permanent condition. But, treating the free-standing isolated nuclear family as the most desirable norm has left American families poorly equipped to cope with the changing economic and social conditions of the past generation. It has also made it more difficult to respond effectively to politically conservative efforts to weaken even further the support systems that families need.

Today's "family crisis" is not about a breakdown of the nuclear family and the collapse of moral values. Rather it is a story of the collapse of community systems of support for families at a time when the economic gap between the prosperous few and the working majority has widened precipitously. For instance:

— A majority of women have always engaged in productive labor. But today, in an advanced capitalist economy, work increasingly means wage labor outside the home. Without the presence of extended kinship systems, community services to care for children, or generous family leave policies, households in which both parents work face enormous stresses.

— Female-headed households are not a new phenomenon. Through death, injury, or desertion, women in the past often found themselves with the responsibility to support their families financially. In fact, the desperate plight of mothers with children was responsible for the creation of a welfare system in the first place. But two decades of decrying female-headed households as symptoms of immorality and irresponsibility have led not to a more humane public policy, but to a welfare reform that shredded the already threadbare safety net.

— Teenage pregnancy was more common in many eras of the past than it is today. But, in today's economy, which requires high levels of formal education and training in order to earn a living wage, teenage parenthood now often means permanent poverty and economic struggle. Where are the social and economic policies designed to help young parents have a decent life?

This revised understanding of American family traditions — of family relationships defined broadly and inclusively, of family as embedded in community, and of family as needing economic and social support systems — offers an essential context for examining the rise of family issues within the lesbian and gay community and for seeing their potential as catalysts of change.

Lesbian and Gay Family Issues: Why Now?

Lesbians and gay men have all come from families. Even in eras when the oppression was most intense and unrelieved, they have established households and constructed webs of intimate relationships, including lovers, former lovers, close friends, offspring, and members of families of origin, that have constituted family. But, in the past decade or so, family issues have emerged on a large scale as an area of collective organizing and advocacy.

Why is this happening now? The answer lies, in part, in the changing public face of the lesbian and gay community and the impact this has had on the movement's agenda for action.

In the 1970s, in the wake of Stonewall and the rise of a mass social movement, the emphasis on coming out as the central focus of activism privileged those groups within the population for whom visibility posed the least risks. Not surprisingly, the visible community that the media spotlighted was urban, middle class, college-educated, white, and male. The agenda most closely associated with this segment of the broader community was one that focused on a libertarian ethic of sexual freedom, curtailing police harassment, and influencing middle-class mental health professionals. Though the movement was never monolithic or homogeneous, these were the voices that most shaped public perceptions of who gay people were and the policy goals of the movement.

In the 1980s and 1990s, this changed dramatically. Lesbians, who had organized separately in the 1970s, moved into positions of leadership in gender-mixed organizations. People of color created a network of autonomous organizations that provided a base for a distinctive multi-issue agenda. There was also an upsurge, especially after the 1987 March on Washington, of organizing outside large urban areas, in smaller sized cities and towns throughout the United States. The AIDS epidemic injected the urgency of political action into networks of middle-class white men who had remained outside the orbit of public advocacy and activism. It also brought notions of family to the center of consciousness of almost anyone touched by the epidemic.

In different but complementary ways, each of these changes has served to move family issues into the foreground of the agenda of the lesbian and gay movement:

— Lesbians have been organizing around issues such as child custody since the early 1970s. Because of the gendered division of labor that, historically, has associated women with children, lesbians have been in the forefront of public battles to ensure that sexual orientation does not serve as a barrier to parenthood. They have also brought to the politics of family issues a perspective deeply informed by feminism.

— Because of the multiple oppressions that gays and lesbians of color face, and because of the historical importance of kinship ties and community solidarity in the resistance to racism, lesbians and gays of color have articulately argued that the path to gay liberation cannot be one that involves exile from family and the rejection of community ties.

Lesbians and gays of color have sought to integrate public gay identities with the maintenance of family connections.

— As lesbians and gay men come out in smaller communities, where
family is often just down the road, the need to incorporate notions of
family into ways of being gay has assumed new importance. In small
towns and rural areas, gay community and families of origin cannot be
kept apart.

— Important events have conspired to highlight the perils of not having gay and lesbian family ties recognized by law. In the 1980s, lesbian communities around the country mobilized in support of Karen
Thompson, a lesbian whose seriously disabled partner, Sharon Kowal-
ski, was removed from her care by court order and put, against Kowal-
ski's wishes, under the custodial care of her parents. Meanwhile, the
AIDS epidemic dramatized the costs, emotional and otherwise, of
one's intimate relationships having no standing in law. Partners and
close friends could be denied access to someone who was sick or the
right to make important decisions about life and death. The AIDS
epidemic highlighted the family nature of the social relationships in
the gay community.

Finally, a younger generation of lesbians and gay men simply have a more
demanding set of expectations than the community did twenty or thirty
years ago. For those who have come of age at a time when a gay liberation
movement already existed, it is not enough just to have the space to be gay or
lesbian free of harassment. They want more, and rightfully so. They want the
right to celebrate their relationships in formal public ways. They want the
basic benefits and responsibilities that marriage brings. They don't believe
they should have to choose between their sexual identity and a desire to
parent. They refuse to accept a marginalized place in their society. They have,
in other words, expanded the agenda of what freedom, justice, and respect
should encompass.

The Potential Impact of Family Issues

The constellation of family issues has the potential to move the lesbian and
gay freedom struggle forward in interesting ways. For one, it challenges

homophobia in ways that simply coming out and asserting the right to be gay or lesbian does not. In a sense, important as coming out has been, it unwittingly has served to reinforce myths about gay men and lesbians that reproduce homophobia. Because the public representation of gay life in the 1970s and early 1980s emphasized freestanding adult males in an urban subculture, it preserved the stereotypical — and oppressive — boundary between homosexuality and a world of children and families. The vision of gay freedom, in other words, was a sharply constricted one. Asserting a claim to family ties, with or without children, pushed the struggle for equality and justice forward on to new and broader ground.

Laying claim to family also addresses issues that speak to the needs of a broad constituency within the lesbian and gay community. Though the invisibility of sexual identity makes it impossible to take a census of the gay and lesbian population, there is enough evidence to suggest that large numbers are already parents, that many of them are raising children, and that more would do so if access to parenting were not restricted on the basis of sexual identity. Data gathered from exit polling after the 1992 presidential election found that while one-third of heterosexual voters had children under eighteen living with them, one-quarter of lesbian, gay, or bisexual voters did as well. In other words, a population not thought to be at all involved with parenting is only 25 percent less likely to be raising children than are heterosexual adults.

Family issues also bring economic questions closer to the foreground. Everything we know about lesbians and gay men suggests that they are distributed across class, racial, and ethnic groups. Thus, while some are economically privileged, most are not. For lesbians of whatever race who are raising children, whether in a couple or alone, the economic effects of gender discrimination are magnified when children are added to the picture. And, the impact of racial oppression amplifies the economic hardship even further. Organizing for family rights has particular salience as a workplace issue. Campaigns for family recognition have helped to create a visible, organized lesbian, gay, and bisexual presence in workplaces around the country, as employees have sought benefits for family members on a par with those received by heterosexual employees.

In a politically reactionary era, when the power of the Right is still growing, family concerns have special potential as coalition-building issues among progressives: around access to health care and expanded Medicaid funding;

around public schools and the right to a quality education; around a broad range of welfare programs that address the needs of families; around the attacks on single-parent and other nonnuclear and nonmarital family structures; around the sexist, racist, and homophobic family rhetoric of the extremist Right. Within the lesbian and gay community, a focus on family issues will also tend to push forward the needs and the voices of lesbians, people of color, and those outside major metropolitan areas.

A Utopian Speculation

Where can this discussion take us? If we think of the first quarter century after Stonewall as twenty-five years in which large numbers of lesbians and gay men succeeded in coming out of the closet on their own terms, I am absolutely confident that the next twenty-five years will see the acceptance of lesbian and gay families as an integral part of American society. By this I mean the formal recognition of our spousal relationships, the acceptance of the right to parenthood regardless of sexual identity, and the readjustment of family-related institutions, like the public schools, to incorporate these changes.

I do not think these changes will come easily or automatically. We have seen in the nineties how the Christian Right will fight tooth and nail against the prospect of same-sex marriage and lesbian or gay parenting. Bills to prohibit recognition of same-sex marriage have sped through state legislatures faster than the eye can see. Nonetheless, gay and lesbian family issues are moving with the stream of American society, in which family forms are becoming more diverse and more complex. In other words, rather than set us apart, our family issues further integrate us into an increasingly heterogeneous society.

Because I am confident that we will ultimately win in our quest for family recognition, I am more concerned, and more intrigued, with how we succeed than whether we succeed. Here is what I mean: Agree to entertain my interpretation that a core piece of traditional American family values is the close connection between family and community. And entertain as well my analysis that the so-called contemporary crisis of the American family has to do with the weakening of community ties in much of the nation. If so, then gay and lesbian family issues might have a meaning that stretches beyond the aspirations of this one social group.

Much of the struggle for spousal recognition and much of the bearing and raising of children among us is occurring within the context of a social movement with a high degree of collective community consciousness. Our commitment ceremonies often have a refreshing inventiveness that disrupts the conventionality of many weddings and allows participants to marvel at the power of human caring. Our parenting often involves complex arrangements in which many adults who are not blood kin assume responsibilities for childrearing. Could it be that, in our quest to create and sustain lesbian and gay families, we are reinventing a very long and old American tradition in which family and community are deeply connected to one another? If this is true, then the fight for the recognition of our families is a fight that has meaning for everyone.

PART III   *Reflections*

13

Visions of Leadership:
Remembering Ken Dawson

Each one of us here has had to find our own way of dealing with the mountains of grief that the AIDS epidemic has thrown at us. For myself, as acquaintances and movement buddies and close friends have died, I have managed my grief by collectivizing it. I've shed tears for the terrible loss to the community, and to the movement. At other times I've convinced myself that I have been grieving over the pain and the anguish of friends whose lovers have died.

With Ken's death I can't pretend any longer that the loss is someone else's. We knew each other across too many years and in too many ways. We played and worked and traveled together. We fought in the way that only very special friends can fight, and we knew the places where each of us had had to struggle.

Ken was something of a fixture in the New York City community. For half a dozen years he was the executive director of Senior Action in a Gay Environment (SAGE), at a time when few individuals had jobs that paid them to be gay activists. Later, he was a partner in Strub–Dawson, when Sean Strub was doing pioneer work as a gay direct-mail maven. In the last few years of his life, Ken worked as a consultant to community organizations, here and around the country, creating a career out of strengthening the infrastructure of our still fragile institutions. He always seemed to be just ahead of the curve of gay community development. He was constantly pushing the frontiers of what it meant to be openly gay.

These remarks were delivered in June 1992 at the Lesbian and Gay Community Center in New York City, at a memorial service for Ken Dawson.

Through all this work he extended his reach widely and powerfully. He presented himself with self-assurance, as someone who knew his own mind, and was sure of what he was doing and where he was going. Lots of us trusted him, benefitted from his counsel, and borrowed his confidence when we could. And that was true for me, too. I trusted him, I asked him for advice, and I gained enormous strength from his example.

But that doesn't explain why I loved him as much as I did. I cared for Ken, I cherished him, because he opened himself to me and let me see the struggles that were the source of his strength. It is those struggles, and the strengths that came from them, that I want to talk about tonight.

Ken and I were both just old enough to have confronted our gayness before Stonewall, before gay liberation washed over our lives. Being gay may have come naturally to us, but pride took a lot of work. Ken's conflicts with his gayness were not unique to him, but there were ways that he seemed to be locked in combat with his identity that went deeper than what many of our friends experienced. The confident self-assured exterior coexisted with a good deal of inner doubt. He was fascinated, for instance, by discussions about what made us all gay, and he was drawn to any shred of evidence that suggested biology, that claimed we were born this way. He just couldn't fathom what I and other historians meant when we wrote about queer identities as "socially constructed," as products of history and culture unique to particular times and places. It drove him crazy when I would talk about gayness as a choice that we made, as the accumulation of an endless series of experiences and events, often serendipitous, that we chose to keep building on. I think it upset the lingering Catholic in him to believe that any willfulness of his own could have contributed to something he had been taught was so wrong.

I don't know that Ken ever put that struggle to rest, but I do know that no matter how fiercely it raged at times, Ken was always clear that the source of the struggle came from the outside, from the hatred, the cruelty, the lies, the criminal acts of intolerance that we face every day. He transformed his inner struggle into a public commitment to activism, into a determination that he renewed every day to see to it that the hatred and persecution would some-day stop. I remember how much he loved the closing of the pledge of membership of the Mattachine Society, one of the earliest gay activist orga-nizations in the United States. It was written in 1951 when Ken was only five years old: "We are sworn," those pioneering activists wrote, "that no boy or girl, approaching the maelstrom of deviation, need ever make that crossing alone, afraid, and in the dark ever again." In the end, Ken's interior struggle was less important than the commitment to justice that he forged from it.

Ken was also cautious. This may sound like a strange thing to say about him, since he put himself so far out there as an openly gay man fighting for justice. But there was a deeply implanted streak of caution in his personality. He did not like to make mistakes. He knew mistakes were inevitable. It was part of his routine as an organizational consultant to tell others endlessly and soothingly that making mistakes is the only way we learn and grow. But he preferred that others make them. He hated mistakes that were his own and he especially hated to make decisions that might have irrevocable consequences.

I remember when he applied to be executive director of SAGE. At the time, he had spent the previous dozen years as an educator. Right out of college he had joined in the radical education movement of the late 1960s, working in Harlem and East Harlem in parent-run alternative schools. Later, he went on to become the headmaster of a private school on Manhattan's West Side. He had already been slowly coming out in his work environment, in face-to-face relationships with staff and parents, a pretty brave thing to be doing in the 1970s. Still, he was worried about what it would mean to take a job that would so obviously define him as gay. I remember how as he came closer and closer to getting the job, he approached each of his friends to seek advice about what he should do. What if SAGE folded? What would he do then? Would he ever get another job as an educator?

Ken was a very smart guy. He could build a convincing case for almost anything. After listening to him spin out all the hazards of becoming a professional homosexual, it was very easy to believe that only a fool would take the job. Finally, I and another of his friends, Donna, together challenged him. We told him that he was too conservative and cautious, that he needed some excitement and uncertainty in his life, and that he should take the damned job and worry about the future later. I don't think Ken ever regretted that decision.

The caution didn't leave him, but Ken learned to use it creatively. It explains one of his trademarks, his belief in long-term planning. Ken didn't mind spontaneity, but he knew that you couldn't build a liberation movement, or a community organization, on the random activity of masses of individuals. He believed in setting goals, in charting a direction for several years down the line, confident that he could change a goal to fit new circumstances, but knowing that he would never reach a goal that he hadn't set. He was always on people's backs to get them to think beyond the immediate task, to have a vision that would keep us on a proactive track instead of being held hostage to yesterday's tragedy. It was this quality of careful planning that allowed him to build SAGE into a model community institution and that made so many of us turn to him for advice.

Ken's deepest personal struggle, I think, was with loneliness. This, too, may sound strange, since Ken was so well connected to so many people. He had the largest Rolodex I've ever seen. He was in touch with people from every stage of his life and spent hours every day on the phone, nurturing and strengthening relationships with friends and colleagues around the country. But the loneliness was there. More even than most gay men I've known, Ken yearned for a lover, a life partner with whom to share tender intimacies. Yet the loneliness could make its presence felt whether he had a lover or didn't, whether he was in a group of close friends or was alone. It was a powerful force in his life and made it difficult at times for some of us to know how important we were to him.

I remember vividly an incident that happened in 1983, when I was getting ready to leave New York for a job in North Carolina. Ken and I went out of town for Memorial Day Weekend, on a peer counseling retreat with a group of gay men. In the course of the weekend, we all had a chance to talk about what was going on in our lives. When Ken had his turn in front of the group, he barely started when he began to cry. Ken didn't cry often and, believe me, when he did, it was unforgettable: big, heaving sobs that were as strong as he was and that filled a room. And what he was crying about that night was my leaving New York. He didn't want me to go.

We had known each other at that point for seven or eight years, and I certainly counted him among my friends. But I had no idea that I meant so much to him. We bonded that night in a way that was permanent and, though I couldn't excise that core of loneliness, I could let Ken know that he wasn't alone.

When Ken became executive director of SAGE, he felt his loneliness with a special force: here he was, an openly gay man in a visible position of leadership, responsible for the survival of an organization, at a time when the community wasn't providing the resources to sustain very many men or women in such roles. Out of his loneliness came the commitment that was at the heart of Ken's work and that I know is what he wanted to be remembered for: his commitment to the development of leaders and to a new model of leadership.

Ken had a very simple definition of leadership. A leader was someone who had made the decision to set things right in the world and who acted on that decision. A leader looked beyond his or her own self-interest and tried to think about the bigger view. The forms that leadership might take were as varied as the scope of human life. Leadership could be exercised within a family, a workplace, a school, a neighborhood, a church—anywhere that brought human beings together for common purposes. A leader wasn't always the top dog. It could be a secretary rather than the boss, or a teacher's aide rather than the school principal. But in whatever guise it appeared, leadership—and leaders—was something that Ken believed needed to be nurtured, nourished, and cherished. "Leader" was not a dirty word to Ken. He believed we would never succeed in making permanent progressive change in society without an abundance of leadership. He believed it was a capacity and a need that everyone had, and that there were enough problems in the world to occupy the talents of all of us. In Ken's view our movement and our community needed more leaders, not fewer.

Ken also hated the conditions under which leaders had to work and the way they were treated. Leadership ought to provide the opportunity for closeness and connection, as people worked together to achieve lofty goals, but too often it meant isolation. Leaders ought to be appreciated for the work they did, but too often they were the targets of carping, mean-spirited criticism. Ken hated the mudslinging that left leaders maimed and exhausted. As far as I know, he never publicly attacked another community leader. He might take issue with a decision or criticize a point of view, but the person, the individual, always remained a potential ally, an object of respect and caring.

In the past three years, Ken traveled around the country as a consultant working with community-based gay organizations. He anticipated the explosion of staffed organizations that the AIDS epidemic enabled, and knew from his own struggle building SAGE that the boards and staff of these organizations would need help. Ken worked, especially, to propagate his model of leadership. He was responsible for convening annual retreats of executive directors of organizations from around the country, believing that everything would work better if movement leaders built face-to-face relationships. He made himself available to the activists of different cities, as he facilitated tension-filled gatherings of angry impassioned people. He wanted more than anything to unleash the potential for leadership in the activists with whom he worked, to heal the wounds and repair the rifts that divided community members, and to build the metaphorical army of lovers that he knew would be needed if we were going to succeed in our efforts to remake the world. Even as he fought the virus that would eventually kill him, these last years of work were, I think, among the most satisfying of his life. He was doing what he most wanted to do and, no surprise, the bonds that he helped build among activists did much to cut through his loneliness.

Ken and I spent endless hours thinking about social movements, social change, and social justice. We talked and we planned and we plotted and we schemed together. Our conversations often came back to the civil rights movement and to the figure of Martin Luther King. Ken had devoured the biographies of King that came out in the 1980s. He was fascinated by and drawn to a phrase that King used many times: "The universe," King said, "is on the side of justice." It took quite a leap of faith for King to say that in the American South in the 1950s, and it takes a leap of faith to say it today in the face of this epidemic. Ken made that leap, over and over and over again. I think, ultimately, the reason I cherished him so much was that he was some- one who had decided to throw his weight, to throw the full force of his talents and his life, on the side of the universe and of justice.

14

My Changing Sex Life

One of the earth-shaking assertions of the women's liberation movement in the late 1960s was its claim that "the personal is political." Today, the slogan evokes puzzled stares. Does it mean that the pursuit of personal goals is really a form of political activity? Is the pursuit of happiness political? Is career ambition political?

Like all rhetorically compelling turns of phrase, "the personal is political" was always subject to multiple interpretations. But at the time of its coinage, it also elicited an almost immediate stunned recognition of its profundity. Two of the meanings that it had for me, as I encountered young radical feminists and read their polemics, were these: Issues, or problems, that our culture defined as personal, or private, or individual, often had political roots, and thus required public, collective solutions. And personal experience could be effectively mined for valuable insights about politics, social structures, and the need for collective action to make change.

It is in that spirit, a generation later, that I want to talk about my sex life, though without any of the graphic details. Specifically I want to talk about how it has changed over time, and how my thinking about gay issues and politics have also changed because of this.

My Coming Out

I came out in New York City, in the mid-1960s, a few years before Stonewall. I use the phrase "coming out" in the way that it was employed at that time — to signify that I was willing to admit to other gay men that I, too, was like

This essay grew from a set of remarks that I made at an NGLTF Town Meeting on Sex and Politics held in St. Louis in 1992.

them, that we shared some kind of secret bond. Coming out was really more like a "coming into" a semi-secret world. Coming out publicly, as a form of resistance to oppression, was an innovation of Stonewall-era activists not yet on my horizon.

The engine that drove my coming out process was sex. From my early teenage years, I found myself possessed by sexual desires far beyond the power of my adolescent will to shape in any way at all. Like many boys who have just passed through puberty, I always seemed to be on the edge of sexual arousal. An acutely embarrassing bulge in my pants might appear, unbidden, at any moment. But unlike most of my peers, at least as far as I could tell, my desires were directed mostly toward men.

Since this was happening to me in the early part of the 1960s, before gay liberation began to change both the context in which many gay men lived and our attitudes about ourselves, sexual experience was not so easy to come by for an adolescent living at home. I couldn't go to the local gay youth group to meet my peers, or to a Saturday night gay dance on a college campus. There were no big street festivals or parades through New York's gay neighborhoods, where I might hang out, strike up a conversation, and make some friends. I couldn't consult the gay yellow pages, or the listings in my local gay paper, to find an organization to work with, or a recreational group — of runners, bowlers, or bridge players — where I would meet men to have fun and find myself a date. At my neighborhood library, there was no shelf of good gay mysteries or romances for me to browse through.

Instead, driven by desire, I found sexual partners through a time-consuming process of trial and error. I found them on the subway, on certain city streets at night, in the balconies of movie theaters in the afternoon, along the edges of public parks. The desperation attached to these desires, whether for sexual release, for physical closeness, for human connection, or some combination of all three, was so intense that I was willing to have sex in whatever places were available — in public toilets, in secluded sections of parks, in alleys and vacant lots, in the basements of apartment buildings.

All these experiences were with strangers, and all the men were older than I. For the first two or three years, I never had sex with a man a second time (good Catholic boy that I was, I was always promising God that I would not sin again), and I never gave my partners my real name. I was afraid that any bit of knowledge that I shared about myself would be a route to exposure. As a teenager I'd read novels like *Advise and Consent* and, from them, had absorbed ideas about extortion and suicide as conditions of queer life.

Segments of gay male culture have come over the decades to eroticize both "public" sex and sex with strangers. I can certainly testify from my own adult experience that each — and both in combination — can provide an extraordinarily thrilling erotic charge. But I want to assure you that, as a teenager, I was not happy with this state of affairs. There was no joy attached to my being gay — or homosexual, as I thought of it then. The way I came out isn't the way that *any* adolescent boy should experience his initial encounters with the joys and the pleasures and the mysteries of sexual connection.

Besides this male adolescent sense of being sexually driven and out of control, these early experiences added two other elements to my learned understanding of sex. They fused sexual desire with an aura of danger and with the emotion of fear. For years, I felt constantly vulnerable and always terrified. Terror attached itself to every corner of my queer self. I lived in terror of what any sexual encounter might bring — the physical risks of perhaps having cruised a psycho, the worry of being discovered by the police, the dread of having my life utterly ruined because I had followed the trails of my desire. And so to avoid this, I became an adept carrier of secrets. My sexual self remained deeply hidden and protected.

At some point the sheer repetitiveness of these experiences started to make this state of affairs so familiar that it bothered me less. Or, to put it another way, I had to go pretty numb. As a high school student, I had been a star debater and public speaker. I had learned, somehow, to contain the violent shaking that threatened to overcome me as I stood before a large audience. So, too, I can remember struggling to contain my trembling as I searched for sex. Trust me — it wasn't the trembling that came from anticipated pleasures.

I must have a strong instinct for survival. I look back on those years and am amazed that they didn't send me, a somewhat shy pimply faced kid from a deeply religious family, over the edge. The annals of queer history in the twentieth century are filled with life stories of those of us who didn't make it at all, or who had long harrowing stretches in comparison to which my teenage years seem, retrospectively, like a cakewalk. At some point I just made the decision that being gay was who I was, and that danger and terror were things I would learn to live with, or manage. I can't say that, at the time, I was thrilled about this. To me it meant that I would have a difficult life. But I was also relieved by the decision. My sexual feelings seemed so deep and were so persistent that it seemed fruitless to try to deny them.

I still think of this decision as the single most important in my life. One can understand, as I do now, that coming out stories are "constructed narratives," and yet still claim that this moment of coming to terms with my sexual desires changed everything. Most immediately, it seemed to lift a great invisible weight from my shoulders. It allowed me to begin to figure how I would actually go about constructing a worthwhile life, instead of struggling all the time against feeling thoroughly worthless and depraved.

It is probably worth mentioning here that I also experienced sexual attraction to and feelings for females as well as males. From early on in my childhood, I was curious and fascinated by little girls as well as little boys, and I hugged, kissed, and rolled around with both. In high school I began to date, and during my first two years in college, I dated a lot. I experienced sexual arousal in these dating relationships as we hugged, kissed, and petted. I even felt powerfully attracted to and desirous of some of the young women I went out with. But I was aware of a difference during my years of adolescence. While I was attracted to *particular* women, I desired men almost indiscriminately. Ironically, there were also barriers to having sex with women that weren't there with men. The teenaged girls I went out with were all Catholic, and they weren't about to have sex; on the other hand, the men I met were as desperate or eager as I was. Women can get pregnant; men can't. This may sound bizarre, but somehow the fear of impregnating a girlfriend was a more powerful inhibitor than the fear of blackmail, exposure, and arrest.

One result of the decision to be gay rather than resist it was that I also began coming out in our contemporary sense of the word. One by one, I confided in a handful of close friends. This cut considerably the isolation I felt. Another result was that I could search not just for sex but for a relationship. During my last two years in college I had a lover, a graduate student at the same university I attended. Billy had a wide circle of gay friends and acquaintances and was familiar with New York's gay male subculture. Through him, I discovered a much larger gay world than I had ever known existed. When our relationship ended, I met another man, Carlos, with whom I fell passionately, wildly in love. There is nothing like the raptures of true love to confirm the absolute rightness of a decision to embrace one's homosexual desires.

After Stonewall, Before AIDS

Life histories don't unfold in a vacuum. During the years I lived with Carlos, our lives intersected with two of the movements that shaped the consciousness and the experience of a segment of my generation: the counterculture and gay liberation.

Mention the counterculture to today's undergraduates and the word immediately conjures up visions of Woodstock, of hippies living in group households far from the city, of long-haired freaks communing with nature. But Carlos and I — and almost everyone we knew — thought of ourselves as part of a counterculture without ever leaving the island of Manhattan. For us and our friends it involved, unquestionably, a rejection of much that we had been taught to value — career, material prosperity, the acquisition and accumulation of things, notions of family as a fortress against the world. But it also impelled us toward a host of other values, among them the embrace of sex as good in and of itself, of sexual pleasure as transformative of individual lives and social structures.

Translate this into the lives of two youngish gay men and suddenly sexual expressiveness was now infused with political ideology. It became both a form of rebellion and part of a noble quest for freedom and the good society. So, when we struggled, as gay men did then and still do now, over the conflict that our sexual desires posed to the monogamous relationship that true love seemed to require, sexual desire won out. It seemed irrefutably logical that since sex and love were both good things, they shouldn't be restricted to just one person. Having sex with others almost seemed a mandate. And so we did — a lot. We had sex with other partners at home. We had group sex. We had sex in public places. We brought some of our partners into the relationship we had with each other. Gay friends, friends of friends, acquaintances, strangers on the street — all were potential sexual partners.

Gay liberation, which was sweeping through New York City in these years, only added to these countercultural and hormonal inclinations. Gay liberation taught — and it was a most welcome lesson — that it was okay to feel good about our particular brand of sexuality. It created a movement out of sexual desire, an intensified sense of brotherhood that added an erotic charge to almost any encounter with another gay man. For participants like myself, it also made gay life even denser. Now we were gay not only when we went looking for sex, but during those endless hours when we were activists as well.

Gay liberation did something else during these years. In a fairly short period of time, it dramatically changed police practices. Police harassment never ended completely. On Times Square, in hustler bars, in subway toilets, and along the waterfront in Manhattan, arrests continued sporadically. But suddenly there was a large geography of gay male life in New York that to me seemed utterly safe. Bars, bathhouses, sex clubs, and adult bookstores proliferated, while certain urban spaces for sexual connection were ignored by the police. The opportunities for sex were expanding exponentially, while the level of danger and fear plummeted.

Put these changes together and, over the course of a decade, everything about the sex life of a once-terrified teenager changed. The fear and trembling were gone. The uncertainty about where or how to find sex was eliminated.

My relationship to the baths can provide a glimpse into how the broader changes provoked by these social movements translated into one man's sex life. With the AIDS epidemic, gay bathhouses have become almost as extinct as the dinosaur, but in the 1970s they flourished. One paid a few dollars to enter, and for the next several hours moved about in a great pleasure palace of sex, filled with other gay men wearing only a towel. There were steam rooms and saunas and hot tubs, long corridors with small cubicles on each side fitted with a bed, and large, dimly lit rooms. Sex occurred in any of these places; the possibilities were endless. There were also TV lounges, snack bars, massage rooms, and dance floors, so that one could take a break from sexual encounters, socialize with a new found playmate, watch TV, or chat with a friend or acquaintance who might happen to be there that night.

Even as gay liberation had been offering me new ways of understanding, experiencing, and feeling my sexual desires, old patterns of behavior had continued. The early cruising for sex in public places, which I once did because it was my only option and because I was desperate to meet others, had continued. It didn't seem to matter that all sorts of other ways of meeting men had materialized or that my life was rich with gay friendships and sexual opportunities. More than I was able to acknowledge, I felt myself out of control, still the prisoner of desires and impulses that were running me. At an earlier stage in my life, successful cruising brought me some level of comfort. Now, it was making me miserable, yet I felt powerless to stop.

The baths changed all that. My first trip to a bathhouse, when I was twenty-five, was like a revelation. Here was a place that was commercial but not public. It was secure from the police. There was no ambiguity about the identities of the men who were there, or why they were there. It was like discovering Shangri-la. For several years, the baths were an important part of my life. I sometimes stayed for as long as sixteen hours, would have sex with several men, take a nap to revive myself, and start again. But the heart of this discovery involved more than stumbling on a new venue for sexual experience. The baths somehow changed my own psychology of sex. Knowing that they were there, that there was this dependable venue for sexual delight, allowed me to stop — instantly — my cruising in public places. The baths seemed to detach from sex much of the fear and danger that I had come to associate with the experience, shifting the balance in ways that were satisfying.

Mind you, I don't want to create the impression that my bathhouse experience, or any of the other forms of sexual expression that filled my life in the 1970s, was unalloyed joy. Certainly there were experiences and relationships that were wildly memorable and that deserve all of the superlatives that attach to descriptions of sex. But it was also true that sex was sometimes quite ordinary and unremarkable, sometimes unpleasant and conflict ridden, sometimes frustrating and forgettable.

But, by and large, my friends and I moved in a social world in which sexual expression figured differently than it had in years past, both quantitatively and qualitatively. Quantitatively, because the opportunities were multiplying, and qualitatively, because we felt much freer, because our sexual desires were now enmeshed in a community we were creating and were suffused by an ideology that associated sex with liberation. Because of this dramatic sudden shift from repression and fear to freedom and exuberance, because my experience of sex was so wrapped up in gay liberation and gay community, I was absolutely clear that the essence of gay liberation, its heart and soul, was a quest for sexual freedom, and that gay oppression was fundamentally about the control and repression of sexuality.

Into the 1980s

By the beginning of the 1980s, the shape of my sexual life was changing. There were lots of reasons for this, and I'll give them not in the order of their importance, but in the sequence in which they happened:

First of all, the novelty of new sexual partners wore off. At a certain point, I noticed that I was able to make the choice not to have sex, which also meant that I could choose to have it just at those times when that's what I wanted to do. The nonsexual needs my erotic adventures had been filling — whether for intimacy, or to assuage loneliness, or to distract me from work and other issues — were somehow finding resolution. I also had found for myself what in those days we called "fuck buddies," other gay men with whom there was a compatibility of sexual desires and an enjoyment of one another's company but no inclination for a settled coupled relationship. I don't want to give the wrong impression. It's not that I had become chaste, but the sense of frenzy had definitely gone.

Soon after the decade turned, I met someone with whom I had a uniquely intense sexual connection as well as a compatibility of personality and values. Jim and I began dating, and soon it was clear that we were an "item." While my attachment to the sexual freedom of gay liberation made me insist, for a long time, that we were not in a monogamous relationship, in fact my sexual interest in others was fading.

Then there was AIDS. By 1982, a year into my relationship with Jim, AIDS had become this inescapable presence in my world. Although my network of friends and acquaintances were not, initially, those most struck by the epidemic, it was close enough, and the uncertainty great enough, to bring the return of fear and terror to sexual encounters. I spent the summer of 1982 in the San Francisco Bay area, away from Jim, and during those weeks I made a trip to the baths for the first time in over a year. Afterward, it left me crazed. This was before HIV had been identified, when knowledge of transmission was zilch. I realized that no amount of sexual desire, no complex of emotional needs, was strong enough for me to put my life at risk, and so Jim and I decided that there would be no sex outside the relationship. Placed alongside my sexual history, the agreement to be monogamous was about as implausible a course of action as one could imagine. Nothing in my previous history suggested that I could successfully do this, yet it proved very, very easy.

About a year after this, we moved, for work reasons, to Greensboro, North Carolina. Even without AIDS and without a pledge of monogamy, there were now far fewer opportunities for sexual adventure. The gay geography of the North Carolina Piedmont was barren when compared with Manhattan's. To my surprise, the absence of incessant opportunity made desire seem less urgent, not more insistent. Fewer occasions for adventure translated into even less interest.

Finally, my work and home life together were becoming more important to me and hence more time consuming. I was in my first academic job, learning to teach, continuing to engage in research and writing, and maintaining something of an activist life in this less hospitable environment. Jim and I were living together, which we had not in New York, and the intimacies of home and coupledom did not come automatically. They took time and emotional energy to nurture. We were also having to construct a new social world for ourselves. Even if I had wanted some new sexual adventures, I have no idea how I would have found the time.

All these developments laid the groundwork for a change more startling to me than the decision to be monogamous: my perfect sexual relationship became celibate! Jim and I remained physically close and affectionate; we continued to sleep together every night. But sex, as we knew it and defined it, was gone. This was not done through my initiation. It was sparked by the surfacing of complicated emotional issues that Jim needed time to work through, and at first we thought it would just be for a delimited period of time. But this state of affairs ended up continuing indefinitely. And because this was happening within the context of a relationship that had defined itself as monogamous, I remained celibate even when my work took me away from Jim for a year, and relocated me close to San Francisco, the gay male world's mecca.

Interestingly, my celibate life proved to be very similar, emotionally, to my sex life in the 1970s. There were times when celibacy induced an amazingly satisfying sense of intimacy and connection. There were times when it was ordinary and unremarkable. And there were times when it was ridden with conflict. Tensions over other needs and other issues easily got attached to it. In other words, whole worlds of emotion, meaning, and experience took shape around it. The absence of sexual engagement, I was discovering, could induce as much soap opera as its enactment.

In duration, this time has lasted as long now as the sexual cornucopia that the flowering of post-Stonewall gay liberation had made possible for me. These years have given me much to mull over. They have made me reconsider my understandings of what gay oppression and gay liberation are about. Though I have been living without a gay sex life, my encounters with the pulsating reality of gay oppression have not ceased. For instance, during these past few years, Jim has experienced a number of medical crises. As a gay couple in North Carolina, our encounters with the health care industry have forcibly brought home to us just how disrespected, unacknowledged, and illegitimate our relationship is. At times when I should be thinking about how best to support Jim, I have to fight for the simplest kinds of access to him in hospitals. These crises also coincided with periods of unemployment, and the issue of health insurance for Jim, which I would not have to worry about had he been my legal spouse (or, admittedly, if I lived in a country in which health insurance was universal), has been a serious one. Or, consider the effects of my activism. Almost every time I have done something that made me visible as a gay activist in Greensboro — a mention in a newspaper article or on the local news — I have received harassing phone calls, sometimes laced with ugly obscenities and occasionally including threats of physical harm.

To me, gay oppression no longer seems to be about constraints on sexual expression, and I would no longer define gay liberation as, primarily, a quest for sexual freedom. I have come to the conclusion that, even if I completely renounced sex publicly and repeatedly, I would still be the target of hostility, and I would certainly still be subject to a range of institutional practices that were unjust.

Oppression is about injustice. For gay men, our sexuality is at most an excuse that is used to target us. Because sex is such a flash point of conflict in our culture, because it is so laden with meanings, it is ready-made to serve this purpose well. But sexual behavior is not the reason, any more than the reason for anti-Semitism is Jewish dietary law or the reason for racism is skin pigmentation. These are excuses that are used to rationalize and perpetuate injustice.

What is the essence of injustice? In a society that lays claim to democratic ideals, one key aspect of injustice is the insistent requirement of conformity. This can take the form of expectations about behavior, about ideas and values, about appearance, about speech. It can attach itself to religious practice, or living arrangements, or artistic creation and expressive culture. In all these areas we, as gay men, have proved ourselves to be "deviant," some more than others and some in one way rather than another. But, no matter how hard we might try, we simply do not fit into the box that is labeled "male heterosexuality." Our unwillingness to fit into that box is a good thing, and it's what we need to be fighting to protect. For some of us, sexual desire figures prominently in our self-definition, but for others not. Our freedom struggle stakes its claim to significance because we are, importantly, a litmus test for the capacity of a democratic system to put its money where its mouth is — not merely to tolerate but positively to affirm the value of nonconformity, of difference.

Oppression also has a strong material component. It is about the denial of access to social, economic, cultural, and political resources. Historically, gay oppression has restricted access in all sorts of ways. The wealth and conspicuous consumption of a few of us shouldn't obscure this fact. Sometimes the restrictions have been overt, in the form of clear and unambiguous exclusions from major segments of the labor market. Sometimes the restrictions have been indirect: the arrest and conviction of so many gay men through police practices have compromised our ability to move through school and work. Sometimes we ourselves have cooperated in the imposition of restricted access. Our fears of exposure have led us to make choices in our lives that have kept us quiet, in the background, unobtrusive, unwilling to push for what we want or need. However it has happened, gay oppression has unjustly constrained us.

There are aspects of gay male sexual culture that are precious. We have figured out how to validate the exuberance that sexual connection can unleash. We have elaborated the joys of sexual pleasure in wondrous ways. In the past, we have had to fight for even the barest shred of sexual satisfaction. And, today, in the wake of AIDS and in light of the recent attacks on the National Endowment for the Arts, we still have to defend the right to our sexual selves. These fights can make it seem, as it certainly once did for me, that our rationale as a movement is sexual freedom, whatever that means. But if experience has taught me anything, it is that we do ourselves wrong if we only imagine gay liberation as a sexual freedom struggle.

15

Then and Now: The Shifting Context
of Gay Historical Writing

Everyone should have something they can call "a first," no matter how slight. Mine came in 1983 when the University of Chicago Press published my dissertation as *Sexual Politics, Sexual Communities: The Making of a Homosexual Minority in the United States*. At the time, there were perhaps a handful of books on gay and lesbian history.[1] *Sexual Politics, Sexual Communities* was the first monograph in U.S. gay history. It told the story of the first generation of gay and lesbian activists in the United States, the men and women who shaped a gay politics before Stonewall.

In this chapter, I reflect on the conditions that went into the making of the book. What provoked me to research and write it? What experiences shaped it (and me)? What assumptions propelled the work forward? In what context were the questions framed, the research done, the answers puzzled through? I also consider how the passage of time since its publication has changed my outlook and understanding. In particular, in what ways has subsequent gay and lesbian historical writing modified my interpretation of the homophile movement and the post–World War II era? How does the longer view, at the start of the new millennium, complicate assumptions that guided me two decades ago?

* * *

This essay originally appeared as the preface and afterword to a second edition of *Sexual Politics, Sexual Communities: The Making of a Homosexual Minority in the United States, 1940–1970* (Chicago: University of Chicago Press, 1998). My thanks go to Doug Mitchell for encouraging me to write it.

Though published in the 1980s, *Sexual Politics, Sexual Communities* was a product of the 1970s, the historical "moment" bounded by the Stonewall Riots in New York City and the onset of the AIDS epidemic. For many gay men and lesbians in the United States, and especially in New York City where I lived and was going to school, the decade brought a dramatic experience of change that daily left one almost giddy with hope and an expectant sense of possibility. *Something* had happened, was happening all around us.[2]

Of course, that "something" seemed to depend on one's experience. By the time I came into the gay liberation movement early in 1973, I had managed to construct for myself a very full gay life. I had a lover, a wide circle of gay male friends, and a broad familiarity with the public institutions of the gay subculture in New York City—from bars, restaurants, and cruising strips in the Village, Times Square, and Third Avenue, to parks, the West Side docks, the subways, and the ticket line for the Metropolitan Opera. Entering the orbit of the movement broadened my world in two very important ways. It gave a political edge to my identity as a gay man. And, despite the reputation of the seventies as the separatist decade, I met lesbians for the first time and formed a significant number of important relationships with them.

By the mid-1970s, virtually every gay man or lesbian I knew, whether through social, sexual, or political activities, had a few characteristics in common. We were born in the second quarter of the twentieth century and had consequently come of age—as the work of historians of sexuality now informs us—at a time when a particular form of identity, revolving around same-sex desire, was coming to the foreground, and when the conditions of gay life offered a mix of both opportunity and constraint. We all had experienced some kind of struggle, or difficulty, related to our homosexuality. For some, the struggle had been external, an overt conflict with authority of one sort or another, such as family, church, or medical experts. For others, the difficulty had been largely internal, one of having resisted the desires and yearnings that seemed to spring from the core of our selves. For still others, the problems were primarily practical in nature, involving a search for information, understanding, companionship. And for many, it encompassed all three. Despite these struggles, we had also all made the leap toward acknowledging, to ourselves and others in the gay world, that we were homosexual. Finally, almost everyone who filled my gay universe had been touched in some way by the sixties, by the complex of social, cultural, and political upheavals that called into question most forms of authority, knowledge, and institutional arrangements.

Bring those shared characteristics together in the context of a radical liberation movement and one can begin perhaps to apprehend how easily politics came to infuse the very essence of our queer souls. By politics I don't mean elections and candidates and campaigns and voter mobilization. Rather I mean it in the way that word was most often used by radicals of the sixties and early seventies: as collective action for the purpose of changing institutions, power relationships, beliefs, and social practices, whether at the level of the national government and the corporation or at the level of family relationships, schools, and neighborhood institutions.

Because I came to gay liberation through the Gay Academic Union (GAU), an effort to mobilize faculty, staff, administrators, and graduate students to make colleges and universities into environments hospitable to lesbians and gays, it was natural that movement work for me and many others in the group should involve the generation of new knowledge.[3] An important strand of the radicalism of the 1960s had focused on what might be called the "politics of knowledge." Knowledge, or scholarship, did not exist in a vacuum of objectivity but instead was enmeshed in, subservient to, productive of, or resistant to power relationships and institutional structures. Whether it was the antiwar movement exposing the ties between university researchers and the Pentagon, or the Black Power movement decrying the Eurocentric nature of the curriculum, or radical feminists attacking the gendered assumptions of psychoanalysis, the radical forebears of gay liberation had trained a spotlight on the power of knowledge — to corrupt, to oppress, to empower, to free.

What this meant to me, and to others with whom I collaborated, was that research, writing, and scholarship became activities that counted for something, though not in their own right or detached from the world around them. They mattered because there were connections between knowledge and power, between consciousness and experience, between ideas and action. For instance, the psychological research of someone like Evelyn Hooker in the 1960s showed lesbians and gay men to be emotionally adjusted, finely functioning human beings; it became the foundation for the American Psychiatric Association to eliminate the sickness classification of homosexuality. The elimination of medical stigma in turn weakened arguments used to justify the exclusion of gays from a range of jobs. Thus, changing ideas through intellectual labor was one way to provoke change, while the actions that we, collectively as a movement, were taking made it easier for some of us to have the freedom to do more of this kind of research and writing. In other words, it was hard, for me at least, to imagine any kind of gay scholarship without the movement that supported it, while the production of new knowledge seemed an essential component of a successful social change movement.

At the same time, intellectual work, at least in the domain of history, seemed hopelessly handicapped by one of the forms that gay oppression took. Sometimes we framed the problem as one of silence imposed by an oppressive society. At other times we expressed it as an issue of lies and myths about us, not noticing the contradiction between these two ways of describing our challenge. In either case, it made the prospect of writing a dissertation on some aspect of the history of homosexuality, which is what, in 1974, I proposed to the history department of Columbia, a daunting task. At the time, Martin Duberman was the only professional historian I knew of who had come out of the closet, but he was just embarking on research into the broader history of sexuality which, at that time, was itself an almost completely untouched subject.[4] Jonathan Ned Katz, an activist and scholar with whom I had become friends through the GAU, had written a play, *Coming Out!,* which had been produced Off-Off Broadway.[5] The dialogue all came from documents, which Katz had collected as part of his continuing research for what became, in 1976, *Gay American History.* His discoveries were thrilling, but also sobering. If it was taking so much effort to find documents scattered across four centuries, how was I going to find the material to be able to write a focused piece of gay and lesbian history, the kind of monographic study that a dissertation is supposed to be?

*   *   *

Deciding to write about the gay movement seemed the perfect choice. It appealed to my interests and to the "moment": in the wake of the 1960s, the study of social movements had generated interest among historians, sociologists, and political scientists; besides, since gay liberation was profoundly changing the world around me, what could be more important than studying it? Studying the movement also had utility: uncovering the pre-Stonewall legacy of struggle would provide contemporary activists with a wider angle of vision. Above all, it might actually be achievable. In a past that seemed characterized by silence and invisibility, a movement to make change could at least be found. Movements, after all, are composed of organizations with memberships, goals, newsletters, activities. Even so, because I had so internalized the gay liberationist view that the Stonewall Riots started every-thing, that before Stonewall was a bleak wasteland with few stories to define the landscape, I assumed I would be writing a work of contemporary history. As I originally conceived the project, perhaps half the work would be about pre-Stonewall life and activism; but the heart and soul would be the events of the 1970s.

So the research began. The process was both exhilarating and laborious, with more of the latter than the former. Had I been working on a standard topic in U.S. history — for instance, some aspect of the New Deal or the coming of the Civil War — I would have been able to read a huge literature and absorb the general contours of my topic even before stepping into an archives. I would know, in other words, that I was entering a long-standing scholarly conversation in mid-sentence. But writing gay history, a phrase without any currency in the mid-1970s, felt like an act of invention. True, in the wake of Stonewall, there were a few books by gay and lesbian liberation-ists that touched in small ways on pre-Stonewall politics, but otherwise the slate was blank.[6]

Though I received support for the work from the usual places that gradu-ate students look (an extremely helpful faculty adviser and fellow students at Columbia who were eager to read my drafts), what kept me going and what was responsible for much of the early published work on lesbian and gay history was a parallel intellectual structure that community-based activist scholars were creating in the 1970s. In New York I joined first a gay men's study group that explored the utility of Marxist theory for understanding the political economy of sexuality, and then a gender-mixed study group on the history of sexuality that met for several years. As the 1970s progressed, groups like these sprouted in a number of cities, creating a network of gay and lesbian community history projects that kept in close touch and fed one another's thirst for knowledge. The movement in the 1970s also sustained a set of high-quality newspapers and magazines that printed work of sub-stance. Publications like the *Body Politic, Sinister Wisdom, Gay Sunshine, Con-ditions,* and *Fag Rag,* to name just a few, allowed emerging queer writers to find an audience for work that was intellectually, culturally, and politically

provocative. There is nothing comparable in the print world of today, dominated as it is by glossy magazines obsessed with gossip, celebrity, and "life-
styles," and shaped by advertisers.

Only very slowly did the contours of the book emerge. Early on in the
research I made contact with the New York Mattachine Society, one of the
important organizations of the pre-Stonewall years. Its director, Richard
Wandel, gave me free run of their library and old office files. Four weeks later,
when he informed me that the organization had gone belly up and was
closing, he allowed me to move some file cabinets and stacks of periodicals
into my apartment, so my research could proceed. Over the course of a year,
I worked my way through every issue of *ONE, Mattachine Review,* and *The
Ladder,* the chief publications of the homophile movement. The reading was
helpful in the sense that it gave me a feel for what lesbians and gay men in the
orbit of this tiny social movement were thinking, but I still had little sense of
what they were actually *doing.* And, for the most part, I still had no idea of
who they were, since most writers in these publications used pseudonyms
until well into the 1960s.

Meanwhile, from Jonathan Katz, who was nearing completion of *Gay
American History,* I learned a seemingly incredible story of a small group of
Communist Party members in southern California who founded the Mat-
tachine Society at the onset of the McCarthy era. He had heard this from
Harry Hay, one of the founders whom Katz had interviewed for his book.[7]
Hay had also given him names and phone numbers of other activists from
the 1950s so at the end of the summer in 1976 I headed toward California for
a round of research and interviewing.

The several months I spent in Los Angeles and San Francisco finally gave
me a story to tell. I plugged into a network of older California activists, many
of whom had known each other for two decades or longer and virtually all of
whom were eager to talk. Already, by 1976, most of them were feeling that
history had passed them by; the young whippersnappers of gay liberation
and lesbian feminism seemed to have no use for the work they had done in
harder times. The fact that I was willing to listen, that I deemed their stories
important enough to tape and, eventually, to recount as history, was enormously validating to them. In the course of the fall I interviewed about three
dozen participants. Some lasted only an hour. Others stretched into several
sessions spread over days.[8] More importantly, perhaps, some of these individuals, notably Jim Kepner, Dorr Legg, and Don Lucas, opened to me the

extensive personal archives they had kept over the years. These documents were critical because they allowed me to test my oral histories, taken many years after the events from individuals who did, after all, have an interest in magnifying the importance of their work, against a paper trail from the past.

At some point during this research trip, the organizing concept of the project shifted dramatically. I realized that the pre-Stonewall events, which I had originally imagined as somewhat akin to a preface to the "real" story of gay liberation, had a historical integrity of their own. They were, in short, significant enough to be placed at the center of what I was writing. The homophile movement, as the participants called it, had many of the ear-marks of other social change movements in their early phases: visionary founders; hard times and tribulations; serious debates over philosophy, strategy, and tactics; victories that mattered. Hence, I determined that the book ought properly to stop with the Stonewall Riots in order to highlight more effectively the distinctive character and contribution of the activists of a preceding generation.

Two other aspects of the intellectual genesis of *Sexual Politics, Sexual Communities* deserve comment. The first speaks directly to the ways the present can shape our view of the past. In 1979 I made a second extended trip to San Francisco, intending to write while I continued to do research there. My stay coincided with important events in the life of the city. In November 1978, Californians rejected at the polls a statewide antigay ballot initiative that would have, among other things, prevented any gays or lesbians from teaching in the state's public schools. A few days after the election, Dan White, a conservative member of the San Francisco Board of Supervisors, assassi-nated George Moscone, the mayor, and Harvey Milk, the city's first openly gay supervisor and an outspoken proponent of gay rights. White's trial was wrapping up as I arrived; a few days later, the jury returned a voluntary manslaughter verdict. It meant that White could be free after less than five years in prison. That night, thousands of lesbians, gay men, and their sup-porters rioted at City Hall, smashing windows and setting fire to police cars. The police responded by invading the Castro, the main gay neighborhood in San Francisco, and indiscriminately assaulting pedestrians on the street and patrons of gay bars.[9]

What I witnessed that night, as well as over the succeeding days and weeks, allowed me to read my historical research in a new light. I saw how dependent the movement was on the subculture; in reality, the subculture, or community, was the sea in which activists swam. Much of the crowd that gathered in front of City Hall had poured out of the bars when they heard about the jury's verdict.

In my research I had noted how the movement before Stonewall seemed to develop further in San Francisco than in any other city—an interesting fact for which I had only the circular explanation that San Francisco was, after all, the gay capital of the United States. Now, with my interest piqued by contemporary events, I began to search more deeply. Clues whose meaning had eluded me became significant. I uncovered an interlocking set of events and circumstances—the Beat subculture in San Francisco and its gay subtext, patterns of state harassment, and gay-related scandals involving police corruption—that provoked activism within the pre-Stonewall bar world. Out of this I was able to fashion an interpretation of San Francisco's gay social and political history. I was also able to emphasize throughout the book the critical nature of the movement's relationship to the subculture, or what we now call the community. To the degree that the movement remains separate and the community estranged from activism, advances will be slow in coming. To the degree that the relationship between movement activists and the broader gay community is strong, change will be expansive.

A second aspect of the book's intellectual origins involves the broader historical framework into which I set the homophile movement. During this same stay in San Francisco, I had the privilege of being closely involved with a group of community-based intellectuals who had gathered together in the San Francisco Lesbian and Gay History Project. Many of them—Allan Berube, Jeffrey Escoffier, Estelle Freedman, Eric Garber, Amber Hollibaugh, Gayle Rubin—went on in the 1980s and 1990s to produce significant work in gay history, sexuality, and sexual politics. Combined with the intellectual stimulation and encouragement of my study groups in New York, this made for a situation in which we were all encouraging one another to think big and creatively. Since the movement of which our research and writing and forums and slide shows were a part was so evidently remaking the world around us, it seemed inevitable that we would strive to connect our work to broad themes and large social processes, that we would seek to invest it with significance. Thus, it made sense to me to ask questions about how events such as World War II and political trends like McCarthyism impinged on gay life and activism. It also made sense to play with taken-for-granted concepts like sexual orientation and ask whether they had always

218 THE WORLD TURNED

existed, whether they described the essence of human beings, whether perhaps they were "creations" of history that came into being under one set of social, cultural, and economic conditions and that might remake themselves in yet other ways in the future. Hence, the opening chapters of *Sexual Politics, Sexual Communities* attempt to build a large historical stage on which the specific story of lesbian and gay activism played itself out.

* * *

Much has happened since the winter of 1982, when I completed the final revision of the manuscript for *Sexual Politics, Sexual Communities*. A vibrant historical literature of the gay and lesbian experience emerged, along with a provocative interdisciplinary field of queer studies. Add two additional decades of "living" gay and lesbian history — of movement building, community development, political engagement, cultural change, and everyday life — and the world and our understanding of it look as different from the early 1980s as that moment did from pre-Stonewall life. How have the new historical writing and the longer view at the turn of the millennium altered, enriched, or upended my view of the story I wrote with such confidence two decades ago?

First, let me make explicit what I understood to be the key themes in this history. As best I can reconstruct my thinking from that time, I had five major points of emphasis: (1) Gay and lesbian life didn't start with Stonewall. Rather, there was a rich history of social experience and political struggle in preceding generations; (2) gay and lesbian identity as we then knew it in contemporary America was not a universal, transhistorical and cross-cultural category but rather the creation of a particular time and place, culture, and society; (3) the mid-twentieth century, through its mixture of freedom and oppression, was a key moment in the creation of a collective consciousness among gays and lesbians; (4) the specific legacy of homophile activists mattered; their work made a difference; and (5) in making change, those armed with a radical analysis of society and a willingness to engage in militant collective action proved most effective and made the most enduring contributions.

It Didn't Start with Stonewall

Today this point seems so obvious that it is almost startling to realize that it needed to be made. Unlike two decades ago, we now have at our disposal a substantial body of historical writing about the pre-Stonewall generations, with more on the way. Allan Berube has produced a sophisticated study of gays, lesbians, and the military during World War II. In rich detail, he describes the shifting approaches of the military to the queer presence in its midst, and the ways that gays and lesbians made use of that experience to forge a group identity under both exhilarating and threatening conditions. Elizabeth Kennedy and Madeline Davis have written a detailed, nuanced history of working-class lesbians in Buffalo, New York, and the public bar culture they created between the 1930s and the 1960s. Their discussion illuminates not only the place of butch-femme roles in pre-Stonewall life, but also the ways that lesbians fought to create access to public space. Esther Newton has chronicled the evolution, over the course of two generations, of a gay and lesbian community in the vacation resort of Cherry Grove, Fire Island; through oral histories, she is able to chart important shifts in the way gays and lesbians understood their identity, shifts that help explain the post-Stonewall world. In *Gay New York*, George Chauncey describes the changing institutions, norms, experiences, and sexual identities of men who were attracted to men in the nation's largest city between the 1890s and the 1930s. He detects important class differences in the understanding and experience of sexual relations between men, and a remarkable move toward visibility as early as the 1920s. John Howard has provided a remarkable account of queer life in Mississippi in the mid-twentieth century. Challenging commonplace views of same-sex relationships as an urban phenomenon, he finds men loving men in the state's churches and schools, in its parks and along its highways. Marc Stein has uncovered a complicated story of gay and lesbian public culture in Philadelphia after World War II, and explains how it fed a militant local activism before Stonewall. John Gustav-Wrathall has directed his gaze toward a key American institution, the YMCA, describing how it fostered a culture of male romantic attachments and passionate commitments. Lisa Duggan has painstakingly constructed the sensationalized representation of the lesbian in popular culture between the 1890s and the Great Depression. Lillian Faderman has provided a broad account of the evolution of lesbian life and culture in the twentieth century.[10]

Those are just the key book-length historical studies in print. Others are either in press or close to completion.[11] There are also several collections of articles or documents on gay and lesbian history: *Hidden From History*, which ranges widely across time and continent; *Creating a Place for Ourselves*, a collection of historical articles on various gay and lesbian communities including Detroit; Philadelphia; Birmingham; Flint, Michigan; and Washington, D.C.; *Carryin' On in the Lesbian and Gay South,* which, as the name reveals, is a regional anthology; *We Are Everywhere,* a massive collection of documents on gay and lesbian politics over the past century.[12] Historical writing on same-sex desire and identity can also be found in the growing number of anthologies on the history of sexuality and gender; in those emanating from the interdisciplinary field of queer studies; and in the pages of scholarly journals that are more receptive than ever before to the new gay history.[13]

The recovery of gay and lesbian historical experience is proceeding in at least two additional ways: in books on other topics in which homosexuality plays a part, and in the writing of biography. As examples of the former, Leisa Meyer integrates a discussion of lesbians into her careful study of women and the military during World War II. Susan Cahn includes an insightful discussion of lesbians and homophobia in her history of women and sports in twentieth-century America. Kevin Mumford's book on early twentieth-century vice districts and interracial sex includes analysis of same-sex relationships and homosexual identities.[14]

Meanwhile, the growth of interest in gay history has coincided with a revival during the past decade of the genre of biography. Biographers increasingly have departed from the bowdlerized telling of life stories that erased gay content and are now not only acknowledging the passions, intimacies, and inclinations of their subjects, but exploring how those desires and identities gave shape to public life, too. The lives range across a broad spectrum of social worlds and include Ruth Benedict, a pioneering anthropologist; Eleanor Roosevelt, the illustrious first lady and a political activist in her own right; Billy Strayhorn, a musician and songwriter close to Duke Ellington; Miriam Van Waters, a leading criminologist and prison reformer; Virgil Thomson, a composer; Billy Tipton, a transgender band leader who performed in small towns from the Ozarks to the Northwest in the mid-twentieth century; and Liberace, a popular culture phenomenon of the 1950s and 1960s.[15] As of yet, the biographical and the historical often function as two disconnected genres of scholarly study. But individual lives can be mined for clues about consciousness and experience that can illuminate more than the one life under scrutiny.

It would take the better part of another book to elucidate the full meaning and significance of this work. But, suffice it to say, in the years since I wrote *Sexual Politics, Sexual Communities*, we have moved far beyond "it didn't start with Stonewall." At least for the twentieth century, historians are creating a multilayered, many-voiced account of a collective gay and lesbian life as complex and subtle as those we already have for ethnic and racial groups in the United States. And, as it develops, gay history is demonstrating its connections to and influence on other important matters: topics such as World War II, the Cold War, and McCarthyism; fields such as urban history and popular culture; our understandings about the ties between sexuality and other social categories such as race and class.[16]

Gay Identity Is Socially Constructed

In making this argument, I was building on the work of other writers and applying their perspective on homosexuality to a particular problem posed by my own research: how to explain the fact that, although key elements of gay oppression had existed for centuries, a gay freedom movement only came into being after World War II.[17]

The debate over whether the homosexual is a universal category or a socially constructed one raged throughout the 1980s.[18] Simply put, the two positions go something like this: "Essentialists" would argue that, whether or not a society has a word to describe homosexuality, individuals who are primarily attracted to members of the same sex are to be found in every society, every culture, every era of human history. Just as nature seems to produce humans who are male or female, with some in between, so too does it reliably produce heterosexuals, homosexuals, and some in between. There is a universal character to this core of sexuality that makes it essentially comparable across time and space, no matter how different it may look to us today. It is meaningful, in other words, to speak of a gay minority as a percentage of the population no matter what the era or the society; the historian's task is to find it. On the other hand, "social constructionists" would say, in effect, that difference is everything. Human sexuality is amazingly malleable and can organize itself in many sorts of ways. How that desire is understood and hence experienced is what counts. Only in some societies and eras do desires coalesce into a social role, or identity, that gets labeled homosexual, or gay, or lesbian, and that corresponds to how individuals organize their emotional, intimate, and erotic lives. And, for reasons that still can only remain speculative, the modern West appears to be one such place and time.

While ink was spilled and conferences held over these contrasting intellectual approaches to the understanding of human sexuality, in some fundamental sense the disagreement is unresolvable. Neither view can be proved in the way that a mathematical theorem or scientific proposition can be demonstrated as true or false. Essentialism and social constructionism are ways of approaching the history of sexuality, of analyzing evidence and elaborating plausible interpretations of the past.

The ground has shifted somewhat in the 1990s. Intellectuals from outside the fields of history and sociology have trained a whole set of theoretical approaches on to the study of sexuality. The complex of perspectives described as postmodern and poststructural, including the writing of theorists such as Foucault and Lacan who emphasize the importance of language, or discourse, in shaping human experience, has given added life to the social constructionist position, but without the name and in different guise. In the United States, writers such as Judith Butler, for instance, have argued for the malleability of gender, for an understanding of it as "performative."[19] In fact, at the heart of the whole enterprise of the new cultural studies of the 1980s and 1990s in the United States is the idea that identities — whether gendered, racial, ethnic, national, or sexual — are fluid and created, not fixed and stable. This notion, as much as anything, helps bind together the widely disparate work labeled "queer studies."[20] And it tends to push scholarly inquiry away from the search for a gay and lesbian history, or community, or identity, toward an exploration of how the concepts, or understandings, of sexuality as divided into homo and hetero have come to infiltrate the whole culture.[21]

Ironically, even though social construction and its intellectual progeny seem, over the past two decades, to have swept essentialism from the playing field of humanistic and social scientific study, the essentialist notion that gays constitute a distinct minority of people different in some inherent way has more credibility in American society than ever before. It is the routine assumption of most gay and lesbian activists. It has sparked a mass of scientific research in search of the gay gene, the gay hypothalamus, gay twins, or other such biological evidence concerning the origins of homosexuality.[22] Liberal allies of the gay community, including national politicians like Al Gore and publications like the *New Yorker,* phrase their support of civil rights in terms of the belief that homosexuals are born that way, that there always were and always will be gays and lesbians. In other words, the core assumptions at the heart of *Sexual Politics, Sexual Communities* and most of the more recent historical studies are ignored, even as the content of the history—the fascinating lives, the heroic struggles, the fierce oppression—are embraced and absorbed.

*The Middle Decades of the Twentieth Century Were a Key Moment
in the Emergence of a Gay and Lesbian Minority*

Newer work in gay and lesbian history both confirms this view and complicates it in important ways.

On the one hand, it seems even clearer than it did before that the 1940s and 1950s are significant decades for understanding the emergence of an articulate, self-conscious, visible lesbian and gay community, national in its reach and connectedness. Allan Berube's work on World War II, based on numerous oral histories, extensive archival research, and the chance discovery of a large cache of correspondence between gay GIs, has given us a detailed look at how the experience of total war expanded the sites for homosexual experience *and* for a coming to terms with one's desires as a form of social identity. The three-way struggle between the military, the psychiatric profession, and gays and lesbians to define the meaning of homosexual desire gave greater coherence to these desires even as men and women had more opportunity to act on them. Community studies, such as ones of Buffalo, Cherry Grove, and Washington, seem to confirm the war years as a moment of change: in the war's aftermath, the public gay world seems to have grown more dense.[23]

We also have more evidence of the persecutions of the 1950s and the extent to which state power was mobilized to label, isolate, and punish gays and lesbians. Material appearing in biographies and memoirs adds to the stock of examples I had. For instance, Estelle Freedman's work on the career of Miriam Van Waters, a criminal justice reformer, describes the effective use of lesbian baiting and labeling in the postwar decade. John Howard's study of Atlanta in the 1950s points to intense police repression. Alan Helms's autobiography of life in New York City in the 1950s calls attention to the ways that university administrators tracked information about the sexual orientation of their students. Martin Duberman's and Audre Lorde's own memoirs of the 1950s, Donna Penn's portrait of the new visibility of the lesbian as sexual deviate, Freedman's discussion of the prison lesbian, and biographies of Cold War figures such as Joseph Alsop and Tom Dooley all add to the picture of the postwar decade as a time of virulent persecution and intensifying attacks, from the national government on down to the local cop and city journalist. The work of David Johnson, soon to be published, will give us a full-length study of homophobia and McCarthyism in the nation's capital.[24]

At the same time, other work scrambles a bit this periodization of gay history. Without denying either the importance of the war or the magnitude of the Cold War attacks, some historians have uncovered evidence that the turn toward an active, aggressive, even hysterical stance of attack began earlier. Freedman's look at the evolution of the concept of the sexual psycho-path finds its roots in the 1930s, in a panic over sex crimes that extended into the postwar era. The conflation of the psychopath with the homosexual meant that gay men in particular were being targeted both by law enforce-ment agencies and elements of the psychiatric profession even before the scapegoating associated with McCarthyism. Chauncey's study of New York City gay life found that, in response to the growing visibility of the subcul-ture, law enforcement in the post-Prohibition years began taking a more aggressive stance toward public manifestations of homosexuality. Thus, the persecutions of the McCarthy era built on tendencies already underway in some locales, with roots in law enforcement practices rather than national security concerns.[25]

More work is needed before one can confidently generalize. Were the attacks on gay male life in New York City in the 1930s typical, or the result of a higher level of visibility than elsewhere? Did a revised definition of sexual psychopathology have a substantial impact not only on the law but on its enforcement? Meanwhile, the existing literature on the 1930s makes World War II seem even more significant. By destabilizing the routines of hetero-sexual socialization and hence opening space for homosexual experience, and by creating, through the geographic mobility that military service and civilian war work afforded, a stronger sense of a national gay culture, the war years may have left the developing gay community better fortified both to survive and resist the persecutions of the 1950s.

The Work of Homophile Activists Mattered; They Set the Stage
for Stonewall and Gay Liberation

It would be very hard, I think, to dispute the first half of this proposition after having read *Sexual Politics, Sexual Communities.* But the issue is not whether the work made a difference, but how and to what degree. Can one claim, as I did, that the roots of Stonewall and gay liberation can only be understood in the light of homophile activism? Is there a direct and strong line of influence between the work of this first generation and what occurred in the wake of Stonewall?

This is one area where the growth of gay history has sparked interesting debate. For instance, Kennedy and Davis have argued that the consciousness forged among working-class lesbians who participated in the bar culture of the 1950s and 1960s in Buffalo (and presumably in many other cities as well) made the rapid spread of gay liberation possible. Though they speak of this consciousness as "prepolitical," it shared key characteristics with what we associate with the post-Stonewall movement: a willingness to fight in order to have access to public space; a defiant pride in one's identity; the assumption that one has a right to be lesbian or gay. Lesbians in Buffalo were ready for the more overtly political message of Stonewall because they had been living it for two decades. Allan Drexel makes similar arguments for the significance of the tradition of public drag balls among working-class black men in Chicago in the 1950s. This, he argues, more than the activities of middle-class white homophile activists, should be seen as ancestral to the Stonewall revolt and its aftermath.[26]

While Drexel's claims for a ritualized annual event that operated with the support of the police department seem suspect, Kennedy and Davis are on stronger ground. They point us toward something that I suggested in my discussion of San Francisco and that needs explicit commentary: neither activism alone nor subcultural participation has the capacity to make substantial change in law, public policy, and institutions. Instead, only when those two spheres intersect, as they did in San Francisco in the 1960s, and as they did in *many* American cities in the 1980s in the wake of the AIDS epidemic, do powerful forces for change get launched.

But still more needs to be said about the issues of causation and antecedents that both I and Kennedy and Davis were struggling with. A similar paradox courses through our work. Each of our books is attempting to give credence to the importance of what came before Stonewall. Yet, by stopping our accounts roughly at the time that Stonewall happened, we unintentionally preserve — even strengthen — the notion that the riots marked a critical historical divide. Retrospectively, I am now able to see the almost schizophrenic way I dealt with this issue. For instance, at both the beginning and end of my conclusion, I affirm in unambiguous language that homophile activism was a necessary prelude for the emergence of gay liberation. Yet, just before that, at the close of the penultimate chapter, I also confidently state that Stonewall "marked a critical divide in the politics and consciousness of homosexuals and lesbians."[27]

I point this out less as an exercise in self-ridicule than to call attention to an important issue that still needs exploration: Stonewall, its cause and significance. Because of the mythic status and continuing symbolic power of the riot, any historical studies of this era necessarily have to ask how important was it and where did it come from.

Let me suggest two different — and somewhat contradictory — ways of addressing the problem that draw on newer historical writing as well as the longer view that the passage of time offers. One approach might be to challenge altogether the significance of the Stonewall Riots and gay liberation. A second contrasting approach might hold on to the notion that Stonewall and gay liberation marked a major rupture in gay life, but insist that we keep looking for an explanation robust enough to have produced it.

What, then, if Stonewall and the radicalism it spawned was just a momentary blip on the radar screen of history rather than the great divide we assume it to be? What, in other words, if there is greater continuity between pre- and post-Stonewall life and politics than we usually acknowledge? Reading Esther Newton's account of the resort community of Cherry Grove, one of the few historical studies whose time frame bridges the Stonewall divide, I was impressed with how much change was already occurring there in the 1960s. In fact, Newton titles the section on the 1960s "The Nation Takes Shape," a metaphor that incorporates notions of solidarity, visibility, public recognition, and pride that are commonly seen as post-Stonewall characteristics. Marc Stein's work on Philadelphia also suggests important elements of continuity between the 1960s and the 1970s. By the same token, the view from today makes it plausible to argue that we have tended to overestimate the depth of change provoked by Stonewall. Already by 1973 or 1974, the radicalism associated with gay liberation was on the wane. Until the rise of militant AIDS politics in the late 1980s, gay and lesbian activism in the 1970s and 1980s tended to look very much like what Frank Kameny, Barbara Gittings, and the members of the Society for Individual Rights in San Francisco were doing in the 1960s. The difference was primarily quantitative. The activists of the late 1970s far outnumbered those of the 1960s and hence were able to achieve more; activism also spread beyond a few very large cities. Visible, self-confident, and collective, the work of both groups of activists resembled those of a long line of American reformers seeking definite but limited institutional change. From this vantage point, homophile activists, working-class bar patrons, and other still-to-be-studied groups of lesbians and gay men in the 1950s and 1960s each contributed to a broad process of incremental change occurring over many decades. Some moments, like Stonewall, were certainly dramatic, but overall the continuities are more impressive than not.

While I believe there is wisdom in this version, it also does not completely satisfy. How do we account for the widespread folk wisdom that Stonewall *was* a big deal? Perhaps by reinterpreting Stonewall not as an event of great historic significance but as a kind of queer shorthand for a larger historic phenomenon: "the sixties." In an essay evaluating the legacy of one of the radical movements of the decade, Maurice Isserman and Michael Kazin wrote: "It is striking that while 'nothing' was accomplished by the New Left in its short life, everything was different afterward."[28] Certainly the huge waves of radical protest that washed over the nation from the beginning of the sixties to their end *must* have impinged on gay men and lesbians more than did homophile pickets and weekends in a bar. Key sources of political power and cultural authority — the military, law enforcement, elected officials, traditional church teaching, mental health professionals — were challenged. Surveying the history of gay New York since the 1940s, Charles Kaiser perceptively noted about the sixties that "because everything was being questioned, for a moment anything could be imagined — even a world in which homosexuals would finally win a measure of equality."[29] Almost every aspect of American experience looked, by the early 1970s, significantly different from what had passed for commonplace in the late 1950s. This was especially true of matters connected to sociability and sexuality, broadly understood. From the declining formality of dress, symbolized by women's abandonment of hats and gloves and men discarding the ubiquitous jacket and tie, to the rise in divorce, cohabitation, and contraceptive practice, to the sexual content of mass culture, the 1960s stand as a watershed decade. From this angle, Stonewall becomes emblematic of the gay world absorbing this panoply of changes, and beginning to act accordingly. And, in ways not yet fully analyzed by historians, the emergence of gay liberation undoubtedly affected the trajectory of the decade's radicalism.[30]

Does this mean that the homophile movement was irrelevant to the processes of change? Not at all. But attention to the world outside of both gay activism and the gay subculture alerts us to something that, though obvious, is well worth stating: Gay history does not stand independent of the society of which it is part. At some moments, the experience of gay men and lesbians will be decisively shaped by the larger currents of change swirling around them. At others, events and actions within the gay world will have important ramifications for the whole society.

Radical Analysis and Militant Collective Action Work Best

Though I strove to be evenhanded in my evaluation of the careers of the homophile activists and empathetic in my assessment of the challenges they faced, some figures more than others are treated as heroic in this story. Harry Hay and the Mattachine founders; Kameny, Gittings, and East Coast militants in the early 1960s; Jose Sarria in San Francisco: all emerge as crucial players pushing the quest for freedom forward. Behind this treatment of individuals lies an analysis of the dynamics of movements for social change. The biggest leaps forward occur at the hands of individuals whose understanding reaches to the roots of social problems, whose vision of change is far reaching, and who are willing to engage in militant collective action to achieve their goals.

Although these views still make sense to me, the passage of time has given me a more nuanced and complicated view of how change happens over the long haul. As marked by the founding of the Mattachine Society, the lesbian and gay movement is now almost half a century old. The shifts that have occurred, particularly in the 1990s, reach far beyond anything that happened in the two decades of homophile activism. And almost all the changes — the spread of political organizations and other community institutions; changes in law and public policy; the greater visibility and the broader range of cultural representation; the shifts in public opinion; the legitimacy that gay issues have in the political sphere; and, above all, the large number of men and women who have come out — have come during an era of deepening political conservatism.

At different points in the past three decades, the dynamic edge of activism has been either radical or militant or both. The handful of years after Stonewall saw a major infusion of energy and activity as large numbers of younger gays and lesbians, shaped by the radicalism of the 1960s, poured their hearts into gay liberation and lesbian feminism. At the end of the 1980s, a new wave of direct action politics emerged out of the gay community in response to the accumulated grief and anger that the AIDS epidemic produced. At particular moments in many cities, events ranging from an incident of antigay violence to the homophobic actions of politicians or public officials have provoked a militant response that leaves the gay community better organized and more visible.

But these moments have been exceptional and sporadic rather than typical and sustained. In the intervening years, large numbers of activists, in national, state, or local organizations, plod along, working in undramatic, routine ways. They meet with legislators, newspaper editors, school officials, television producers, police captains, and government bureaucrats. They register voters, work on electoral campaigns, and lobby. They volunteer their time at any one of the many organizations that provide services to the lesbian and gay community. Even larger numbers of gays and lesbians, in the course of their everyday lives, come out to co-workers, hold hands while walking down the street, or bring their partners home to meet their family of origin over Thanksgiving dinner. Surely all this activity, some overtly political and some not, counts in the ledger of history.

With five decades of history to draw on, I am now more impressed with the alternating cycles of "leaping" and "creeping" that the gay movement displays. There are moments when events, circumstances, and personalities combine to spark a great deal of change in a compressed period of time. These moments of leaping ahead are always accomplished through some combination of militant collective action and radical visionary outlook. But in between are longer stretches of just creeping along. They display less drama and excitement; the kind of change that occurs often escapes notice at the time. But the work of these eras is critically important nonetheless.

Fortunately, part of what makes historical studies exciting is that history never ends. The story of the gay movement remains unfinished while the evolution of sexual identities continues. New experience will allow us to keep reinterpreting the meaning of homophile activism while our continuing excavation of the past will provide richer, fuller contexts for understanding its significance.

16

A Biographer and His Subject:
Wrestling with Bayard Rustin

Four years ago, the Center for Lesbian and Gay Studies at the City University of New York sponsored a conference on the state of gay and lesbian history. I was one of several presenters in a session on biography. None of us on the panel had consulted beforehand. But by the beginning of the third or fourth presentation, a common pattern had emerged, and the audience erupted with laughter. Each one of us had opened our remarks with a mixture of apology and denial: we each were not, we assured the audience, writing a biography!

At the time the motives behind the denial seemed pretty obvious to me. Most of us on the panel would have defined ourselves as activists and scholars. We saw the work we did as intellectual endeavors closely tied to a project of social change. In writing about Bayard Rustin, for instance, I was much less interested in recounting the life of an individual than I was in exploring a period of radical social movements. To see my purpose as the telling of one man's life story seemed unworthy of the years of effort that a biography takes. Beyond that, gay and lesbian scholarship in the nineties was falling under the sign of the queer. Its methods were those of the intellectual avant-garde while biography was as traditional and boring a genre as one could

This essay was delivered as the eighth annual David R. Kessler Lecture, sponsored by the Center for Lesbian and Gay Studies, City University of New York, on December 10, 1999. It was held that year at Columbia University, which explains some of the references to the Columbia campus. I want to thank Jill Dolan and Alisa Solomon, as well as all the staff and board members who contributed to the pleasures of the evening. Allan Berube, Lisa Duggan, and Urvashi Vaid opened the evening with flattering introductions of me, making it especially memorable for me.

imagine. From the obligatory opening about the grandparents of the subject to the closing at the memorial service, biographies unfold in a fashion too linear and predictable for the end of the millennium.

Some time after the conference, I began to have dreams about Rustin. This invasion of my psyche gave me another angle for understanding the refusal to own up to my status as a biographer. I have cared passionately about everything that I have researched and written, but for the most part, I have been able to write history from a comfortable emotional distance. Yes, I can remember feelings of disgust as conservative gay men in the McCarthy era stole the Mattachine Society from my beloved Communist founders. But this was a short-term encounter with characters and episodes that I left behind quickly as I moved on to the next chapter in the story. Not so with Rustin. We have been living together now for most of this decade. He's there when I wake up in the morning and when I go to bed at night. We have a long-term committed relationship, and I haven't been able to treat his life and his experience with the kind of detachment that I've brought to the study of history.

In our postmodern world where fractured selves and fluid identities somehow keep peskily asserting themselves, it is hardly original to acknowl-edge that biography is never just about the life whose story gets told. The experience, the concerns, the identities — the subjectivity — of the author are also always present, weaving their way into the structure, presentation, and content of the biography, even when invisible. Biography fails when this dual subjectivity goes unacknowledged — when we delude ourselves into believing that we can reconstruct another life uncontaminated by our own. But it can succeed amazingly well when the passions of the biographer are thoughtfully mobilized, when identity and difference, empathy and in-comprehension, work dynamically with and against each other to produce flashes of insight and sparks of tension on the page.

Last spring, when Jill Dolan let me know that I had been selected to give this year's Kessler lecture, it came not only as an honor, but as an oppor-tunity. I don't want to go so far as to claim that Rustin and I had been engaged in mortal combat. But the easy part of his life — easy at least for me — was over. As I approached the period that had most drawn me to the project in the first place, I found myself stuck in a way that is unusual for me. I was trapped in a place for which "writer's block" is not an accurate description.

My dreams about Rustin, which had stopped long before this, offered something of a clue to what was going on. The setting was always a rattily furnished, frenetically busy activist office. The emotional tone was one of urgency. The plot line was always the same. Bayard and I were both there, he was engaged with something, and I was desperately trying to get his attention.

My reaction to the first dream was something like "Oh, Jesus. What kind of biography will I write if I'm this obsessed with pleasing my subject?" But by the third or fourth replay, it became clear that approval was not the issue. Rustin and I were in struggle. I am trying for force *him* to stop and pay attention to *me*. The urgency, the desperation is about my perception that something is terribly wrong.

All the research I've done has grown from very immediate concerns. My projects have mixed political and personal interests that have struck close to home. I decided to write about the pre-Stonewall movement because of the experience of being an activist here, in New York City, in the early and mid-1970s. Those days were thrilling, but also bewildering. The excitement of reimagining and, in the process, reinventing our lives was balanced at times by a sense of being rudderless, of having not a clue as to what we were doing or where we were going, of having no history or tradition in which to anchor our activities.

Bayard Rustin captured my interest because of how his life and his career seemed to speak to issues that were absorbing me at the turn of the past decade. At the end of the 1980s, something fairly remarkable — and almost never commented on — was happening in the lesbian and gay movement. The executive directors, the key staff, and sometimes the board leadership of many major organizations were men and women who, if asked, would have identified themselves as of the left. Yet there they were, running large community centers that provided social services and were dependent on government contracts, or at the helm of organizations that lobbied legislatures and worked through the courts.

To paraphrase a nineteenth-century homosexual emancipationist, they were radical souls trapped within the bodies of reformers. At a time when American civic culture left little room for an oppositional politics, here was a serendipitously creative effort by an assortment of movement types to experiment strategically. Women and men committed to a transformative social vision were engaging institutional structures in ways that seemed, at quick glance, as traditional as one could imagine. But look more closely, and you would have noticed a more complicated scenario. For instance, in the context of the National Gay and Lesbian Task Force, whose board I chaired, it seemed that insider and outsider tactics were intentionally being played off one another. Street activists and lobbyists, the Stonewall generation and its successor, were in dialogue, and were choreographing a new kind of social movement dance. They were mobilizing and insinuating, rabble-rousing and negotiating, dreaming boldly and plodding methodically, simultaneously. And it seemed to me that there weren't many models for this kind of movement activism. Instead, the history of social movements more often reflected the tensions that erupted when self-defined radicals and reformers squared off against one another.

Meanwhile, my teaching had been evolving so that half of what I was doing was connected to the 1960s. If any of you have worked with students on the sixties, you know how exciting the classroom can become. Undergraduates who gravitate toward these courses tend to be young women and men who are in some way at war with contemporary America. They are struggling to resist the conservative times in which we live. They are looking for any handle they can grasp to support their desire to care. They love the optimism, passion, and hopefulness of the sixties. They love the sense of community. They love the idea that students like themselves were making history.

But pedagogy alone wasn't drawing me to the sixties. The trajectory of my own life was forever altered by those times. The personal transformations set in motion by the radical politics and culture of the sixties were what made me receptive later to the message of gay liberation.

My awakening happened here at Columbia. I arrived on Morningside Heights in 1966, an overly intellectual boy from the Bronx soaked in the patriotism of Cold War Catholicism. My first week here I learned from the Protestant campus minister that God was dead. The senior who was assigned to orient me to campus life turned out to be a Dorothy-Day-style Catholic who took me on retreats filled with renegade priests and nuns contemplating marriage and agonizing over the war in Vietnam. Before long I was booing Selective Service representatives who visited the campus and had eggs thrown at me by campus jocks who were angry for different reasons. In this building I learned conversational Italian with an instructor who had us talking about student strikes in Rome and factory takeovers in Turin.

Meanwhile, late at night in what passed for the campus coffeehouse, I met and talked with men who wanted men. In the corridors of Butler Library I cruised the man who became my first lover. I made my first gay friends on the sixth floor corridor of John Jay Hall where I was living. When students shut down the university for several weeks in 1968, I divided my time between heated political discussions in the dorms and equally heated explorations of the West Village, which I was discovering for the first time. Becoming gay and becoming a political radical are inseparably linked in my experience — and completely bound up for me with the 1960s.

If my imagination presents the sixties to me as a moment of awakening, the classroom exposed a different subterranean emotional drama. No matter how I planned the course, somehow what emerged was a story of loss and devastation, a declension narrative that took my students through the rise — and then fall — of hope and optimism. The "good sixties" of sit-ins, freedom rides, and a war to end poverty were followed by the "bad sixties" of burning cities, Watergate, and a war in Asia. The good sixties are uplifting, while the bad sixties are wrenchingly demoralizing — even as they also thrill.

This is not a narrative that I invented. It defines much of the historical writing on the 1960s, and it is the story that a subset of my generation has spun out over and over and over. In my work on gay history I have certainly proved that I can disrupt other "traditional" or well-established narratives. But the means to disrupt this one were eluding me.

And so I came upon Rustin with a set of hopes and expectations. At the time I began researching his life, almost nothing historical had been written about him. Mostly he had a brief walk-on part as the man who organized the historic 1963 March on Washington. But he was the centerpiece of one chapter in a journalistic account of protest in the sixties, and what was there intrigued me. Rustin's life looked to be the ideal material for constructing a different narrative of the sixties at the same time that his career resonated with the contemporary concerns of the queer movement. Rustin bridged two generations of radicalism in the United States. To the new youth activists of the late fifties and early sixties, he brought the experience of having organized during the heady years of the 1930s. His activism was suffused by deep moral conviction. He wove Quaker traditions and Gandhian principles into a seamless ethical system that shaped his dealings with Southern sheriffs, American military officers, and restaurant owners in northern cities. Rustin, more than anyone, brought Gandhi to the United States. He presided over the transformation of direct action tactics from the cherished possession of a few initiates to its embrace by masses of Americans.

Of most interest to me was the way Rustin's concerns shifted in the 1960s. He had spent almost two decades refining direct action *tactics* until they perfectly comported with a moral philosophy of how human beings should be treated. Now he was turning his attention to questions of strategy: how to make the tactics of protest serve a grander design of political, economic, and social revolution. At the moment when the "good sixties" were at a crossroads, Rustin was addressing to his comrades in the peace, civil rights, and economic justice struggles a strategic manifesto that broke dramatically with the orthodoxy of these social movements.

If an interest in the 1960s drew me to Rustin, his early life is what captivated me. A biographer—or at least this biographer—could not ask for a more compelling subject. His story is heroic and harrowing. It abounds with triumphs and trials. It combines the narrative contours of the saint and the sinner.

Many young white boys today are coming of age immersed in the fictional world of Harry Potter. The stuff of prepubescent fantasies of masculine courage and strength are wizards and potions and magic wands and broomsticks that race through the air. I, on the other hand, was nurtured on the lives of the saints. I ingested the stories of Francis of Assisi, Ignatius Loyola, Xavier, and Augustine. They were men of passion, talent, and intellect, and they all led oversized lives. They perfectly embodied a Catholic plot line that inverted the Puritan declension narrative. These were accounts of a fall and then a rise. In Catholic storytelling, even the grisliest deaths transmuted into heroic events, victories in a cosmic struggle.

Of course, a good Catholic—and believe me, I was a good Catholic boy—reads these stories not with a sense of identification, but with yearning. The reader of these lives does not get to claim sainthood, but instead must pray and wish for the moment when the power of temptation yields to an almost gentle decision to follow a path of goodness. Though Rustin came from a different religious tradition, through the first four decades of his life one can see played out a grand struggle—between a desire for greatness and the troubles brought on him by his sexual yearnings.

His desire for greatness was not conventional. It was not for fame or fortune or success as American society normally measures such things. It emerged and took shape gradually, as a black adolescent of extraordinary talents came face to face with the constraints of white racism. A personal, individual decision to resist gradually evolved into something larger, to be like an Old Testament prophet leading his people to freedom.

Southeastern Pennsylvania, where Rustin grew up, resembled much of the North in the first third of this century. While it lacked the South's solidly built edifice of Jim Crow laws and customs, it practiced segregation nonetheless. Many times the racist practices of the North must have seemed even more infuriating because of the inconsistency of their application. In Rustin's hometown of West Chester, the elementary school was segregated, but the high school was not. The public library was open to everyone, but the gymnasium at the YMCA and the downtown soda fountain were for whites only.

Rustin excelled in high school. He won just about every honor the school offered — prizes for essays and oratory, his poetry in the school magazine, county and state honors in football, track, and tennis. His grandmother reminded readers of the local press that he was "the first colored youth to have won [the school oratory prize] in 40 years." The town's newspaper often featured on its front page his exploits on the football field. When Bayard graduated, he was a speaker at commencement, and his yearbook shows him with a longer list of awards and activities than any other senior. But while his best friend, who was white, graduated with a scholarship to an Ivy League college, Bayard closed his triumphal high school career with *no* college prospects.

Despite the fame that Rustin later achieved, reconstructing the early life of an African American from a working-class family in a provincial town is not easy. The Chester County Historical Society flows over with meticulously accumulated files about white Quaker families whose doings were significant only to themselves. Not so for the Rustin clan.

And yet, despite the paucity of evidence, I *know* that sometime in high school, a decision formed, a moral resolve was made, *never* to accept from white America the restrictions it sought to impose on his person. Rustin would go where he pleased. He would claim any one he chose as his friend and intimate. He would have access to the intellectual traditions and the cultural resources that the world had to offer. In high school he enacted this determination through the friendships he formed, through his refusal to leave a restaurant that denied him service, through his challenge to the authority of his athletic coach.

Although I am framing this resolve in racial terms, because this was the context in which it evolved, Rustin was an equal opportunity flayer of tradition. "He did not suffer fools gladly," more than one of his associates told me. Anyone or anything could become his target. Many who encountered this side of Rustin have spoken to me of his arrogance, a quality that does not sit well with a Quaker or Gandhian. I prefer to think of it as a suit of armor that protected him against the racist and, later, the homophobic assaults, that came at him early and often.

Let's jump ahead a decade and change our locale. In the early 1940s, Rustin was living in Harlem, socializing in the Village, attending Quaker meetings on the East Side, and working on the Upper West Side. As a field secretary for the Fellowship of Reconciliation, a Christian-pacifist organization whose office was located three blocks from here on Broadway, he traveled from coast to coast. He lectured and organized not only in large cities like Philadelphia, Chicago, and San Francisco, but in the small towns of the plains, the mountain states, and the south. He was an apostle of world peace in the midst of a global war, and of racial justice before the civil rights movement commanded national headlines.

There is something about beginnings that entrances me: the beginnings of a life before its direction is firmly set, of a career before it peaks, of a social movement before it can claim many successes. How else can I explain the fact that I devoted seven years of my life to studying a homophile movement whose adherents barely exceeded in number the audience in this room! So it is with the Rustin biography. I could rummage through the 1940s forever, turning up another memory, another set of notes from one of his lectures, another clipping from a small-town newspaper.

The Rustin of those years is extraordinary. The folks who knew him then, no matter what happened in later years, recall him with awe. Norman Whitney, one of his Quaker mentors from this era, was reported to have said of Rustin that "if ever he doubted the existence of God, he always thought of Bayard." "An electrifying presence," another informant told me. "Such charisma that you cannot imagine," said a third. "A prophetic type." "There was a magic about Bayard."

Above all, in stories that tumbled from their mouths, they talk about his courage. A courage called forth because of the decision *never* to collude with racism by acquiescing to its demands. Courage on a bus trip through Tennessee when he refused to sit in the back and was dragged off alone and beaten by police. Courage as he walked down the main street of a Montana town with a white pregnant woman. Courage when he was trapped in a house in Chapel Hill, North Carolina, surrounded by cars filled with angry white men who were armed with clubs and throwing rocks. Courage as he stood eyeball to eyeball with a screaming Cold Warrior on Times Square during the height of the Korean War and displayed not an impulse to defend his person.

These stories circulated through the peace and Northern civil rights movement, making Rustin seem larger than life. Meeting him, one woman told me, "was like being in the presence of history." Young activist wannabes encountering Rustin for the first time would imitate his speech, his gait, his gestures, as if by doing so they could absorb some of his powers. And yet in all these stories is the unmistakeable sense that he always remained eminently reachable, especially to the young students whom he mentored. Rustin made a commitment to social justice seem natural, an understanding of political economy accessible, and courage as something to be found inside everyone.

Twenty-plus years ago, when I interviewed Harry Hay and corresponded with Chuck Rowland about the founding of the Mattachine Society, I fell in love with each of them. As a young gay man trying, somehow, to be a gay socialist, I was touched beyond words to know that, a generation earlier, gay Communists in Los Angeles were plotting the liberation of a little boy in the Bronx who would one day be gay. Now I encounter the Rustin of the 1940s, and I yearn for him. I want him in my life. But not in the life of a fifty-something man who gives Kessler lectures, writes books, and teaches gay studies.

As I work on this biography I find myself time traveling emotionally to an earlier me. I want Rustin in the life of the fragile adolescent who came to this campus more than a generation ago and found himself confronted by unexpected challenges, without any of the usual moorings. An adolescent who needed a mentor and needed, badly, to borrow someone's courage. I want him with me at the one and only meeting of Students for a Democratic Society that I ever attended, across the street in Fayerweather Hall, and that I fled feeling stupid and inadequate. I want him with me as I sat down in the middle of West 47th Street, protesting a speech by the Secretary of State, praying that the charging police horses will stop before they reach me. I want him with me as I leafletted army recruits in front of the Whitehall

Induction Center and an angry crowd gathered across the street. I want him as a reassuring presence during the hair-raising, ear-splitting fights with my god-and-country, Cardinal-Spellman-style Catholic parents over my decision to file as a conscientious objector. I want him near as I sat quivering in front of the members of my draft board on Arthur Avenue in the Bronx, trying to persuade them to grant me CO status while they signed induction orders.

The gays-in-the-military debate of the nineties has obscured a different kind of military drama of a generation ago, when many young men were searching for ways to stay out of the military. Desperation was rife, and a cottage industry of draft counseling grew up to help them. I remember one teenager I counseled at the center here on campus asking me without blinking an eye how many knuckles he needed to lose in order to be draft exempt.

Most conscientious objectors and draft resisters in those years, sexually speaking, were straight as an arrow. And my own relationship to the draft certainly had roots in a catholicism that was getting reconfigured because of my experiences on Morningside Heights. But it was also being shaped, in ways that were both cliché ridden and not, by my rapidly accumulating gay experiences. Warfare was revolting to the emotional sensibilities that drove me toward men. But it was also petrifying to imagine myself in the military's domain during wartime. I couldn't tell if it was more terrifying to imagine doing what they wanted me to do, which was to kill, or doing what I knew they didn't want me to do. Then there were the terrors of being denied CO status — the prospect of jail, the overheated melodramatic visions of prison: not the fantasies of Jean Genet, but the violence of *Fortune and Men's Eyes*, which was playing in New York in those years.

A generation earlier, Rustin had embraced terrors of a magnitude that made mine seem inconsequential. Early in 1944, he surrendered himself to federal marshals to begin serving twenty-seven months for refusing to cooperate with the Selective Service system. This was in the middle of "the good war." There was no mass movement to support his resistance. As a Quaker, he could easily have qualified for alternative service as a religious pacifist, but he chose instead to have no truck with military authority at all.

For Rustin, as a black man, to *choose* prison flew in the face of the logic of African American experience. After emancipation, incarceration became the successor institution to slavery. If the plantation could no longer serve as a prison-without-walls, the prison could become a forced labor camp. State legislatures revised their criminal codes to make it easier to lock up black men for petty offenses, and then used them on forced labor gangs. Jails were also places that black men sometimes did not leave alive. They were institutions where racist brutality could be enacted with almost no constraints. Rustin was sent to a federal prison in Kentucky, south of the Mason-Dixon line, at a time when the penal system enforced racial segregation.

And, of course, he was also a gay man. "Triple jeopardy" barely suggests how dynamics of race, sexuality, and political identity played themselves out during Rustin's incarceration. He was physically attacked by white southern inmates for his challenge to prison segregation. He was resented by guards because of the perceived moral superiority he projected. He was despised by just about everyone — including himself — for the sexual desires he could not suppress and that brought him disgrace.

Rustin's time in prison was a nightmare of harrowing proportions. He spent long stretches in solitary confinement. He suffered through hunger strikes and forced feedings. He fought with guards. He faced the humiliation of confinement in a psychiatric prison facility. He felt the shame of his exposure as a deceitful homosexual before the community of pacifist militants. The photographic evidence from these years is striking. A picture of him taken before the start of his sentence records a sweet tranquillity that is captivating. Another taken midway through his ordeals reveals him bitter, resentful, and sullen.

Yet he came out of prison not broken but toughened, not weakened but determined, the courage he displayed earlier now so magnified that he knew he could face anything. He would have to summon up this fortitude often over the succeeding years. Cold War America was not a propitious time for a black Gandhian militant, publicly branded a sex pervert, to be agitating for world peace, racial justice, and a socialist vision of economic democracy.

Let's jump ahead again, this time to the mid-1960s, the moment of my awakening to a radical politics of dissent, and the historical moment that has led me to Rustin's life in the hope that it will illuminate the mysteries of how to make change.

In the years between his wartime incarceration and the flowering of sixties protest, Rustin and his political comrades had lived through what, for shorthand, we can call McCarthyism. The isolation that they experienced politically was compounded for Rustin by the controversies that kept erupting around his sexuality. From the late 1940s through the mid-1960s, Rustin's homosexuality rarely receded from the consciousness of the peace movement and the civil rights struggle. He was jailed for it once, and arrested a number of other times. He lost one job and had his services rejected by organizations he loved. He found himself abandoned by one mentor, A. J. Muste, and by a man whom he had mentored, Martin Luther King Jr. Politicians as different as Adam Clayton Powell and Strom Thurmond deployed Rustin's sexuality to discredit him. Right-wing organizations like the American Legion, the Minutemen, and the John Birch Society seemed at times to be trailing him, making his speaking engagements flash points for homophobic panics.

But by 1964, Rustin's world was very different. The grim years of the early Cold War and the witch-hunts of the McCarthy era seemed to be in the past. Protests over atmospheric testing, intercontinental missile systems, and civilian defense drills had brought the peace movement out of the shadows. Dramatic events in the South—from the sit-ins of 1960 to the battle of Birmingham in 1963—had made racial equality the most insistent social and political issue of the times. Through the vehicle of the 1963 March on Washington, Rustin, too, was able to move out of the shadows. The success of the march made his place no longer seem tenuous or contingent.

In the expansive freedom that his newly found status brought him, Rustin experienced a season of strategic creativity. He was shaping ideas about politics and change that were new both to the civil rights movement and the peace movement. They grew out of his assessment of what the March on Washington and the civil rights movement meant for America. Despite the sarcasm of Malcolm X's description of the march as the "farce on Washington," Rustin believed that the march had legitimized mass action. Organizations like the NAACP and the Urban League, which looked askance at collective action, had endorsed and supported it. The march also broadened the coalition of forces engaged in the struggle for racial equality by drawing to it white-dominated religious denominations and labor unions. At the same time, Rustin believed the civil rights movement was changing the whole political climate of the nation. The insistent demand for freedom and justice had broken the logjam to progressive change created by Cold War anti-Communism. Rustin saw in the civil rights movement an engine powering the nation toward the kind of social and economic programs that the Johnson administration was soon to propose.

Rustin's strategic perspective, which he expounded in speeches, movement gatherings, and writings, revolved around a few simple propositions. The first was the belief that the historical moment was both propitious and transitory. For the first time since the 1930s, enough Americans were mobilized around calls for equality and justice that the possibilities for change were expansive. But moments like this were evanescent, and all around him Rustin could see the signs of incipient backlash. The second proposition, addressed to black America, was that success in the freedom struggle would come only through espousal of a program of change far more substantial than the demand for legal equality; Rustin used the word "revolution" when he spoke of this. The third proposition was that revolutionary change will only come to black America through a process of securing allies and building coalitions; it could not come through the efforts of African Americans alone. Rustin also urged movement activists to push beyond their reliance on protest tactics which, no matter how successful, kept them perpetually reproducing outsider status, and instead pressed them to directly engage the institutions and structures of the American political system. Finally, and most concretely, Rustin urged the elements of the progressive coalition he was calling for to see the Democratic Party as the institution they needed to transform.

Depending on the setting, Rustin's proposals today can seem boring, controversial, or naïve. For contemporary progressives, who regularly work with the Democratic Party, the only thing the party has going for it is that it is not the Republican Party. The idea that it might be the vehicle to take us to a paradise of social and economic justice seems ludicrous. But 1999 is not 1964. When Rustin was writing, the Democratic Party was pushing past the edge of the centrist agendas that have typified two-party politics. He was saying: "Let's push harder. Let's make it ours. Let us be the ones to redefine its soul."

For progressives today, especially those located in identity-based movements, the call for coalition politics has become normative. But that wasn't always so. When Rustin was arguing for what we might call a multi-issue agenda, neither the NAACP, nor Martin Luther King and the Southern Christian Leadership Conference, nor the militants in SNCC and in CORE thought that minimum wage legislation, or a full employment bill, or the right of workers to bargain collectively belonged on the agenda of the civil rights movement. If multi-issue coalition politics now seems foundational to some of us, that conviction pays tribute to the power of Rustin's historical legacy, whether we know it or not.

And yet, at the same time, these ideas are still controversial and are fought over every day. They are fought out in a gay movement that seems to have no trouble seeing that the military exclusion policy is a gay issue, but that can't seem to grasp, for instance, that the demonization of immigrants damages to the core the well-being of our community.

In proposing this course correction, Rustin was implicitly arguing against several distinct, but powerfully related, strands of thought in the world of American dissent. He was rejecting romanticized leftist notions of a seizure of the state, a moment of dramatic crisis when control over the levers of power shifts suddenly and decisively. He was rejecting a long tradition of American perfectionism that privileged the unbending adherence to absolute moral principle, that defined being right as more important than — and at odds with — being effective. He was rejecting a culture of marginality that took pride in being on the outside, one in which radical dissenters could not imagine themselves doing anything other than protest. He was rejecting the single-issue politics that characterized much of the peace and civil rights movements in this era.

Despite the fact that historians rewrite history all the time, the trajectory of past events doesn't shift simply because we find new ways of looking at them. But as I investigated Rustin's life, there was something tremendously comforting about the way he was trying to rethink radical politics in the heat of struggle. Just when these times were at the cusp of shifting from the "good sixties" to the "bad sixties," Rustin was proposing a strategic reevaluation that promised to build rather than fracture an inchoate progressive coalition. Rustin was challenging the orthodoxy of his political world. He was opening a door to let me revisit what happened in the sixties. He was making his biographer happy, satisfied, and fulfilled.

But subjects can't be counted on to cooperate so neatly with their biographer's wishes. They especially can't be counted on when those wishes are embedded in subterranean veins of emotion. I said at the beginning of this talk that the life of the biographer inevitably informs the biography he or she writes. Let me take that one step further. For me, the work of biography has become most difficult where my subject's history most challenges the unexamined assumptions of my own life. I have gotten stuck in the places where

Rustin's life and mine are in conflict. And nowhere is this clearer than in relation to the war in Vietnam.

From what I've said earlier, it must be abundantly clear that the antiwar movement served as my coming-of-age ritual. It figures as powerfully in my self-definition as my sexual coming out in those same years. In the three decades since then, I have never seen a need to look with detachment at the antiwar movement and reevaluate it. It has always seemed self-evident that the only questions to ask were whether we all worked tirelessly enough to end that abomination, and whether more effort would have brought more results sooner.

Scan the key public events associated with Vietnam-era protests — scan the antiwar movement's greatest hits — and you will not see the figure of Bayard Rustin. The pacifist who chose jail as D-Day was approaching in 1944 was not on the platform in front of the United Nations in April 1967 when Martin Luther King gave an impassioned speech against the war; he was not present at the confrontation at the Pentagon in October 1967; he did not participate in the moratorium protests in 1969; he was not engaged with the turmoil unleashed by the American invasion of Cambodia.

To hear some of my informants tell it, Rustin was more than absent from these events. The pain and resentment of what long-time pacifists experienced as his apostasy during the Vietnam era has transmuted over time into a belief that he actively supported the war. With the anger over his defection has come a search for explanations. I've been told that he became the paid help of the AFL-CIO labor aristocracy. I've been told that he became a captive of the Shachtmanites, a tiny group of leftists with roots in the Trotskyist movement of the 1930s. I've been told that he was in the thrall of a young former lover, Tom Kahn. I've been told that he became a shill of the CIA.

How they've come to make and believe these claims is a whole other story about how the American left constructs identities and exclusions. Their claims evoke underground strands of class, race, and sexual prejudices that infected the peace movement of these decades. For now let me do the short response: it's not true that Rustin supported the war. In fact, in 1965, as opposition to the war began to crystallize, Rustin was articulating a vigorous pacifist response. At a major rally in Madison Square Garden, Rustin gave a speech that one member of the audience described as "by far the most inspired, principled denunciation of our foreign policy. . . . It brought sharply into focus the connections between the struggle for civil rights and the need for an end to militarist actions abroad." During that summer and fall, he worked closely with King and the Southern Christian Leadership Conference to craft an antiwar stance for King whose stature made his voice particularly critical for the peace movement. But as the war escalated, and the antiwar movement mushroomed, Rustin distanced himself from it.

Rustin's reservations came in a complicated package. Some of them were framed in purely moral terms. The pacifism that he and others tried to craft in the 1940s blended Gandhi and Jesus in ways that made means and ends, words and actions, inseparable. If the evil of violence was that it ruptured the wholeness of the human community, opposition to violence always had to repair the damage. Respect for the perpetrator was as important as the demand to stop the violence. Motive and process were as critical as outcome. These were the beliefs that shaped Rustin's pacifist agitation in the forties, and his insinuation of nonviolence into the heart of the civil rights movement in the fifties.

Rustin looked at the antiwar movement after 1965, and saw it polluted by an anti-American rhetoric. He saw it morally corrupted by its endorsement of the violence of the National Liberation Front and North Vietnam. He saw a movement compromised by the unmediated rage of its leaders and participants, a movement that had little in common with the pacifism that once made him choose jail.

Rustin had another beef with the antiwar movement. He objected mightily to its demonization of Lyndon Johnson and to its insistence that the war, and nothing else, should determine one's stance toward the Johnson administration. Make Johnson and American liberals the enemy, Rustin warned, and support for changing the racial status quo would unravel. Support for a social and economic agenda that uprooted inequality would evaporate. Rustin was keenly attuned to history. He knew the difference it made that, under Lyndon Johnson, for the first time since Reconstruction, the power of the federal government was wielded on behalf of black Americans. He knew how fragile and tenuous such commitments could be. And he was not willing to aid and abet a conservative backlash that was waiting for any opportunity.

Of course, these were the very arguments that got Rustin into trouble. They clinched, for his former comrades, the belief that he had sold his soul for a mess of pottage, for invitations to White House meetings and presidential pens from legislative signings. But, though Rustin himself often framed his comments in the language of pragmatic politics, his views rested on a moral basis — his insistence that one treat opponents respectfully, that criticism *and* support could be combined, that pathways to communication must always remain open.

I, too, react viscerally against what Rustin had to say about the antiwar movement. The emotionalism of those years was intense. A common chant at antiwar demonstrations was "Hey, hey, LBJ, how many kids did you kill today?" I hear Rustin's nitpicking criticisms of the antiwar movement and I want to tell him to get over it: "Don't you *know* what's going on over there?" I hear his call for critical support of the Johnson administration and I want to lecture him about the police power of the state: "Don't you know what's going on over here?" With the self-righteous certainty of a new convert to radical politics, I want to explain the world to a man who had endured Northern and Southern racism, who had seen first hand the effect of colonization in Africa and Asia, and whose encounters with homophobia make life since Stonewall a cake walk.

Except in my dreams, these conversations can never happen. But if I had to imaginatively construct what he might have said, I can almost hear the clipped diction, tinged with the arrogance that sometimes leaked from him in political debates:

"Don't you think it odd," he might say, "that the American war that produced the most vigorous sustained opposition in the nation's history, lasted longer than any other American war? Do you think that perhaps the way you opposed the war might have subverted your own goals? Do you take no responsibility for the election of Richard Nixon in 1968? Do you not see that while you were ranting and raving outside the citadels of power, while you were vilifying Lyndon Johnson, political demons you could barely imagine were plotting a slow but systematic rise to power? Do you not see that, a generation later, we are still living with the political results of your self-righteous emotionalism?"

Contrary to what you might be thinking, I'm not especially trying to demonstrate that Bayard Rustin was correct. I'm not trying to transform myself into his defender. I still don't know *what* I think about all this, and I will only find out what I think as I write this period in his life.

I do know that Rustin's career offers as much to chew on about our own times as it does about the sixties. Rustin challenges us to scrutinize orthodoxy in whatever form we encounter, or defend, it. He challenges us to recognize the emptiness of rhetorical militancy. He challenges us to take the call for coalition seriously, and apply it in ways that make many leftists, and progressives, uncomfortable. He asks us to discipline our untamed emotions, not so that we become like unfeeling robots, but so that our politics are shaped by critical thinking. He insists that there is a universalism that can flatten the differences of identity, and that this universalism will be found on a field of justice.

I also know that the opportunity to deliver this year's Kessler lecture has pushed the envelope for me — for which I thank you. Wrestling with this lecture has allowed me to discard emotional baggage that stood between me and an open-ended appraisal of Rustin's life. It has made it much more likely that the biography I finish will be about him, and not about me.

And the wrestling, so far, has been very much worth it. For in this life that began obscurely in a small Pennsylvania town, almost a century ago, is a wealth of wisdom and courage and moral integrity that deserves transmission as Bayard Rustin's legacy to us.

Notes

1. Homophobia and the Course of Postwar American Radicalism: The Career of Bayard Rustin

1   See Jonathan Katz, *Gay American History* (New York: Thomas Crowell, 1976), and *Gay/Lesbian Almanac* (New York: Harper and Row, 1983); John D'Emilio, *Sexual Politics, Sexual Communities: The Making of a Homosexual Minority in the United States, 1940–1970* (Chicago: University of Chicago Press, 1983); Martin Duberman, Martha Vicinus, and George Chauncey, eds., *Hidden From History: Reclaiming the Gay and Lesbian Past* (New York: New American Library, 1989); Allan Berube, *Coming Out Under Fire: The History of Gay Men and Women in World War II* (New York: Free Press, 1990); Lillian Faderman, *Odd Girls and Twilight Lovers: A History of Lesbian Life in Twentieth-Century America* (New York: Columbia University Press, 1991); Martin Duberman, *About Time: Exploring the Gay Past* (New York: Penguin, 1991), and *Stonewall* (New York: Dutton, 1993); Elizabeth Lapovsky Kennedy and Madeline D. Davis, *Boots of Leather, Slippers of Gold: The History of a Lesbian Community* (New York: Routledge, 1993); Esther Newton, *Cherry Grove, Fire Island: Sixty Years in America's First Gay and Lesbian Town* (Boston: Beacon Press, 1993); George Chauncey, *Gay New York: Gender, Urban Culture, and the Making of the Gay Male World, 1890–1940* (New York: Basic Books, 1994); Brett Beemyn, ed., *Creating a Place for Ourselves: Lesbian, Gay, and Bisexual Community Histories* (New York: Routledge, 1997); John Howard, *Men Like That: A Southern Queer History* (Chicago: University of Chicago Press, 1999); Jennifer Terry, *An American Obsession: Science, Medicine, and Homosexuality in Modern Society* (Chicago: University of Chicago Press, 1999); Marc Stein, *City of Sisterly and Brotherly Loves: Lesbian and Gay Philadelphia, 1945–1972* (Chicago: University of Chicago Press, 2000); Lisa Duggan, *Sapphic Slashers: Sex, Violence and American Modernity* (Durham, N.C.: Duke University Press, 2000).

2   Bayard Rustin, "From Protest to Politics," *Commentary*, 39 (February 1965): 25–31.

3   Material on Rustin's first twenty-nine years, until he joined the staff of the Fellowship of Reconciliation in 1941, is sparse. For information about his years in West Chester, see Rustin interview, Columbia University Oral History Project (hereafter

CUOHP). See also the following material in the Chester County Historical Society collections, in West Chester, Pennsylvania: Rustin Family file in clippings collection; issues of the *Garnet and White,* the yearbook of West Chester High School, 1930–32; and coverage of athletic events and commencement exercises in the West Chester *Daily Local News,* 1930–32. The only significant biographical account of Rustin in print may be found in Milton Viorst, *Fire in the Streets: America in the 1960s* (New York: Simon and Schuster, 1979), pp. 197–231. A full biography of Rustin by Jervis Anderson is currently near completion.

4 For contextual information on the Communist Party and on the student movement of the 1930s, see Mark Naison, *Communists in Harlem during the Depression* (Urbana: University of Illinois Press, 1983); and Robert Cohen, *When the Old Left Was Young: Student Radicals and America's First Mass Student Movement, 1929–1941* (New York: Oxford University Press, 1993). On his work with the American Friends Service Committee (AFSC) see "Peace Section Institutes: 1929–37" and "Peace Section: Mexico and Puerto Rico, 1939–41" in AFSC Archives, Philadelphia.

5 Rustin discusses his initial contacts with Randolph in his oral history at Columbia. The circumstances under which he met Muste remain unknown to me, but by the summer of 1941 they were corresponding and arrangements had been made for Rustin to begin working at the FOR. See Muste to Rustin, July 29, 1941, and Rustin to Muste, August 5, 1941, in Fellowship of Reconciliation Papers, Document Group (DG) 13, Series D, Box 21, Puerto Rico Folder, Swarthmore College Peace Collection (hereafter SCPC). On Randolph's career, see Jervis Anderson, *A. Philip Randolph: A Biographical Portrait* (New York: Harcourt Brace Jovanovich, 1973); William H. Harris, *Keeping the Faith: A. Philip Randolph, Milton P. Webster, and the Brotherhood of Sleeping Car Porters, 1925–37* (Urbana: University of Illinois Press, 1977); and Paula F. Pfeffer, *A. Philip Randolph, Pioneer of the Civil Rights Movement* (Baton Rouge: Louisiana State University Press, 1990). On Muste, see Jo Ann Ooiman Robinson, *Abraham Went Out: A Biography of A. J. Muste* (Philadelphia: Temple University Press, 1981); and Nat Hentoff, *Peace Agitator: The Story of A. J. Muste* (New York: Macmillan, 1963).

6 On Rustin's activities, see FOR Papers, DG 13, Box 3, Executive Committee Meeting Minutes; Box 3, Reports; Box 10, Rustin Folder; and Series D, Box 1, Writings and Speeches, all in SCPC. On the peace movement, see Lawrence J. Wittner, *Rebels Against War: The American Peace Movement, 1933–1983* (Philadelphia: Temple University Press, 1984), especially chapter 2.

7 On the early years of CORE, see August Meier and Elliott Rudwick, *CORE: A Study in the Civil Rights Movement, 1942–1968* (Urbana: University of Illinois Press, 1975), chapter 1; and James Farmer, *Lay Bare the Heart: An Autobiography of the Civil Rights Movement* (New York: Penguin, 1985).

8 Rustin to Muste, February 22, 1943, in FOR Papers, DG 13, Box 10, Rustin Folder, SCPC.

9 Material on Rustin's time in federal prison may be found in the file of his letters to Davis Platt, in Platt's possession, New York City, and in General Correspondence,

1944–45, Reel 20, Bayard Rustin Papers, University Publications of America (UPA) Microfilms (1988). For other discussions of conscientious objectors in prison during World War II, see James Tracy, *Direct Action: Radical Pacifism from the Union Eight to the Chicago Seven* (Chicago: University of Chicago Press, 1996); and David Dellinger, *From Yale to Jail: The Life Story of a Moral Dissenter* (New York: Pantheon, 1993).

10   Detailed accounts of the Journey of Reconciliation may be found in the "Log of the Journey" and in "Journey of Reconciliation: A Report by George Houser and Bayard Rustin," both in FOR Papers, DG 13, Series D, Box 1, SCPC. See also the brief account in Meier and Rudwick, *CORE,* pp. 33–40. Rustin wrote a report on jail conditions in North Carolina, where he was sentenced, in which he discussed the subject of homosexuality in prison. See Rustin, "A Report on Twenty-Two Days on the Chain Gang at Roxboro, North Carolina," typescript, 1949, in Rustin File, Collected Document Group-A (CDG-A), SCPC.

11   On the campaign to end segregation in the military, see the material in A. Philip Randolph Papers, Boxes 15 and 16, Library of Congress (hereafter LC).

12   See, for example, the account of a month-long campaign in Washington, D.C., during July 1947: "The Interracial Workshop: A Report by George Houser and Bayard Rustin," in FOR Papers, DG 13, Series D, Box 1, SCPC.

13   Quotations are from my interviews with Roy Finch, March 8, 1993, and Glenn Smiley, November 14, 1992. For one account of Rustin's courage under pressure see "Non-Violence vs. Jim Crow," *Fellowship,* July 1942, p. 120.

14   On Rustin's thinking about Africa, see "Report on Trip to Africa," October 20, 1952, in FOR Papers, DG 13, Series D, Box 1, SCPC; and Rustin to Muste, November 30, 1952, in War Resisters League Papers, DG 40, Series B, Box 18, SCPC.

15   "Lecturer Jailed on Morals Charge," *Los Angeles Times,* January 22, 1953, and "Lecturer Sentenced to Jail on Morals Charge," *Los Angeles Times,* January 23, 1953, both in *Congressional Record,* Senate, August 13, 1963, p. 14837.

16   Information in this paragraph comes from the following interviews: Davis Platt, July 17, 1992, and December 14, 1993; Shizu Proctor, October 10, 1993; John Swomley, November 18, 1993; and Doris Grotewohl Baker, June 19, 1994.

17   Rustin to Platt, April 5, 1945, and April 20, 1945, in the possession of Davis Platt.

18   Muste to Rustin, June 18, 1945, and July 4, 1945, both in Bayard Rustin Papers, Reel 20, Correspondence—1945, UPA Microfilms.

19   Information on the 1946 incident comes from a lengthy FBI memorandum on Rustin, dated August 16, 1963, detailing his political affiliations, record of arrests, and foreign travel, obtained by the author through a Freedom of Information Act (FOIA) request. With regard to other incidents, see Rustin to Judge James Lanzetta, October 28, 1947, and Rustin to Dear Friend, October 10, 1947, both in FOR Papers, DG 13, Series D, Box 1, SCPC, and the author's interviews with John Swomley and Glenn Smiley.

20   FOR statement, adopted January 28, 1953, in FOR Papers, DG 13, Series D, Box 1, SCPC. For reactions to it, see the correspondence in General Administration,

Individuals—Bayard Rustin, 1953, AFSC Archives; and the two memos of Roy Finch to the Executive Committee and National Advisory Committee of the War Resisters League (WRL), one from August 25, 1953, and the other undated, in WRL Papers, DG 40, Series B, Box 1, SCPC.

21 Rustin to Swomley, March 8, 1953, in FOR Papers, DG 13, Swomley Collection, Box 2, Rustin Folder, SCPC. Ironically, Rustin's arrest occurred at a moment when the Mattachine Society was growing rapidly in Los Angeles, because of its challenge to police entrapment practices. Gerry Brissette, a young pacifist from Northern California, heard of Rustin's arrest, wrote to the Mattachine Society, and proceeded to organize the first chapter of the Mattachine in the Bay Area. See Brissette to Mattachine Foundation, February 15, 1953, and Freeman to Brissette, February 23, 1953, in James Kepner Papers, Los Angeles.

22 See the memos of Roy Finch to the Executive Committee and National Advisory Committee of the War Resisters League, one from August 25, 1953, and the other undated, in WRL Papers, DG 40, Series B, Box 1, SCPC.

23 For a discussion of both initiatives, see Maurice Isserman, *If I Had a Hammer: The Death of the Old Left and the Birth of the New Left* (Urbana: University of Illinois Press, 1993; originally published 1987), chapter 4.

24 Two important accounts of the Montgomery bus boycott, King's career, and Rustin's relationship with King are David J. Garrow, *Bearing the Cross: Martin Luther King, Jr., and the Southern Christian Leadership Conference* (New York: William Morrow, 1986); and Taylor Branch, *Parting the Waters: America in the King Years, 1954–63* (New York: Simon and Schuster, 1988).

25 For reactions to Rustin's trip to Montgomery, see Smiley to Swomley, February 29, 1956, Swomley to Riles, February 21, 1956, Swomley to Smiley, February 29, 1956 (three letters), and March 1, 1956, all in Swomley Papers, Box 2, SCPC. See also Swomley to Walker, no date, Rustin Papers, Reel 4; and James Farmer Interview, CUOHP.

26 On Rustin's role in Montgomery and his early work with Martin Luther King, see Rustin to Brown, February 23, 1956, and Rustin to Brown and DiGia, both in CDG-A, Rustin File, SCPC; Rustin to King, May 9, 1956, and King to Rustin, September 20, 1956, both in Rustin Papers, Reel 3; Homer Jack Memo, March 9, 1956, in Rustin Papers, Reel 4; Rustin to King, March 8, 1956, Box 5, Folder 29, and Rustin to King, October 18, 1956, Box 64A, Folder 22, both in King Papers, Boston University. Rustin published an account of his first trip to Montgomery. See "Montgomery Diary," *Liberation*, April 1956, pp. 7–10.

27 Rustin to King, May 10, 1957, in King Papers, Box 34, Folder 35, Boston University.

28 For information on the Prayer Pilgrimage and the youth marches, see the material in Rustin Papers, Reels 4 and 6, UPA microfilms; and Randolph Papers, Boxes 30, 33, and 34, LC.

29 See, for example, his article, "To the Finland Station," *Liberation*, June 1958, pp. 9–10.

30 Rustin, "New South, Old Politics," *Liberation,* October 1956, pp. 23–26. Rustin's thinking in this area bears a similarity to ideas associated with Max Shachtman, a Trotskyist active in the anti-Stalinist Left in New York. From the late 1950s onward, two of Rustin's closest associates were Tom Kahn, who became his lover for a time, and Rachelle Horowitz. Both were members of the Young People's Socialist League, and both were close to Shachtman. Whether Rustin's thinking about political realignment, already evident by 1956, influenced Shachtman and his followers, or whether the intellectual influence flowed in the other direction, is still unclear to me, and requires further investigation. For a discussion of Shachtman and his influence on the Left in the 1950s and 1960s, see Isserman, *If I Had a Hammer,* chapters 2 and 5.

31 Peck to Rustin, November 16, 1959, in Committee for Nonviolent Action Papers, DG 17, Box 13, Sahara Correspondence, SCPC. For more on the 1960 project see material in Rustin papers, Reel 1, "Election — 1960" folder; CDG-A, Rustin folder, SCPC; and Student Nonviolent Coordinating Committee (SNCC) Papers, Subgroup A, Series I, Box 1, Folder 20, Martin Luther King Center Archives, Atlanta.

32 On the Powell incident, see Pittsburgh *Courier,* June 25, 1960, p. 3, and July 9, 1960, p. 2; the press release announcing Rustin's resignation, June 27, 1960, in CDG-A, Rustin file, SCPC; Rustin interview, CUOHP; and the accounts in Garrow, *Bearing the Cross,* pp. 138–40, and Branch, *Parting the Waters,* pp. 314–18.

33 Interview with David McReynolds, March 5, 1993.

34 See James Baldwin, "The Dangerous Road before Martin Luther King, *Harper's Magazine,* February 1961, pp. 33–42.

35 On Rustin's European work see Committee for Nonviolent Action (CNVA) Papers, Series VI, Boxes 14–16, "San Francisco to Moscow Peace Walk," SCPC. On his African work see A. J. Muste Papers, Box 40, Folder 6, SCPC.

36 Material on the Birmingham demonstrations and on the March on Washington is voluminous. See the accounts in Garrow and Branch, previously cited. For Rustin's analysis of Birmingham see Rustin, "The Meaning of Birmingham," *Liberation,* June 1963, pp. 7–9.

37 For accounts of the meeting, see Rustin Interview, CUOHP, and Milton Viorst's interview with John Lewis, 1976, in Howard University Civil Rights Collection.

38 See *Congressional Record,* Senate, August 2, 1963, pp. 13968–75; August 7, pp. 14454–63; and August 13, 14836–44. The designation of "Mr. March-on-Washington" comes from the *Washington Post,* August 11, 1963, p. A6. For concerns about Rustin, see the FBI memo, dated August 11, 1963, reporting on a conversation between Martin Luther King and Ted Brown, obtained through FOIA request. For discussion of the FBI and the civil rights movement, see David J. Garrow, *The FBI and Martin Luther King, Jr.* (New York: Penguin, 1983); and Kenneth O'Reilly, *"Racial Matters": The FBI's Secret File on Black America, 1960–1972* (New York: Free Press, 1989).

39 *Philadelphia Sunday Bulletin,* August 18, 1963, p. 1.

40 *Philadelphia Inquirer,* August 27, 1983, clipping in Chester County Historical Society.

41 See Bayard Rustin, "The Meaning of the March," *Liberation,* October 1963, pp. 11–13.

42 *Life* Magazine, for its issue of September 6, 1963, used for its cover a photo of Randolph and Rustin in front of the Lincoln Memorial. *Newsweek* captioned a photo of Rustin, "Out of the Shadows," September 2, 1963, p. 18. King and his associates began discussing whether to invite Rustin to work for the Southern Christian Leadership Conference as early as September 10, 1963. See FBI Memo, New York Office, Bureau File 100-106670, September 11, 1963. One unwelcome sign of Rustin's newly acquired prominence is that the FBI decided, in the fall of 1963, to place him under electronic surveillance.

43 For information on these aspects of Rustin's work, see the following: on the school boycott, Rustin Papers, Reels 11 and 12; on the Albany march, Rustin Papers, Reel 3; on the Freedom Budget, Rustin Papers, Reels 13 and 14; on the "State of the Race" Conference, Randolph Papers, Box 31, LC; on King and Vietnam, see King Papers, Series I, Boxes 29 and 31, King Center, Atlanta. There is also a great deal of information about Vietnam scattered through Rustin's FBI file.

44 Information on Rustin's role in the call for a moratorium and at Atlantic City comes from the almost daily FBI reports filed on Rustin during the summer of 1964. On Rustin's criticisms of the antiwar movement see Rustin Papers, Reel 6, WRL File.

45 "From Protest to Politics," cited above, N3. The choice of *Commentary* as a venue for his ideas was itself significant. Most of Rustin's writing in the previous half dozen years had appeared in the self-consciously radical *Liberation; Commentary* in the 1950s and 1960s addressed an audience of Cold War liberals.

46 For Carmichael's comments, see Milton Viorst, *Fire in the Streets,* pp. 350, 355. See also Staughton Lynd, "Coalition Politics or Nonviolent Revolution?" *Liberation,* June–July 1965, pp. 18–21. David Dellinger was also sharply critical of Rustin. See David Dellinger, "The March on Washington and Its Critics," *Liberation,* May 1965, pp. 6–7. The edge to these articles was so sharp that it provoked a defense of Rustin by David McReynolds: "Transition: Personal and Political Notes," *Liberation,* August 1965, pp. 5–10.

47 On the conflicts over the March on Washington organization, see, for instance, Betti Whaley to Whitney Young, September 27, 1963, and Young to Randolph, January 29, 1964, both in National Urban League Papers, Part II, Series I, Box 25, LC.

48 FBI Memo, New York Office, August 11, 1963, Bureau File 100-106670.

49 Special Agent in Charge, New York, to Director, FBI, Air Telegram, September 23, 1963, in King and Levison FBI File, Box 8, Section 10, King Center, Atlanta. On the Levison-King relationship, see Garrow, *The FBI and Martin Luther King, Jr.*

50 Interview with Shizu Proctor, October 10, 1993.

51 Baumgardner to Sullivan, December 17, 1964, FBI Memo, Subject: Martin Luther King Jr.

2. Placing Gay in the Sixties

1 See, as examples, Kirkpatrick Sale, *SDS* (New York: Random House, 1973); Milton Viorst, *Fire in the Streets: America in the 1960s* (New York: Simon and Schuster, 1979); Allen Matusow, *The Unraveling of America: A History of Liberalism in the 1960s* (New York: Harper and Row, 1984); Todd Gitlin, *The Sixties: Years of Hope, Days of Rage* (New York: Bantam, 1987); James Miller, *"Democracy Is in the Streets": From Port Huron to the Siege of Chicago* (New York: Simon and Schuster, 1987); Terry H. Anderson, *The Movement and the Sixties: Protest in America from Greensboro to Wounded Knee* (New York: Oxford University Press, 1995).

2 John D'Emilio, *Sexual Politics, Sexual Communities: The Making of a Homosexual Minority in the United States, 1940–1970* (Chicago: University of Chicago Press, 1983; 2nd edition, 1998), p. 149. The information on the pre-Stonewall gay movement in this and the following paragraphs comes from chapters 8 through 12. Citations identify the location of quotations.

3 Ibid., p. 153.

4 Ibid., pp. 153, 164.

5 Ibid., p. 143.

6 Charles Kaiser, *The Gay Metropolis, 1940–1996* (Boston: Houghton Mifflin, 1997), p. 138.

7 For details, see Chapter 1 in this volume.

8 James Baldwin, *The Fire Next Time* (New York: Dial Press, 1963; Laurel edition), p. 15.

9 Ibid., p. 21.

10 Paul Goodman, "Being Queer," in Taylor Stoehr, ed., *Crazy Hope and Finite Experience: Final Essays of Paul Goodman* (San Francisco: Jossey-Bass, 1994), p. 109.

4. A Meaning for All Those Words: Sex, Politics, History, and Larry Kramer

1 For a vivid account of ACT UP's style of activism, written by a participant, see Douglas Crimp, with Adam Rolston, *AIDS demo graphics* (Seattle: Bay Press, 1990). For a discussion of other direct action movements, see Barbara Epstein, *Political Protest and Cultural Revolution: Nonviolent Direct Action in the 1970s and 1980s* (Berkeley: University of California Press, 1991).

2 In making this claim, I am painfully aware of how little visibility and public recognition have accrued to *anyone* associated with the gay and lesbian freedom struggle. One person who comes to mind as a point of comparison — Harvey Milk — was hardly known outside California at the time he was assassinated in 1978; recognition and influence came to him more in death than in life. Another, Audre Lorde,

was deeply influential among feminists as a poet, essayist, and theorist of change. But, sadly, the gay men and lesbians who have distinguished themselves through their actions and writings in the gay and lesbian freedom struggle rarely have achieved a profile beyond the boundaries of the gay community.

3   Unfortunately, there is still no thoroughgoing history of the gay and lesbian movement in the decades since Stonewall. Some places to obtain an overview are Urvashi Vaid, *Virtual Equality: The Mainstreaming of Gay and Lesbian Liberation* (New York: Anchor Books, 1995); Barry D. Adam, *The Rise of a Gay and Lesbian Movement*, 2nd edition (Boston: Twayne, 1995); Margaret Cruikshank. *The Gay and Lesbian Liberation Movement* (New York: Routledge, 1992); and my own essay "After Stonewall," in *Making Trouble: Essays on Gay History, Politics, and the University* (New York: Routledge, 1992).

4   I am thinking of a tradition of writing about homosexual desire that includes such diverse products as Thomas Mann's *Death in Venice*, Tennessee Williams's *Suddenly Last Summer*, and Mart Crowley's *The Boys in the Band*.

5   *New York Times Book Review*, January 14, 1979, pp. 15, 40; *New Republic*, January 6, 1979, p. 30; *Gay Community News* review quoted in *New York Magazine*, June 3, 1985, p. 45.

6   For accounts of the gay liberation movement in the immediate aftermath of the Stonewall riot see Martin Duberman, *Stonewall* (New York: Dutton, 1993); Terence Kissack, "Freaking Fag Revolutionaries: New York's Gay Liberation Front, 1969–1971," *Radical History Review* 62 (spring 1995): 104–134; Toby Marotta, *The Politics of Homosexuality* (Boston: Houghton Mifflin, 1981); and Dennis Altman, *Homosexual: Oppression and Liberation* (New York: Avon, 1971).

7   For a collection of representative writings from radical gay and lesbian liberationists see Karla Jay and Allen Young, eds., *Out of the Closets: Voices of Gay Liberation* (New York: New York University Press, 1992; 20th Anniversary Edition).

8   Quoted in Jay and Young, eds., *Out of the Closets*, p. 341.

9   I do not mean to suggest that Larry's novelistic diatribe against the culture of gay male sexuality was rooted in the left-wing anticapitalist politics of gay liberation. Larry wrote from the vantage point of a romantic in a new world of sexual plenty, frustrated in his search for love. Yet, in penning his novel, he was hardly attacking something that other gay men hadn't already taken on. His criticism, in other words, was different; it rested on mainstream values of romantic love. But dissent from the practices of gay male sexuality had precedent in the recent past.

10 Quoted in Larry Kramer, *Reports from the Holocaust: The Making of an AIDS Activist* (New York: St. Martin's Press, 1989), p. 10.

11 *The Nation*, May 1, 1989, p. 600.

12 See Gabriel Rotello, *Sexual Ecology: AIDS and the Destiny of Gay Men* (New York: Dutton, 1997); Dangerous Bedfellows, eds., *Policing Public Sex* (Boston: South End Press, 1996); and Michael Warner, *The Trouble with Normal: Sex, Politics, and the Ethics of Queer Life* (New York: Free Press, 1999).

5. *Cycles of Change, Questions of Strategy: The Gay and Lesbian Movement After 50 Years*

1 For information on the period between World War II and Stonewall see Allan Berube, *Coming Out Under Fire: The History of Gay Men and Women in World War II* (New York: Free Press, 1990); John D'Emilio, *Sexual Politics, Sexual Communities: The Making of a Homosexual Minority in the United States, 1940–1970*, 2nd edition (Chicago: University of Chicago Press, 1998); and Marc Stein, *City of Sisterly and Brotherly Loves: Lesbian and Gay Philadelphia, 1945–1972* (Chicago: University of Chicago Press, 2000).

2 See Alfred Kinsey et al., *Sexual Behavior in the Human Male* (Philadelphia: W. B. Saunders, 1948), and *Sexual Behavior in the Human Female* (Philadelphia: W. B. Saunders, 1953); and Donald Webster Cory [pseud.], *The Homosexual in America: A Subjective Approach* (New York: Arno Reprint, 1975).

3 U.S. Senate, 81st Congress, 2nd Session, Committee on Expenditures in Executive Departments, *Employment of Homosexuals and Other Sex Perverts in Government* (Washington: Government Printing Office, 1950).

4 D'Emilio, *Sexual Politics, Sexual Communities*, p. 9.

5 For information on this period see Sidney Abbott and Barbara Love, *Sappho Was a Right-On Woman* (New York: Stein and Day, 1972); Dennis Altman, *Homosexual Oppression and Liberation* (New York: Outerbridge and Lazard, 1971); David Deitcher, ed., *The Question of Equality: Lesbian and Gay Politics in America Since Stonewall* (New York: Scribner, 1995); John D'Emilio, *Making Trouble: Essays on Gay History, Politics, and the University* (New York: Routledge, 1992); Martin Duberman, *Stonewall* (New York: Dutton, 1993); Karla Jay and Allen Young, eds., *Out of the Closets: Voices of Gay Liberation* (New York: NYU Press, 1992; 20th Anniversary Edition); Randy Shilts, *The Mayor of Castro Street* (New York: St. Martin's Press, 1982).

6 The literature on AIDS is vast. Some useful works include Dennis Altman, *AIDS in the Mind of America* (Garden City, N.Y.: Anchor/Doubleday, 1986); Cindy Patton, *Sex and Germs: The Politics of Aids* (Boston: South End Press, 1985); Simon Watney, *Policing Desire: Pornography, AIDS, and the Media* (Minneapolis: University of Minnesota Press, 1987); Randy Shilts, *And the Band Played On: Politics, People, and the AIDS Epidemic* (New York: St. Martin's Press, 1987); Larry Kramer, *Reports from the Holocaust: The Making of an AIDS Activist* (New York: St. Martin's Press, 1989); Douglas Crimp, ed., *AIDS: Cultural Analysis, Cultural Activism* (Cambridge: MIT Press, 1988); Douglas Crimp with Adam Rolston, *AIDS demographics* (Seattle: Bay Press, 1990); Paula A. Treichler, *How to Have Theory in an Epidemic: Cultural Chronicles of AIDS* (Durham, N.C.: Duke University Press, 1999); and John-Manuel Andriote, *Victory Deferred: How AIDS Changed Gay Life in America* (Chicago: University of Chicago Press, 1999).

7 For developments in the 1990s, see Chris Bull and John Gallagher, *Perfect Enemies:*

The Religious Right, the Gay Movement, and the Politics of the 1990s (New York: Crown, 1996); James Button et al., *Private Lives, Public Conflicts: Battles over Gay Rights in American Communities* (Washington: Congressional Quarterly Press, 1997); Kathleen DeBold, ed., *Out for Office: Campaigning in the Gay '90s* (Washington: Gay and Lesbian Victory Fund, 1994); John D'Emilio, William B. Turner, and Urvashi Vaid, eds., *Creating Change: Sexuality, Public Policy, and Civil Rights* (New York: St. Martin's Press, 2000); Didi Herman, *The Antigay Agenda: Orthodox Vision and the Christian Right* (Chicago: University of Chicago Press, 1997); and Urvashi Vaid, *Virtual Equality: The Mainstreaming of Gay and Lesbian Liberation* (New York: Anchor Books, 1995).

8 Quoted in William Eskridge and Nan D. Hunter, *Sexuality, Gender, and the Law* (Westbury, N.Y.: Foundation Press, 1997), p. 93.

9 See Leila Rupp and Verta Taylor, *Survival in the Doldrums: The American Women's Rights Movement, 1945 to the 1960s* (New York: Oxford, 1987); Frank D. Baumgartner and Bryan D. Jones, *Agendas and Instability in American Politics* (Chicago: University of Chicago Press, 1993), pp. 235–36; and Nancy Whittier, *Feminist Generations: The Persistence of the Radical Women's Movement* (Philadelphia: Temple University Press, 1995), pp. 255–57.

6. Organizational Tales: Interpreting the NGLTF Story

1 The social science literature on organizations is vast. For a recent discussion, see S. Andrews, C. Basler, and X. Collier, "Organizational Structures, Cultures, and Identities: Overlaps and Divergences," *Research in the Sociology of Organizations,* 16 (1999): 213–235. For a recent analysis of the gay and lesbian movement, see Mary Bernstein, "Celebration and Suppression: The Strategic Uses of Identity by the Lesbian and Gay Movement," *American Journal of Sociology,* 103 (1997): 531–565. Nancy E. Stoller has published an insightful comparative study of AIDS organizations, with particular attention to how social identity shapes the culture of an organization and how organizational culture, in turn, shapes the mission, goals, and day-to-day practices of a group. See Nancy E. Stoller, *Lessons from the Damned: Queers, Whores, and Junkies Respond to AIDS* (New York: Routledge, 1998).

2 The information for this history of the task force comes less from research in the traditional sense than from direct participation, with the implications this participation had for observation and for access to documents. In particular, I was a board member of NGLTF from November 1988 to October 1993, and a staff member from June 1995 to May 1997. In addition, as part of a strategic planning process for the organization, I spent a week in the spring of 1989 combing through NGLTF's office files in order to write a brief history. Later, in October 1992, I examined the papers of Charlotte Bunch, who served on NGTF's board in the 1970s; her papers are deposited at the Schlesinger Library of Radcliffe College. Aspects of the task force's history are touched on in the following books: Howard Brown, *Familiar Faces,*

Hidden Lives: The Story of Homosexual Men in America Today (New York: Harcourt Brace Jovanovich, 1976); Toby Marotta, *The Politics of Homosexuality* (Boston: Houghton Mifflin, 1981); Eric Marcus, *Making History: The Struggle for Gay and Lesbian Equal Rights, 1945–1990, An Oral History* (New York: Harper Collins, 1992); Martin Duberman, *Cures: A Gay Man's Odyssey* (New York: Dutton, 1991), and *Midlife Queer: Autobiography of a Decade* (New York: Scribner, 1996); Urvashi Vaid, *Virtual Equality: The Mainstreaming of Gay and Lesbian Liberation* (New York: Doubleday Anchor, 1995); John-Manuel Andriote, *Victory Deferred: How AIDS Changed Gay Life in America* (Chicago: University of Chicago Press, 1999); Dudley Clendinen and Adam Nagourney, *Out for Good: The Struggle to Build a Gay Rights Movement in America* (New York: Simon and Schuster, 1999); and John D'Emilio, William B. Turner, and Urvashi Vaid, eds., *Creating Change: Sexuality, Public Policy, and Civil Rights* (New York: St. Martin's Press, 2000). Of these, Vaid and Clendinen and Nagourney provided the most sustained discussions. Finally, for researchers interested in pursuing in depth the history of NGLTF, the organization's papers have been deposited in the Human Sexuality Collection at Cornell University.

3   For Brown's coming out, see the *New York Times,* October 3, 1973, p. 1.

4   Voeller wrote an account of the founding of the NGTF and his experience as executive director. See Bruce Voeller, "My Days on the Task Force," *Christopher Street,* October 1979, pp. 55–65.

5   See the interview with O'Leary in Marcus, *Making History,* pp. 261–73.

6   See the interview with Brydon in Marcus, *Making History,* pp. 305–13.

7   For the work of the antiviolence project, see Gregory M. Herek and Kevin T. Berrill, eds., *Hate Crimes: Confronting Violence Against Lesbians and Gay Men* (Newbury Park, Calif.: Sage Publications, 1992).

8   For a discussion of Vaid's years at the NGLTF, as well as an analysis of the movement's politics in this period, see Vaid, *Virtual Equality.*

9. Stonewall: Myth and Meaning

1   The best, and most extensive account, is Martin Duberman, *Stonewall* (New York: Dutton, 1993).

2   Some works that include discussions of the resistance embedded in everyday life include Elizabeth Lapovsky Kennedy and Madeline D. Davis, *Boots of Leather, Slippers of Gold: The History of a Lesbian Community* (New York: Routledge, 1993); Allan Berube, *Coming Out Under Fire: Gay Men and Women In World War II* (New York: Free Press, 1990); Esther Newton, *Cherry Grove, Fire Island: Sixty Years in America's First Gay and Lesbian Town* (Boston: Beacon Press, 1993); John Howard, *Men Like That: A Southern Queer History* (Chicago: University of Chicago Press, 1999); and Marc Stein, *City of Sisterly and Brotherly Loves: Lesbian and Gay Philadelphia, 1945–1972* (Chicago: University of Chicago Press, 2000).

10. Born Gay?

1 The quote comes from the much reprinted document, "The Woman-Identified Woman." It can be found in Karla Jay and Allen Young, eds., *Out of the Closets: Voices of Gay Liberation* (New York: NYU Press, 1992; 20th Anniversary Edition), pp. 172–77.

2 See Simon LeVay, "A Difference in Hypothalmic Structure between Homosexual and Heterosexual Men," *Science,* 253 (1991): 1034–37; J. Michael Bailey and Richard C. Pillard, "A Genetic Study of Male Sexual Orientation," *Archives of General Psychiatry,* 48 (2) (December 1991): 1089–96; Dean Hamer et al., "A Linkage between DNA Markers on the X Chromosome and Male Sexual Orientation," *Science,* 261 (1993): 321–27. For accounts aimed at a lay audience, see Chandler Burr, *A Separate Creation: The Search for the Biological Origins of Sexual Orientation* (New York: Hyperion, 1996); and Dean Hamer and Peter Copeland, *The Science of Desire: The Search for the Gay Gene and the Biology of Behavior* (New York: Simon and Schuster, 1994).

3 The articles about LeVay's work appeared on August 30, 1991, as did the *Nightline* broadcast. The article about the gay gene appeared in the *Canberra Times* on July 18, 1993.

15. Then and Now: The Shifting Context of Gay Historical Writing

1 Works on gay and lesbian history published prior to 1983 include Jonathan Katz, *Gay American History: Lesbians and Gay Men in the U.S.A.* (New York: Crowell, 1976); Jeffrey Weeks, *Coming Out: Homosexual Politics in Britain from the Nineteenth Century to the Present* (London: Quartet Books, 1977); John Boswell, *Christianity, Social Tolerance, and Homosexuality: Gay People in Western Europe from the Beginning of the Christian Era to the Fourteenth Century* (Chicago: University of Chicago Press, 1980); Lillian Faderman, *Surpassing the Love of Men: Romantic Friendship and Love Between Women from the Renaissance to the Present* (New York: Morrow, 1981); and Alan Bray, *Homosexuality in Renaissance England* (London: Gay Men's Press, 1982).

2 For insights into the period between the Stonewall Riots and the onset of AIDS, see Dennis Altman, *Homosexual: Oppression and Liberation* (New York: Outerbridge and Dienstfrey, 1971), and *Coming Out in the Seventies* (Sydney: Wild and Woolley, 1979); Sidney Abbott and Barbara Love, *Sappho Was a Right-On Woman* (New York: Stein and Day, 1972); Martin Duberman, *Cures: A Gay Man's Odyssey* (New York: Dutton, 1991), *Stonewall* (New York: Dutton, 1993), and *Mid-Life Queer: 1971–1981* (New York: Scribner, 1996); Donn Teal, *The Gay Militants* (New York: Stein and Day, 1971); Randy Shilts, *The Mayor of Castro Street: The Life and Times of Harvey Milk* (New York: St. Martin's Press, 1982); Karla Jay and Allen Young, eds., *Out of the Closets: Voices of Gay Liberation* (New York: Douglas/Links, 1992), and *Lavender Culture* (New York: Jove, 1978). See also my own collection of essays,

some of which were written in the 1970s and early 1980s, *Making Trouble: Essays on Gay History, Politics, and the University* (New York: Routledge, 1992).

3 For information on the founding and early work of the Gay Academic Union, see *The Universities and the Gay Experience: Proceedings of the Conference Sponsored by the Women and Men of the Gay Academic Union, November 23 and 24, 1973* (New York: Gay Academic Union, 1974).

4 Duberman came out in print in his book *Black Mountain: An Exploration in Community* (New York: Dutton, 1972).

5 See Jonathan Katz, *Coming Out!* (New York: Arno, 1975).

6 See Del Martin and Phyllis Lyon, *Lesbian/Woman* (San Francisco: Glide Publications, 1972); Laud Humphreys, *Out of the Closets: The Sociology of Homosexual Liberation* (Englewood Cliffs, N.J.: Prentice-Hall, 1972), and Kay Tobin and Randy Wicker, *The Gay Crusaders* (New York: Paperback Library, 1972).

7 The interview with Hay appears in Katz, *Gay American History*, pp. 406–20. For more on Hay, see Stuart Timmons, *The Trouble with Harry Hay: Founder of the Modern Gay Movement* (Boston: Alyson, 1990), and Will Roscoe, ed., *Radically Gay: Gay Liberation in the Words of Its Founder, Harry Hay* (Boston: Beacon, 1996).

8 Many of these tapes have been deposited at the New York Public Library and are available to other researchers.

9 For more detail on the events in San Francisco, see Shilts, *The Mayor of Castro Street*, and John D'Emilio, "Gay Politics and Community in San Francisco Since World War II," in Martin Duberman et al., eds. *Hidden From History: Reclaiming the Gay and Lesbian Past* (New York: New American Library, 1989), pp. 456–73.

10 See Allan Berube, *Coming Out Under Fire: The History of Gay Men and Women in World War Two* (New York: Free Press, 1990); Elizabeth Lapovsky Kennedy and Madeline D. Davis, *Boots of Leather, Slippers of Gold: The History of a Lesbian Community* (New York: Routledge, 1993); Esther Newton, *Cherry Grove, Fire Island: Sixty Years in America's First Gay and Lesbian Town* (Boston: Beacon, 1993); George Chauncey, *Gay New York: Gender, Urban Culture, and the Making of the Gay Male World, 1890–1940* (New York: Basic Books, 1994); John Howard, *Men Like That: A Southern Queer History* (Chicago: University of Chicago Press, 1999); Marc Stein, *City of Sisterly and Brotherly Loves: Lesbian and Gay Philadelphia, 1945–1972* (Chicago: University of Chicago Press, 2000); John Donald Gustav-Wrathall, *Take the Young Stranger by the Hand: Same-Sex Relations and the YMCA* (Chicago: University of Chicago Press, 1998); Lisa Duggan, *Sapphic Slashers: Sex, Violence, and American Modernity* (Durham, N.C.; Duke University Press, 2000); and Lillian Faderman, *Odd Girls and Twilight Lovers: A History of Lesbian Life in Twentieth-Century America* (New York: Columbia University Press, 1991).

11 Among books that will appear shortly are Jonathan Ned Katz's study of male-male intimacy in nineteenth-century America and David Johnson's study of McCarthy-era Washington, D.C., both from the University of Chicago Press.

12 See Martin Duberman et al., *Hidden From History: Reclaiming the Gay and Lesbian*

262 NOTES TO CHAPTER FIFTEEN

Past (New York: New American Library, 1989); Brett Beemyn, ed., *Creating a Place for Ourselves: Lesbian, Gay, and Bisexual Community Histories* (New York: Routledge, 1997); John Howard, ed., *Carryin' On in the Lesbian and Gay South* (New York: New York University Press, 1997); and Mark Blasius and Shane Phelan, *We Are Everywhere: A Historical Sourcebook of Gay and Lesbian Politics* (New York: Routledge, 1997).

13 See Kathy Peiss and Christina Simmons, eds., *Passion and Power: Sexuality in History* (Philadelphia: Temple University, 1989); John C. Fout and Maura Shaw Tantillo, *American Sexual Politics: Sex, Gender, and Race since the Civil War* (Chicago: University of Chicago Press, 1993); Joanne Meyerowitz, *Not June Cleaver: Women and Gender in Postwar America, 1945–1960* (Philadelphia: Temple University Press, 1994); Brett Beemyn and Mickey Eliason, eds., *Queer Studies: A Lesbian, Gay, Bisexual, and Transgender Anthology* (New York: New York University Press, 1996); Martin Duberman, ed., *Queer Representations: Reading Lives, Reading Cultures* (New York: New York University Press, 1997); *A Queer World: The Center for Lesbian and Gay Studies Reader* (New York: New York University Press, 1997), and "The Queer Issue: New Visions of America's Lesbian and Gay Past" *Radical History Review*, 62 (spring 1995).

14 See Leisa D. Meyer, *Creating GI Jane: Sexuality and Power in the Women's Army Corps During World War II* (New York: Columbia University Press, 1996); Susan K. Cahn, *Coming on Strong: Gender and Sexuality in Twentieth-Century Women's Sport* (New York: Free Press, 1994); and Kevin Mumford, *Interzones: Black/White Sex Districts in Chicago and New York in the Early Twentieth Century* (New York: Columbia University Press, 1997).

15 See, for example, Margaret M. Caffrey, *Ruth Benedict: Stranger in This Land* (Austin: University of Texas Press, 1989); Blanche Wiesen Cook, *Eleanor Roosevelt: Volume One, 1884–1933* (New York: Viking, 1992); David Hajdu, *Lush Life: A Biography of Billy Strayhorn* (New York: Farrar, Straus and Giroux, 1996); Estelle B. Freedman, *Maternal Justice: Miriam Van Waters and the Female Reform Tradition* (Chicago: University of Chicago Press, 1996); Anthony Tommasini, *Virgil Thomson: Composer on the Aisle* (New York: Norton, 1997); Diane Wood Middlebrook, *Suits Me: The Double Life of Billy Tipton* (Boston: Houghton Mifflin, 1998); and Darden Asbury Pyron, *Liberace: An American Boy* (Chicago: University of Chicago Press, 2000).

16 As one example of an effort to weave gay history and same-sex relationships into a broader historical narrative, see John D'Emilio and Estelle Freedman, *Intimate Matters: A History of Sexuality in America*, 2d edition (Chicago: University of Chicago Press, 1997).

17 Among the earlier works that influenced me are Mary McIntosh, "The Homosexual Role," *Social Problems* 16 (1968): 182–92; Jeffrey Weeks, *Coming Out: Homosexual Politics in Britain from the Nineteenth Century to the Present* (London: Quartet 1977); Robert Padgug, "Sexual Matters: On Conceptualizing Sexuality in History," *Radical History Review*, 20 (spring/summer 1979): pp. 3–23; and Michel Foucault, *The*

History of Sexuality: Volume One, An Introduction, trans. Robert Hurley (New York: Pantheon, 1978).

18 See Edward Stein, ed., *Forms of Desire: Sexual Orientation and the Social Constructionist Controversy* (New York: Routledge, 1992). In the 1990s, the discussion moved beyond academic circles, as seen by its front page coverage in the *New York Times*. See "Study of Sex Experiencing 2d Revolution," *New York Times,* December 28, 1997, p. 1.

19 Judith Butler, *Gender Trouble: Feminism and the Subversion of Gender* (New York: Routledge, 1990).

20 See Michael Warner, ed., *Fear of a Queer Planet: Queer Politics and Social Theory* (Minneapolis: University of Minnesota Press, 1993), and the anthologies edited by Beemyn and Eliason and by Duberman, cited above, n13.

21 Eve Kosofsky Sedgwick makes this call in an especially persuasive way in the introduction to her book, *Epistemology of the Closet* (Berkeley: University of California Press, 1990).

22 For discussions of biological approaches to sexual orientation, see John P. DeCecco and David Allen Parker, eds., *Sex, Cells, and Same-Sex Desire: The Biology of Sexual Preference* (New York: Harrington Park Press, 1995). Some of the key works from scientists espousing biological explanations are Simon LeVay, *The Sexual Brain* (Cambridge, Mass.: MIT Press, 1993) and *Queer Science: The Use and Abuse of Research into Homosexuality* (Cambridge, Mass.: MIT Press, 1996); Dean Hamer and Peter Copeland, *The Science of Desire: The Search for the Gay Gene and the Biology of Behavior* (New York: Simon and Schuster, 1994); J. Michael Bailey and Richard C. Pillard, "A Genetic Study of Male Sexual Orientation," *Archives of General Psychiatry,* 48 (1991): 1089–96; and Richard C. Pillard and J. Michael Bailey, "A Biological Perspective on Sexual Orientation," *Psychiatric Clinics of North America,* 18 (1995): 71–84. For a popularized journalistic account by a nonscientist, see Chandler Burr, *A Separate Creation: The Search for the Biological Origins of Sexual Orientation* (New York: Hyperion, 1996).

23 See the books by Berube, Kennedy and Davis, and Newton, cited above, n10. On Washington, D.C., see Brett Beemyn, "A Queer Capital: Race, Class, Gender, and the Changing Social Landscape of Washington's Gay Communities, 1940–1955," in Beemyn, *Creating a Place for Ourselves,* pp. 183–209.

24 For the biographies of Miriam Van Waters and Tom Dooley, see above, n15. See also John Howard, "The Library, the Park, and the Pervert: Public Space and Homosexual Encounter in Post–World War II Atlanta," *Radical History Review,* 62 (spring 1995): 166–87; Alan Helms, *Young Man from the Provinces: A Gay Life Before Stonewall* (Boston: Faber and Faber, 1995); Martin Duberman, *Cures: A Gay Man's Odyssey* (New York: Dutton, 1991); Audre Lorde, *Zami: A New Spelling of My Name* (Watertown, Mass.: Persephone Press, 1982); Donna Penn, "The Sexualized Woman: The Lesbian, the Prostitute, and the Containment of Female Sexuality in Postwar America," in Meyerowitz, *Not June Cleaver,* pp. 358–81; Estelle B. Freedman, "The Prison Lesbian: Race, Class, and the Construction of the Aggres-

sive Female Homosexual, 1915–1965," *Feminist Studies,* summer 1996, pp. 397–423; Edwin M. Yoder Jr., *Joe Alsop's Cold War: A Study of Journalistic Influence and Intrigue* (Chapel Hill: University of North Carolina Press, 1995). Johnson's book is under contract with the University of Chicago Press.

25   Estelle B. Freedman, "'Uncontrolled Desires': The Response to the Sexual Psychopath, 1920–1960," *Journal of American History,* 74 (June 1987): 83–106.

26   Allan Drexel, "Before Paris Burned: Race, Class, and Male Homosexuality on the Chicago South Side, 1935–1960," in Beemyn, *Creating a Place for Ourselves,* pp. 119–44.

27   See the statements on pages 240, 249, and 239 of *Sexual Politics, Sexual Communities.*

28   Maurice Isserman and Michael Kazin, "The Failure and Success of the New Radicalism," in Steve Fraser and Gary Gerstle, eds., *The Rise and Fall of the New Deal Order, 1930–1980* (Princeton: Princeton University Press, 1989), pp. 212–42.

29   Charles Kaiser, *The Gay Metropolis, 1940–1996* (Boston: Houghton Mifflin, 1997), p. 138.

30   For a recent discussion of the origins of gay liberation and of the ways that historians of the sixties have tended to ignore it, see Terence Kissack, "Freaking Fag Revolutionaries: New York City's Gay Liberation Front, 1969–1971," *Radical History Review,* 62 (spring 1995): 104–34.

John D'Emilio is a prominent gay rights activist and was the first
director of the National Gay and Lesbian Task Force's Policy
Institute. He is the author of several books on civil rights and
sexuality, including *Sexual Politics, Sexual Communities: The Making
of a Homosexual Minority in the United States, 1940–1970,* and *Intimate
Matters: A History of Sexuality in America,* coauthored with
Estelle B. Freedman. He is currently Professor of Gender and
Women's Studies and History at the University of Illinois, Chicago.

Library of Congress Cataloging-in-Publication Data
D'Emilio, John.
The world turned: essays on gay history, politics, and culture /
John D'Emilio.
p. cm.
ISBN 0-8223-2930-1 (cloth : alk. paper)
ISBN 0-8223-3023-7 (pbk. : alk. paper)
1. Gay rights — United States — History — 20th century. 2. Gay
men — United States — History — 20th century. 3. Lesbians —
United States — History — 20th century. 4. Social change — United
States — History — 20th century. 5. United States — Social life and
customs — 1971– 6. United States — Social conditions — 1960–
1980. 7. United States — Social conditions — 1980– 8. United
States — Politics and government — 1945–1989. 9. United States —
Politics and government — 1989– I. Title.
HQ76.8.U5 D454 2002
305.9'0664'0973 — dc21   2002001674